SPYGATE

EXPOSED

The Failed Conspiracy Against President Trump

Svetlana Lokhova

DEDICATION

I dedicate this book to the loyal men and women of the security services who work tirelessly to protect us from terrorism and other threats. Your constant vigilance allows us, your fellow citizens to live our lives in safety.

And to every American citizen who, whether they know it or not, almost lost their birthright government of the people, by the people, for the people—at the hands of a small group of men who sought to see such freedom perish from the earth.

God Bless Us All.

www.spygate-exposed.com

Table of Contents

What happened to the President of the United States was one of the greatest travesties in American history. Without any basis they started this investigation of his campaign. Even more concerning is what happened after the campaign in a whole pattern of events…to sabotage the presidency.

Attorney General William Barr
April 8, 2020

Introduction

I've got a story to tell you. It's all about spies. And if it's true—which I think it is—you boys are gonna need a whole new organization.

—John le Carré, *Tinker, Tailor, Soldier, Spy*

Svetlana Lokhova, supposedly this is Flynn's girlfriend. This is the reason that they open up an investigation on General Flynn.

—Rep. Devin Nunes July 28, 2019.

To me belongeth vengeance and recompense; their foot shall slide in due time: for the day of their calamity is at hand, and the things that shall come upon them make haste.

—Deuteronomy 32:35[1]

Truth is stranger than fiction, but it is because fiction is obliged to stick to possibilities. Truth isn't.

—Mark Twain, *Following the Equator*

S pygate is "the greatest scandal in US political history."[2] After the 2016 Presidential election political opponents attempted to unseat the elected US President Donald J. Trump. The plotters, among them some of the former leadership of Obama's intelligence community

---

[1] Unless otherwise indicated, all Scripture is taken from the King James Version in the public domain.

[2] President Donald J. Trump May 23, 2018.

used information they knew was false and supplied to them by a man with links to an "obviously unethical if not criminal spying operation during the 1980 presidential campaign."[3]

In John le Carré's masterpiece *Tinker, Tailor, Soldier, Spy,* the greatest spy novel ever written, the source codenamed "Merlin" almost destroyed the security services by providing false intelligence. Spygate's "Merlin" was perhaps the long-term CIA and FBI asset Stefan Halper. [4] As with the fictional intelligence organization in the novel, the real intelligence organizations before and especially after President Donald Trump's election were seemingly so desperate for "gold dust" intelligence on campaign figures, they gobbled up the false information on offer, however preposterous. Here is the question; did the spy chiefs either know at the time or should they have known that the "intelligence" they received was concocted by a single unreliable source and unverified? Both the fictional and real intelligence organizations paid a fortune for fake information and the more they rewarded the source the more they relied on the fables.[5] Both the fictional "Source Merlin" and the real life Halper have been described as collectors of intelligence no-one else could get, with "contacts" at the highest level of the Moscow Kremlin.

---

[3] Glenn Greenwald, *The Intercept* (May 19, 2018), https://theintercept.com/2018/0;5/19/the-fbi-informant-who-monitored-the-trump-campaign-stefan-halper-oversaw-a-cia-spying-operation-in-the-1980-presidential-election/

[4] Halper has been named by numerous media outlets including the *Washington Post* and *New York Times* as both a CIA and FBI asset. David Ignatius described him as FBI "trusted source." Tom Hamburger also of the Post described Halper as *"a peripheral figure in intelligence circles — someone who is unofficially "part of the family" and is trusted to take on low-risk tasks at the government's behest."* Halper or someone close to him, I believe is the likely source of this information. Family is a reference to his ex-father in law Ray Cline a legend in the CIA. I call him the Spider, referencing a line from a poem by Sir Walter Scott.

[5] Halper's exact FBI payments are redacted in the Inspector General Horowitz report. It would appear to be a sum in excess of $1million from 2008.

The novel, *Tinker Tailor Soldier Spy* has a good ending: George Smiley, a veteran British intelligence officer, painstakingly investigates and dramatically exposes the entire plot. He proceeds to clean out the stables. Spygate is real-life. Will Attorney General William Barr, who is investigating the origins of Spygate, emerge as the hero?

Myths born in the Cold War espionage battles between the great powers are the origin of the Spygate scandal. For the operation to come so close to toppling President Donald Trump, the Deep State sought to influence American public opinion against him, relying on inherited memories planted deep in the US psyche. "The press is part of the operation, the indispensable part. None of it would have been possible…had the media not linked arms with spies, cops, and lawyers to relay a story first spun by Clinton operatives."[6] The press scam unlocked latent suspicion of Russia. A remarkable and intense media campaign poisoned the minds of the American public to the point many believe their own president, Donald J. Trump, was a "Manchurian Candidate", a Kremlin puppet under the control of a hostile foreign power. The disinformation campaign ran 24/7 for years and was unlike anything seen before.

The Spygate scandal progressed through a series of inquiries. Special Counsel Robert Mueller found no collusion between the Trump presidential campaign and Russia. Inspector General Michael Horowitz uncovered a swathe of FISA[7] abuse, and now Attorney General Bill Barr and US Attorney John Durham from Connecticut are looking at the very origins of the operation. The sordid events of 2015,

---

[6] Lee Smith. The Plot Against the President: The True Story of How Congressman Devin Nunes Uncovered the Biggest Political Scandal in U. S. History. (New York, Center Street 2019)

[7] Foreign Intelligence Surveillance Act

2016, 2017, and 2018 live on, still spinning around us and inevitably feeding into the politics of re-election in 2020.

I am uniquely qualified to explain this horror of government abuse. I am an intelligence scholar, an eye witness and a critical one to the operation against Donald Trump. I know those who are now named and routinely reported on as players in the origins of this story. In this book I provide my own eyewitness evidence of hard facts together with deduction and analysis. Of course, I may be wrong in some of my assumptions as is inevitable in unravelling so much disinformation. I bring my skills as a scholar and my memory to this task. The arduous mission for Attorney General William Barr and US Attorney John Durham is determining the start, the genesis of the whole operation.

My story starts in 2014. I am a scholar, an academic, a mother and certainly not a spy. Long before the Deep State ensnared me in its web, I was innocuously researching espionage history. Following along in the footsteps of the great novelist John le Carré, I made *"the world of spying ... my genre. My struggle is to demystify, to de-romanticize the spook world, but at the same time harness it as a good story."*

Later, my life was taken over by false allegations fabricated in the plot against Donald Trump, that has become the greatest political scandal of US political history. According to the lies, I am General Flynn's "Russian girlfriend" and that lie is the reason that the FBI opened up a counter-intelligence investigation on General Flynn. I have used my research skills honed as a historian to uncover the lies, the leaks, and the fake investigations. I have an advantage over other writer: I am an eyewitness. My story is important to understand the history of the United States of America and to correct those who maintain the narrative of deceit. It does not fit, in fact my story destroys, the established Deep State's narrative and chronology; it is most inconvenient.

In 2014, I was teaching history to undergraduate students at the UK's top-ranked university, Cambridge. It was a tranquil life and a world away from the dark games of Washington power politics. The University of Cambridge is an elite academic institution founded in the Middle Ages in a quiet, sleepy market town in the crushingly flat east of England. I am a leading expert and possibly the only specialist on early Soviet espionage in the United States which began at the start of the 1930s.[8] My area of expertise is not the modern day but an investigation, an expedition back in time into the secret world of spying in the last century.

By 2014, when this story starts, I had long been a British citizen. I spent sixteen years associated with England's most famous university since emigrating from the chaos of Moscow, Russia, to the calm ivory towers and spires of Cambridge—the educator of choice for the British establishment. It is also home to a small, highly prestigious but dying intelligence history group. My Russian language skills and my youth set me apart from the club which is an otherwise stale, male, and pale world of Cambridge-based espionage historians.

Unlike the others in the small, fractious group, I was not a crusty Cold War warrior clinging to the ideas of the Great Game.[9] I am a product of the modern capitalist Russia that emerged after the collapse of the Soviet Union and a Western education. Unlike the others in the Cambridge club I was not a participant in the shadowy, murky

---

[8] Svetlana Lokhova *"The Spy Who Changed History"* (London, Harper Collins 2018)

[9] The Great Game was a political and diplomatic confrontation that existed for most of the 19th century between the British Empire and the Russian Empire over Afghanistan and neighboring territories in Central and South Asia.

operations of the Cold War. I approached the subject of espionage history with the clear eyes of the intellectually curious and not the preconceived notions of a participant.

In the brief hiatus between the end of the first Cold War in 1991 and its sudden resumption in mid 2014, Russia's new capitalist government released files stored from the Soviet era for public view. Most of my research relied on the declassified records of the long disbanded Soviet Communist Party. The documents are open to the public and archived in Moscow. I have no exclusive access. But unlike almost all Western historians, I read Russian and understand Russians. The no-doubt fascinating official Soviet-era spy records remain highly classified, inaccessible, and likely to remain so forever. However, the Soviet state was a bureaucratic monolith, a machine that generated mountains of files and paperwork. I discovered in the now-declassified Communist Party records a treasure trove of clues for my work in the personal papers of Soviet leaders. A diligent researcher will find revelatory information in these dusty files. It is a Herculean task, so I am the only Western-trained historian with native Russian language skills who has analyzed this unique historical source.

Espionage history can be magical. There are undiscovered stories, thrilling and often tragic in equal measure. Using almost a century old documents, I was making fresh, groundbreaking finds in my field, rewriting our understanding of a bygone era. I was uncovering long-secret spy operations. It was my success as a scholar and not a sordid plot that brought me into the inner circles of Cambridge University. Everyone trusted me, and why not? After so many years, I was very much part of the furniture.

My work extended beyond the ivory towers. I helped the British government declassify its spy records—the British National Archive at

Kew in London stores the declassified MI5 files for public view. The most significant stash of KGB records is the archive of the Soviet era defector, Mitrokhin, located in the Churchill Archive Centre in Cambridge. Naturally, in the course of my everyday work, I was introduced to many distinguished senior servants of intelligence services.

Over its long, mostly glorious history, the University of Cambridge has produced Nobel prize–winning scientists, world leaders, comedians, and more than its fair share of world-class spies and traitors. "Spies are a Cambridge tradition. We've produced more of them than any other British university," says Professor Christopher Andrew, the world's leading expert.[10]

Cambridge's reputation as a center of espionage is now a national joke. Stephen Fry, one of the best comedians the university produced, quipped, "When I was at Cambridge it was, naturally enough I felt, my ambition to be approached in some way by an elderly . . . don [professor] and asked to spy for or against my country." [11]

None of the traitors is more famous than the so-called Cambridge Five. In the early 1930s, at least five British undergraduates studying at the University converted to the Communist cause and later became committed Soviet spies. On graduation, the traitors took their places as moles at the heart of the British establishment and betrayed secrets to the Soviets. These spies were not Russian infiltrators but home-grown British converts to the Communist cause.

The most infamous was Kim Philby. He is the only British traitor to be publicly and prematurely cleared in a speech in the House of

[10] https://www.corpus.cam.ac.uk/news/500-years-of-cambridge-spies

[11] Ted Goodman (ed.,) *Forbes Book of Quotations: 10,0000 Thoughts on the Business of Life* (New York: Hachette Books, 2016), 219.

Commons by the then foreign secretary, and later prime minister, Harold Macmillan. On November 7, 1955, Macmillan told the House of Commons, "I have no reason to conclude that Mr. Philby has at any time betrayed the interests of his country. [12]" Ah, a different age when Russia's spies were buried deep in our government system, and no one believed it! Today the reverse is the case; there were no Russian spies at the heart of the newly elected US government but half the population was fooled into believing there was!

During his long career with the British Secret Intelligence Service, Philby came within touching distance of being appointed the head. No one suspected his treachery especially given his privileged social background and Cambridge credentials. The presence of the long-dead Magnificent Five (interchangeable with Cambridge Five) still lingers in memories around the University. A lively cottage industry still pumps out best-selling books each year, each trying to find a fresh angle on the old scandal.

But the University of Cambridge, as a center of espionage, should have remained as a historical anomaly. The Five were members of the upper-class British elite, not infiltrated Russian-trained sleeper agents. After the political turmoil of the 1930s, Cambridge retreated to its traditional role as a quiet backwater dedicated to studying. In my academic career, the only nugget I uncovered on the Cambridge Five was hidden deep within the Mitrokhin Archive[13]. According to Mitrokhin's account, the KGB regarded their recruits' occasional state of drunkenness and amateur tradecraft antics with grave concern. [14] Russians are still bemused today by the British obsession with their

---

[12] Hansard (1955 Parliament meeting), at https://api.parliament.uk/historic-hansard/commons/1955/nov/07/former-foreign-office-officials-1

[13] The papers of the defector and former KGB archivist Vasily Mitrokhin.

[14] From material translated by the author contained in the Mitrokhin Archive.

long-dead spies. A trail of authors heads to Moscow each year in the vain hope of finding something new. The Russians rate Kim Philby, Anthony Burgess, Donald McClean, Anthony Blunt, and John Cairncross much more for their propaganda value as an embarrassment to British intelligence than their covert work. In turn, the British pump out their propaganda; the myth that the Five all died miserably repenting their treachery in their cups.

The sleepy medieval city of Cambridge is a beautiful setting for a fictional spy story because of its historical associations. There is always some whiff of intrigue in the air. But these days it has been reduced to the petty plotting of fierce academic spats fought out at High Table. In academia, where the stakes are very low, and everyone has time on their hands to plot, I have witnessed many long-held grudges and bitter arguments being played out. So when the *Financial Times* reported the fake story in December 2016 of an alleged spy ring operating on Russian president Vladimir Putin's orders at the University, my reaction was "how absurd." No one could even summon the energy to stir themselves to alert the university authorities let alone the security services about the concocted spy ring. [15]

Spies have studied at the University from the Elizabethan days of the playwright Christopher Marlowe. Even the fictional James Bond obtained a First Class degree in Oriental Languages from the University. But it is the unjustifiable spying of the real life American interloper Stefan Halper, which has brought the most shame on the venerable institution. He is the only known foreign spy to penetrate

---

[15] Sam Jones.*"Intelligence experts accuse Cambridge forum of Kremlin links"* (The *Financial Times* December 16, 2016.)

and operate at the University. [16] Cambridge University and bogus professors are forever synonymous with cover for an espionage asset. After recent revelations, anyone introducing themselves as "The name is Bond, Professor Bond" is more dangerous than plain "Bond, James Bond."

John le Carré's spy books sell so well because their plots draw heavily on historical events. The merit of his first dark work, *The Spy Who Came in from the Cold,* was not just that it was authentic, but that it was credible. Le Carré's most famous work, *Tinker, Tailor, Soldier, Spy* is a masterful reworked version of the Kim Philby story. The gritty and squalid tone of the novelist's plots is a credit to the author. Le Carré was an MI6[17], spy whose career was cut short by Kim Philby's betrayal of him. There are many similarities in the fictional plots about George Smiley, Gerald the Mole, the dissolute spy Alec Leamas, and the real Spygate scandal. The black arts and dirty methods spies employ never change. Le Carré's work based as it is on his real-life espionage experience exposes many of them.

A spy is by all accounts the world's second oldest profession. The Old Testament describes the mission of the Twelve Spies (Hebrew: שְׁנֵים עָשָׂר הַמְרַגְּלִים) in the Book of Numbers 13:1–33. A group of Israelite chieftains, one from each of the Twelve Tribes, were dispatched by Moses to scout out the land of Canaan for forty days. They were looking for a future home for the Israelites, wandering in the wilderness following their Exodus from ancient Egypt. It was much later in the twentieth century when what we see today as professional intelligence and counterintelligence services were established. The

---

[16] Halper has been named as a spy by numerous media outlets since being exposed in May 2018. See, Tom Hamburger *"Cambridge University perch gave FBI source access to top intelligence figures — and a cover as he reached out to Trump associates."* (*The Washington Post,* June 5, 2018).

[17] The British secret service.

British invented modern spying just before the start of WWI founding the famous MI6 (or SIS, Secret Intelligence Service), and MI5 (domestic intelligence service). An article in the British tabloid the *Daily Mail's* began a hoax German spy scare, and the government responded by creating a Secret Service. Before the Great War, gentlemen would simply not spy on each other.

It was the czarist-era Russian spy service known as the Okhranka which first perfected the dark arts of spying on political opponents that we see revealed so starkly today. The czar's government deployed "agent provocateurs" to launch disinformation campaigns at home and abroad against his opponents; much of the *Okhranka's* techniques are those used by the CIA in this story. The United States acquired the records of the Paris bureau of the disbanded czarist spies in 1924 and made an exhaustive study of their methods. Helpfully, they later declassified their studies and posted the analysis online.[18]

The mysteries of the Russian intelligence agencies still grip popular imagination. The Communist Revolution was supposed to tear down the structures of the oppressive czarist state but ironically created the most successful intelligence services the world has ever known. The originally planned "temporary commission" or Cheka formed in 1918 evolved into Stalin's feared NKVD[19] and then later the famous KGB. The Soviet achievement of stealing the secrets of the atomic bomb in WWII remains unsurpassed as the greatest espionage feat in history. Although much smaller in size and impact, the Soviet Military Intelligence, known as the GRU, had its fair share of success. The GRU officer Richard Sorge who operated undercover in China and Japan during WWII is Ian Fleming's pick as the world's greatest spy.

---

[18] www.cia.com

[19] The Soviet secret police agency (People's Commissariat for Internal Affairs)

Ian Fleming, who like le Carré worked in espionage, was the creator of James Bond.

The Americans were very slow to the party. The fledgling American colonies and occupying British had deployed spies during the Revolutionary War. The unfortunate young Nathan Hale was one, hanged by the British in New York for spying on behalf of General George Washington. Of course, Washington's spy ring was not a formal organization. But when the United States belatedly embraced intelligence, they soon became the world's biggest and eventually the best. However, the Americans still remain deferential to British intelligence which taught them a crash course in espionage during wartime. America's WWII Office of Strategic Services (OSS) established by "Wild Bill" Donovan became the CIA in 1947. In terms of its history, US spying might be short, but in scale, no other country compares both in success and now scandal.

Despite the end of the Cold War, the collapse of the Soviet Union, and hence its raison d'être, the US intelligence community continued to expand unchecked in size and cost. One critic, General Mike Flynn said, "There is an inherent bias in the intel community because they want to get money, they want to exist, and they want to grow." [20] It is known around the spook trade as "kingdom building". Today, the US spends more on espionage and counter-espionage than the rest of the world combined. In early 2015, retired General Mike Flynn emerged as a potentially credible threat to the continued existence of the CIA.

Gen. Flynn, a former head of the United States military intelligence organization, the DIA[21], gave a series of explosive media interviews

---

[20] Lt. General Mike T. Flynn, https://foreignpolicy.com/2019/12/10/why-the-afghanistan-papers-matter/

[21] Defense Intelligence Agency

delivering a devastating critique of the Agency's many failures in Afghanistan and Iraq. It was not just what General Flynn had said that caused his target, the CIA concern but to whom he was talking. By the summer of 2015, Gen. Flynn began meeting with leading Republican politicians, in particular, the maverick presidential candidate Donald Trump. This was perhaps a meeting "too far" for the CIA leadership; their mission apparently became an effort to stop Gen. Flynn and Donald Trump. Could the response of the CIA's former leadership to their emerging challenge be to launch a covert operation? Did they see the task was not to protect US national security but to preserve the Deep State?

Chapter One: Much Ado about Nothing

And he saith unto them, follow me, and I will make you fishers of men.

—Matthew 4:19

I reserve the right to be ignorant. That's the Western way of life.

—John le Carré, *The Spy Who Came in from the Cold*

On Christmas Eve 1347, King Edward III of England granted Marie de St Pol, widow of the Earl of Pembroke, a license to found a new college, the third in the fledgling University at Cambridge. The University of Cambridge is the second oldest seat of academic learning in the English-speaking world, just a few years more youthful than its fierce rival Oxford. Pembroke was a religious school for training priests, so the founding of the college and the building of the chapel in 1355 required the permission of the Pope. The original name for the seminary was *Custos & Scolares Aule Valence Marie in Cantebrigg* or "The Hall of Valence Mary". The name of the institution finally settled on Pembroke College in 1856.

The founder, Lady Marie, was firmly involved with college affairs. As a strict disciplinarian, she imposed harsh penalties for drunkenness and debauchery. Students were obligated to inform the authorities if they witnessed excessive drinking or if someone was visiting a disreputable house. Given the background of strict historical rules, I can report nothing of such nature occurred around the dinner table in the Master's Lodge on February 28, 2014.

For me, the events of the innocuous evening are fixed forever in two photographs in my possession. Like countless dinners hosted around that same table before, there was no whiff of international scandal or dark political intrigue that evening. I was then an innocent, believing the old men seated around me had long retired from international intrigue. My great mistake was one of youth; to assume these veterans were bereft of ambition, ego, and greed. The host of the party that night was an important character in this tale: Sir Richard Billing Dearlove, KCMG,[22] OBE,[23] Master of Pembroke College. At first glance, like most spies, Sir Richard is an unremarkable man; short, stout and sporting thick glasses. His humble demeanor is his studied art. In the Cold War, Communist counterintelligence agents underestimated Richard Dearlove describing him in reports "as quite clueless, careful, even timid."[24] He has none of those character traits.

Only in some works of fiction are intelligence assets glamorous standouts. Dearlove's position as Master was prestigious, but a non-academic one. The role, a fixed institution dates back 800 years casting a weighty shadow of tradition. The purpose of the office today is ceremonial and Sir Richard Dearlove took his duties very seriously. I recall one formal dinner where he remonstrated with a butler for banging the ceremonial gong incorrectly. Behind his nondescript appearance, Sir Richard Dearlove is the long-retired "C," the former head of MI6, the British CIA. Sir Richard Dearlove was recruited by the Secret Service while studying at the University of Cambridge. Like all British spymasters, he signed his memoranda in green ink—a

---

[22] Knight Commander of the Order of St. Michael and St. George.

[23] Order of the British Empire.

[24] Chris Dyer, *Daily Mail* (March 1, 2020), https://www.dailymail.co.uk/news/article-8061715/How-British-spy-former-MI6-boss-tricked-Soviets-thinking-just-clueless-diplomat.html

tradition established by the first director of the Secret Intelligence Service, Sir Mansfield George Smith-Cumming (the original "C").

Sir Richard was not a career academic but a retired, "highly trained" veteran British spy. He describes himself as a "master of deception."[25] In a long career, he served first in the field, eventually rising in the ranks of Her Majesty's Secret Service to the very top. After being posted behind the Iron Curtain to Prague, Czechoslovakia Sir Richard Dearlove worked in the British embassies in Paris, France and Geneva, Switzerland. In 1991, he became head of MI6's Washington, D.C. station, Britain's most significant intelligence outpost, developing close contacts with the later leaders of US intelligence.

But Sir Richard Dearlove's career ended early and in some eyes, in humiliation. His undoing, by some accounts was, what has become known as the "dodgy dossier,"which provided unverified intelligence on the existence and exaggerated capability of Saddam Hussein's weapons of mass destruction. As the writer le Carré wrote recently during a public spat with Dearlove:

> When the Iraq war came along, I expressed my disgust in an article that was given prominence in the *Times*. I didn't know —but who did?— that raw, single-source, unchecked MI6 intelligence was being passed to Tony Blair, and presumably to George Bush as well, on a regular basis. And that Sir Richard (Dearlove) was instrumental in causing this to happen. To this day, I am told, despite a mountain of evidence to the contrary, he continues to maintain that Saddam Hussein's weapons of

---

[25] Ibid.

mass destruction were the real McCoy. Maybe some distant memory of my article in the *Times* sticks in his craw.[26]

The Dearlove dossier was the catalyst to start the second Gulf War. The ensuing tension with the ruling Tony Blair government ended Sir Richard's career. Rather than enjoying retirement with a starring, monied role in international boardrooms, Sir Richard Dearlove was skulking around Cambridge, giving terrifying lessons to awkward young students on which direction to pass the port at dinner. The British intelligence community expressed unease that their qualified judgments on the existence of Iraq's weapons of mass destruction were presented to Prime Minister Tony Blair by Sir Richard as hard facts. Expecting to face harsh criticism from a lengthy running public inquiry in 2012, Sir Richard Dearlove took a sabbatical from Cambridge University to write an account of events from his perspective at MI6, including coverage of the production of the so-called "dodgy dossier." Sir Richard Dearlove was warning ex-Prime Minister Tony Blair that if he were made the fall guy, he would not go down alone for disseminating the intelligence.

 Sir Richard Dearlove is a very outspoken and, at times, a controversial public figure. [27] Pretending privately the exact opposite, he is a press darling prepared to issue dire warnings both on and off the record. Ahead of the 2017 British general election, he described in newspaper articles the Labour Party leader Jeremy Corbyn, an eccentric radical socialist, as a "danger to national security" who would pose a "present danger to our country" if he became prime minister. If the yesterday's

---

[26] David Wilkes, (*Daily Mail*. October 1, 2019), https://www.dailymail.co.uk/news/article-7527183/John-Le-Carre-hits-ex-MI6-boss-Sir-Richard-Dearlove-branding-spy-books-corrosive.html.

[27] Dearlove is a proponent of Brexit, the UK's exit from the European Union. When allegations swirled that the Russians had influenced the Referendum, he stepped forward to dismiss them.

men in the "Cambridge's Club" led by Dearlove (including most importantly the US intelligence asset Stefan Halper, my former mentor Professor Christopher Andrew and others) simply stuck to venting such opinions at the dinner table, then fine, but they don't; they go further, much further. Secretly, these old men habitually smear those whose political views they oppose as "national security risks" in stark Cold War terms.[28] In 2015 and 2016 some of this Cambridge Club of old men smeared Donald Trump and Gen. Mike Flynn as Russian assets via a backchannel to the delight of the then US authorities.[29] Described by Rep. Devin Nunes as "some type of contract-for-hire spying outfit,"[30] could the Cambridge group's rumors have been seized upon to become "gold dust" intelligence and part of the attempted coup against an elected president and sixty-three million voters?

Standing on historic Trumpington Street a short distance from the iconic King's Parade, Pembroke College occupies the largest land area of any of the thirty-one colleges nestling in the beautiful landscape of Cambridge. Behind the impressive closed gates and walls, within its vast grounds lurk surprises, including a beautiful chapel designed by Sir Christopher Wren and a statue of its most famous alumnus, William Pitt the Younger, the youngest ever British prime minister. Step through its gates, and you will see the treasures within the manicured quads[31] of this medieval masterpiece. The current Master's Lodge, the venue for the ill-fated dinner, is modern by comparison.

---

[28] See for example Mythili Sampathkumar "Former MI6 chief Richard Dearlove says Donald Trump borrowed money from Russia during 2008 financial crisis," (the *Independent* April 4,2017).

[29] Rep. Devin Nunes in conversation with Dan Bongino at CPAC (February 2020).

[30] "Sunday Morning Features" on Fox News (July 28, 2019).

[31] The exquisite lawns are known as quadrangles or quads, for short.

Built in 1937 in faux Gothic style, its walls are adorned with portraits of the Masters of Pembroke since the fourteenth century.

At dinner that night on February 28, 2014, was a highly unusual guest of honor; the serving Head of the US Defense Intelligence Agency. The man was a decorated US combat hero General Michael T. Flynn. Gen. Mike Flynn stood out from the crusty academic crowd. He was a generation younger, informal and friendly and a man of action; the product of a large blue-collar Irish immigrant family of high achievers. No doubt Gen. Flynn was awed, as was the intention by the show of pomp Sir Richard Dearlove laid on for him. From the Latin Grace at the start of dinner to the specially printed menus, nothing was left to chance to woo Gen. Flynn.

Sir Richard Dearlove deployed all his British Secret Service skills and techniques to disarm Gen. Flynn to let his guard down and to make him feel like one of the Club, relaxed, and at home. The Cambridge intelligence group was desperate to keep the flow of funding they received from the DIA over the years. There was a cozy and profitable relationship between the group at the University and the DIA. Gen. Flynn was the key. The elaborate show was put on to raise money. On the table for discussion was a proposal for the US taxpayer to fund a conference in Cambridge that would launch Sir Richard Dearlove's new business venture. If the dinner went well, a lucrative flagship event would go ahead in Cambridge.

Dearlove invited other dignitaries and luminaries of the Cambridge intelligence group to this exclusive private event to help with the plan. There were aged professors and doctors aplenty in the small party around the table. The stand out was the entertaining raconteur Professor Christopher Andrew, Emeritus Professor of Modern and

Contemporary History. Andrew was the ex-official historian of Britain's FBI equivalent MI5. Christopher Andrew is an entertainer. He is full of amusing stories about espionage and history and can be relied on to oil the flow of any conversation, as I know well since he mentored me for twenty years.

There was a problem. In contrast to their vigorous guest, this group was old, borderline ancient. They were all in their seventies, past Cold War dinosaurs holding out-of-date views and seemingly out of touch with modern reality. Gen. Mike Flynn is a reforming radical. He has little time for ancient history; he is a results-on-the-ground guy. The relics around the table would struggle to come up with a view current enough to impress the General. Dearlove invited a smattering of younger researchers to join his party to showcase at least some youth and relevant insights.

I was invited to attend and seated next to the host, Sir Richard which makes me an eyewitness to events. I would love to say that I was seated in this position because I was so important, but it is simply British etiquette. I was the only woman in the group, so according to tradition I sat next to the host. Gen. Flynn was across the table, away from me. As the photographs show[32], the splendid table was filled with white wine glasses, red wine glasses, and coffee cups. From their position on the walls, the past Masters of Pembroke College stared down inscrutably with blank eyes as everyone had a good time.

I must say that I did not want to attend the dinner for a mundane reason. A troublesome student had blighted my whole day. Even in the ranks of privileged undergraduates at Cambridge, there is the odd lazy

---

[32] Available online at www.spygate-exposed.com

and self-entitled buffoon. This particular student played a dumb game with me. Cambridge offers its students solo supervision. The student is supposed to research and write an essay in advance. With a modicum of organization there is plenty of time to accomplish this weekly task. But for the supervisor, the job is poorly paid, less than minimum wage, and a stretch. The student is supposed to submit their work the night before for marking. Well, this dope irritated me the week before by pretending the "dog had eaten his homework" or the electronic equivalent. When his essay arrived, it was just minutes before his supervision. He left the metadata attached to his piece showing he only started working on it two hours before. He produced two pages plagiarized from the work of the chief examiner. At the supervision, the unrepentant soul demanded I tell him the right answer to the question. No chance. I gave him a one-hour life lesson.

The next week on the day of the supervision, no essay arrived. Instead, I received a distressed email from the student while I was on the early train traveling bleary eyed from London to Cambridge. Fearing the worst, I woke up his college head on a very wet, cold February morning and a concerned Dr. Foster, Head of Studies and Deputy Head of Homerton College, cycled five miles to check on the student. It was another stunt. The lazy student had done nothing in preparation for his supervision. I traveled all the way from London to waste a day on a student who did not care. I wanted to go home straightaway but had to attend the dinner. Dr. Foster sat next to me throughout the Gen. Mike Flynn dinner, another eyewitness, to the non-events.

Critical to telling the story of this dinner in 2014 is someone who was not in attendance that evening, the shadowy, US Professor Stefan

Halper.[33] Despite not attending the dinner, Stefan Halper with his long-established connections into the US Department of Defense appears likely to have arranged the event and was certainly copied on all the emails.[34] How Halper later presented a fabricated account of the events of that evening, first to US intelligence and next to the press, is critical in fixing the exact origins of Spygate.[35] The start of Spygate can be traced to the lies that Stefan Halper made up years later about the events that never happened that evening.

Stefan Halper's phony tale was put to me by journalists in March 2017, three years after the event. According to those journalists[36] he claimed to the press in interviews and to the FBI to be an eyewitness to events that simply did not occur and could not have occurred.[37] Despite not attending the event, Stefan Halper stated with authority that he witnessed me approach the Defense Intelligence Agency head, General Flynn, at the start of the evening. He re-characterized the private dinner as a public event. Stefan Halper claimed Gen. Flynn and I sat next to each other at dinner and most outrageously that I left the dinner with the General, traveling with him by taxi and train to London.

---

[33] There is a mountain of evidence that suggests that Halper was not at the dinner including many eye-witness accounts and photographs.

[34] Email is in author's possession.

[35] It has been confirmed to me and others by journalists that Halper was their source. The *New York Times* and *Washington Post* have reported that Halper reported the alleged incident. See, for example, https://www.nytimes.com/2018/05/18/us/politics/trump-fbi-informant-russia-investigation.html.

[36] From the *New York Times, Wall Street Journal and NBC*.

[37] FBI closing report of counter-intelligence investigation into Gen. Flynn dated January 2017 and Department of Justice submission in the case 2020.

The spice in the tale was all that happened on the orders of President Vladimir Putin. Stefan Halper's Cold War–era allegations are worthy of a John le Carré plot. A glamorous Russian spy approaches a top US general and—hey presto!—a romantically fueled conspiracy is unleashed to put a Kremlin puppet into the White House. Halper ended his tall tale with the false claim I could have compromised General Flynn on behalf of Russian intelligence, and specifically military intelligence, the GRU at that.

The truth is I was one of the select few invited to the dinner a month before by Sir Richard Dearlove as someone significant was coming to visit us in Cambridge. I was not told until a week before who the VIP guest was and even when I was informed, I had only a rudimentary idea about the role of the Defense Intelligence Agency. As part of the regular long running Cambridge Intelligence Seminar program, Gen. Flynn first gave a one-hour presentation to the public on the role of the DIA in intelligence affairs. The talk was well attended as everyone involved with the Seminar was instructed to make every effort to fill the room. Gen. Mike Flynn was accompanied by a couple of incongruous shaven-headed security heavies whose tight suits barely concealed their guns and a liaison team.

The public talk took place in the McCrum Lecture Theatre at nearby Corpus Christi College. Gen. Flynn was introduced as a very distinguished guest to the audience by the seventy-five-year-old Professor Christopher Andrew. Andrew gave a brief overview of the general's career, touching on his acts of personal bravery and his role in defeating Al Qaeda. He made one odd comment that sticks in my mind. Andrew remarked that Flynn delighted in being a square peg in a round hole as it was unusual for a serving Intelligence Chief to author a report which was sharply critical of his political master, President Barack Obama.

The General opened his talk by saying how awed he was by all the history of Cambridge before moving on to deliver a masterpiece showcasing the role of the DIA for an hour. He spoke of his vision of the growing global competition for natural resources that, unless addressed, could pose a threat in the future to the security of the United States. Flynn highlighted the importance of intelligence agencies thinking outside the box to find ways to defeat America's enemies. He described the importance of exploiting local intelligence rapidly in winning the battle for hearts and minds. General Flynn was critical of the traditional methods imposing solutions from desks in Washington, thousands of miles away from the sharp end. After questions and a chilly few hundred yards walk, the select few invited to dinner gathered at nearby Pembroke College.

The British Secret Service and American security had cleared each of the guests who attended the dinner weeks in advance. Our names were screened through the many databases the security services have to weed out any hostile threat. It was impossible for a senior figure such as Gen. Flynn to simply turn up at an event to be confronted by goodness knows who. Dearlove had known the members of the group for many years. After such a long period of preparation for this event, there was no security threat or risk at the dinner—from myself or any other attendee.

For a stiff academic event, everyone had a good time. The food was the best the college's kitchens could offer accompanying a very stuffy conversation about world events. The evening passed in a blur. There was one very awkward moment toward the end of the evening when Gen. Flynn and Sir Richard had a falling out. I'm not sure what triggered the sudden heated argument, but the atmosphere suddenly became very tense. At this point, Professor Christopher Andrew broke the ice by suggesting I should show the group a piece of research I recently discovered in the Stalin archive.

As a result of Professor Andrew's attempt to end the argument, I was forced to show the group the historical document I discovered. It was a digital image of a 1912 postcard Joseph Stalin sent from Sweden to his friends in czarist Russia. No one was interested in the classic nude on the picture side of the card; the excitement was to see Joseph Stalin's actual handwriting. It was a piece of historical cognitive dissonance. Everyone knows "Uncle Joe" as the WWII Soviet leader, but this card was written when he was a relatively young man on the run and demonstrating a wicked sense of humor. The postcard was sent to the fiancée of his best friend and contained a coded message that Stalin was safe abroad. Dearlove described the document as "electric."

Why was Mike Flynn, an American general, interested in the old postcard? It transpired that the General was the first serving US intelligence chief to officially visit the Moscow HQ of a Russian intelligence organization in July 2013. Flynn was a guest at what is known in Moscow as "The Aquarium," the headquarters of the GRU. Officially, he delivered a lecture on leadership to the GRU senior echelons. It is likely he was sent by President Obama to begin a dialogue to share intelligence on Chechen terrorists who had just attacked the Boston Marathon.

As was his way, Gen. Flynn befriended Igor Sergun, the GRU Chief and Chechen terrorism specialist. They bonded in Moscow over war stories fighting Islamic terrorism. As part of the official program, Gen. Flynn was taken for dinner at a unique location in Moscow few get to see. "Stalin's apartment" is the height of Soviet elegance at the top of the Sovietsky Hotel. The apartment is a time capsule from the 1950s, although it now boasts a very modern bathroom for guests who book to stay in this piece of history.

At the dinner in Cambridge a year later, Gen. Flynn announced he was hosting a reciprocal visit for the GRU leadership in Washington shortly. He wanted a copy of the postcard emailed to him to surprise his Russian guests. Gen. Flynn did not believe they would ever have seen a document showing a humorous side of Stalin.

At the end of the celebratory and secure dinner, I snatched a memento photograph of the principal guest and his hosts. On schedule, the General was whisked out by his security detail into the cold, dark Cambridge night to be escorted probably to Molesworth military base. Molesworth is a significant US military base in the UK. It is home to three major Command sites: the United States European Command, Joint Intelligence Operations Center Europe Analytic Center, United States Africa Command Intelligence and Knowledge Directorate Molesworth, as well as the North Atlantic Treaty Organization Intelligence Fusion Centre. It is garrisoned by the United States Air Force.

To this day, I have never seen or spoken to General Flynn.

Fixing this dinner as a happy memory is important as the events that flow from it are going to become extraordinary. Remember, we are competing with le Carré in telling the most excellent spy story, except in my case, this story is true.

Chapter Two: Meet the Spy

What do you think spies are: priests, saints, and martyrs? They're a squalid procession of vain fools, traitors too, yes; pansies, sadists and drunkards, people who play Cowboys and Indians to brighten their rotten lives.
— John le Carré, *The Spy Who Came in from the Cold*

Woe unto you, scribes and Pharisees, hypocrites! for ye are like unto whited sepulchers, which indeed appear beautiful outward, but are within full of dead men's bones, and of all uncleanness.
— Matthew 23:27

On May 17, 2018, President Donald Trump started dropping Spygate truth bombs on Twitter: "Wow, word seems to be coming out that the Obama FBI SPIED ON THE TRUMP CAMPAIGN WITH AN EMBEDDED INFORMANT." He continued, "This is bigger than Watergate!"

On May 18, Donald Trump teased out more pertinent facts:

> Reports are there was indeed at least one FBI representative implanted, for political purposes, into my campaign for President. It took place very early on, and long before the phony, Russia Hoax became a "hot" Fake News story. If true— all-time biggest political scandal!

By May 22, 2018 President Trump made this killer point:

> If the person placed very early into my campaign wasn't a SPY
> put there by the previous Administration for political purposes,
> how come such a seemingly massive amount of money was
> paid for services rendered—many times higher than normal . . .
> Follow the money! The spy was there early in the Campaign
> and yet never reported Collusion with Russia because there
> was no Collusion. He was only there to spy for political
> reasons and to help Crooked Hillary win—just like they did to
> Bernie Sanders, who got duped!"

A day later, he followed up succinctly: "SPYGATE could be one of
the biggest political scandals in history!"

President Trump is right. I uncovered evidence that suggests a spy,
perhaps best described as an evil spider, was at work weaving a dark
web in and around his presidential campaign. The spy appeared to
have worked for many months, even years to undermine the campaign
and administration apparently earning a huge taxpayer funded personal
payday. The president was referring of course to Stefan Halper. As he
was under pressure from the intelligence community he stopped short
of naming him.

Donald Trump's tweets rounded off a quite extraordinary two-week
period of fighting in Washington politics even by the standards of
Spygate. Glenn Greenwald wrote in *The Intercept*, the whole farce

revolved around preventing naming "the long-time, highly sketchy CIA operative, Stefan Halper."[38]

Several weeks earlier, House Republicans spotted that the FBI had used an asset to spy on the Trump campaign, and sought to learn more about his activities. The controversy escalated when President Trump joined the fray with his tweets. The DOJ and the FBI quibbled not with the facts, only the language: was Halper a spy or an informer? Most bizarrely opponents of exposing him began using increasingly strident language to warn that exposing his identity would "jeopardize his life and those of others, and also put American national security at grave risk."[39] The extraordinary defense raises multiple red flags when you know they are trying to hide Halper.

Why would *Washington Post* journalist Robert Costa, an ex-student of Halper's, rush to shield his old professor saying he was "a top-secret intelligence source" and citing unknown DOJ officials as arguing the disclosure of his name "could risk lives by potentially exposing the source, a US citizen who has provided intelligence to the CIA and FBI" ?[40] In the same week Christopher Wray, the FBI director, testified before Congress, "informants take great risks when working for intelligence service. Their identities must not be exposed. The day that we can't protect human sources is the day the American people start

[38] Glenn Greenwald, *The Intercept* (May 19, 2018), https://theintercept.com/2018/05/19/the-fbi-informant-who-monitored-the-trump-campaign-stefan-halper-oversaw-a-cia-spying-operation-in-the-1980-presidential-election/

[39] Ibid.

[40] Robert Costa, *Washington Post*, May 8, 2018, https://www.washingtonpost.com/politics/risk-to-intelligence-source-who-aided-russia-investigation-at-center-of-latest-showdown-between-nunes-and-justice-dept/2018/05/08/d6fb66f8-5223-11e8-abd8-265bd07a9859_story.html

becoming less safe."[41] The *New York Times* article implied that Wray's broad statement about the FBI policy relating to the safety of informers was somehow referring to the specific furore raging about Halper.

The top Democrat on the Senate Intelligence Committee, Mark Warner, threatened his own colleagues in Congress with criminal prosecution if they tried to obtain the identity of the informant. "Anyone who is entrusted with our nation's highest secrets should act with the gravity and seriousness of purpose that knowledge deserves."[42] What on earth was this all about; was there a real master spy at risk of exposure and a potential risk to his life?

The episode came to a truly bizarre conclusion one Friday night in May 2018 when the *Washington Post* and *New York Times* made an about-face and published stories to make sure everyone knew the spy's name. Far from those who named him being prosecuted, it is now Halper's extraordinary activity in 2015 and 2016 that is reportedly under criminal investigation.[43]

By hiding Halper's name were the FBI trying perhaps to conceal another scandal? For while Halper was busy weaving his web, the FBI asset was earning a huge, possibly fraudulent, taxpayer-funded payday from Pentagon contracts. At the same time, the Crossfire Hurricane team at the FBI were paying him for his work as well. The Defense

---

[41] https://www.nytimes.com/2018/05/18/us/politics/trump-fbi-informant-russia-investigation.html

[42] Mark Warner, Twitter May 18, 2018, https://twitter.com/markwarner/status/997626543139639298?lang=en.

[43] Sara A Carter, "Durham Probe Expands to Pentagon Office That Contracted FBI Spy Stephan Halper" November 21, 2019.

30

Department contracts apparently form part of several probes according to reports.[44]

Just when did Halper begin organizing his spy work? One possibility is September 2015 when the first lucrative contract was awarded. By that date Donald Trump's campaign was gathering significant momentum to make him the front runner in the race to become the Republican candidate. Although constrained by a strict prohibition on revealing classified information, Rep. Devin Nunes stated on April 11, 2019 that it was "in late 2015, early 2016, spying began on the Trump campaign" and then leaked.[45] Later Nunes said "the first Trump associate to be investigated was General Flynn."[46]

When Halper was finally named in the press as the mysterious FBI asset, did anyone die? No. Could it be all the fuss about concealing the identity of the spy was for a much simpler reason? If anyone looked closely into Halper's background would the Russia hoax be exposed for what it was: a fabricated plot which no-one should have believed? Was the fuss due to the fact that Halper's bogus "intelligence" was the foundation on which the whole Russia investigation was built? After the election the coup plotters and the former leadership of the intelligence organizations invested heavily in the hoax to the extent that the shaky origins had to be forever concealed. By making Halper at the outset a confidential human source for the intelligence service and his product classified, Halper is still cloaked and legally protected to this day. Despite the major role he played in the hoax, Halper has escaped serious media attention owing to his legal status as an

––––––––––––––––

[44] Ibid.

[45] Interview on the Hannity Show (Fox News).

[46] Congressional Record of Special Counsel Robert Mueller

informer. Indeed those who promoted the Russia hoax from within the security services are protected from exposure.

All Washington journalists knew but few would publish as Glenn Greenwald pointed out:

> As it turns out, the informant used by the FBI in 2016 to gather information on the Trump campaign was not some previously unknown, top-secret asset whose exposure as an operative could jeopardize lives. Quite the contrary: his decades of work for the CIA—including his role in an obviously unethical if not criminal spying operation during the 1980 presidential campaign—is quite publicly known. Whatever else is true, the CIA operative and FBI informant used to gather information on the Trump campaign in the 2016 campaign has, for weeks, been falsely depicted as a sensitive intelligence asset rather than what he actually is: a long-time CIA operative with extensive links to the Bush family who was responsible for a dirty and likely illegal spying operation in the 1980 presidential election. For that reason, it's easy to understand why many people in Washington were so desperate to conceal his identity, but that desperation had nothing to do with the lofty and noble concerns for national security they claimed were motivating them.[47]

So why when conducting a highly sensitive investigation did the FBI turn to Halper, who is described as a notoriously dirty political operative with strong intelligence connections associated with a lifetime of scandal and rogue operations? The Crossfire Hurricane

------

[47] *The Intercept* May 19, 2018

team made Halper their chief Russia investigator and even made him a witness for the Mueller investigation into "Russian interference in the 2016 election".

Many media commentators now call Stefan Halper the Walrus owing to his physical appearance.[48] I describe him as "The Spider" based on the famous quote of Sir Walter Scott who in 1808 wrote in his epic poem "Marmion: A Tale of Flodden Field": "Oh, what a tangled web we weave, when first we practice to deceive!" Widely known in Washington swamp circles, seemingly everyone involved in US foreign policy met Stefan Halper— but when asked about him, in my experience these same experts and elite players always look away and quickly change the subject.

No one will dispute, based on the FBI evidence alone, that Stefan Halper is a deceiver. At the very least, he set out to deceive a number of campaign officials by luring them outside the United States and secretly recording conversations—and perhaps deceiving the taxpayers as well. The reported investigations may well ultimately show if any part of Halper's deception was benign. But at present there are dark clouds of suspicion.

Attorney General Barr shared his common sense suspicions about the spying on the Trump Campaign with Congress. He pointed out the obvious disconnect between the resources deployed by the massively equipped and financed intelligence community which were "a single confidential informant [Halper] and a FISA warrant" and the scale of the threat which was no less than the end of the US Constitutional Republic. He concluded "It strikes me as a fairly anemic effort, if that

_____

[48] The Daily Mail for example.

was the counterintelligence effort designed to stop the threat as it's been represented."[49] The investigations apparently come down to answering questions about the mysterious Halper who has seemingly disappeared off the radar except to pop up to viciously attack this author.

The key question this book answers is why was the frontline in fighting the alleged great Russian election threat located not in the United States, but the backwater of the University of Cambridge? At the end of the day it was proved after years of expensive investigation that all the Russian collusion allegations were a huge sham. No Americans were ever charged with collusion, and "Russian" interference was all invented by the investigators. So what was going on in Cambridge?

Halper seemingly not only has the uncanny knack of Forrest Gump to pop up everywhere at the right time but as the *American Spectator,* who once employed him to contribute articles, says "We know from existing press accounts that Halper, who ran a forum for British spies at Cambridge University, had ties to many, if not all, of the sorry players in this London-to-Langley farce."[50]

Distinguished attorney Jonathan Turley, the Shapiro Professor of Public Interest Law at George Washington University, was one of the first to point out in *The Hill* on May 22, 2018, that we are right to have suspicions but also to be concerned about the legal consequences of the reported activities of Stefan Halper. Professor Turley points out that Halper

---

[49] AG William Barr Testimony on Mueller Report Before Senate Judiciary Committee C -Span (May 1, 2019).

[50] George Neumayr, "Who Hired Stefan Halper?" The *American Spectator* August 7, 2018.

was called the "Walrus," but Cambridge University professor Stefan Halper seemed remarkably agile and active in making contacts with Trump campaign officials in the summer and fall of 2016. Indeed, he not only actively consulted with at least three Trump campaign advisers but appears to have sought a position in the Trump administration.

Many media sources revealed at the time of his exposure that Stefan Halper was an informant for both the FBI and CIA for many years.[51] In Jonathan Turley's opinion, Halper's role in the investigation triggered a justified referral by Deputy Attorney General Rod Rosenstein for investigation by the Justice Department inspector general. "The allegations fall into a gray area of Justice Department guidelines which limit 'overt' acts before an election but are ambiguous on covert acts like running the Walrus."[52] That was before the details of his activities became known. Today few would dispute spying did occur.

The reported activities of Stefan Halper remain the subject of several investigations. Jonathan Turley pointed out at least three strong reasons: no one is clear when exactly he started his work; what are the legal implications of using government money both on and potentially off the books to pay a spy to target a political campaign; and finally, was there a political motivation for ordering the intrusive surveillance conducted by Halper into the Trump campaign? These questions remain unresolved.

---

[51] Inspector General Michael Horowitz's report confirmed Halper became a paid informant for the FBI in 2008.

[52] Jonathon Turley, *The Hill* (May 22, 2018), https://thehill.com/opinion/judiciary/388785-FBI-source-in-Russia-probe-raises-alarms-over-political-surveillance

Following the publication on December 9, 2019 of the much-delayed report by Inspector General Horowitz report we still have more questions than answers about Halper. The man has refused to answer any questions. When I attempted to force him to justify his actions against me in a US court, he claimed "sovereign immunity." All Americans irrespective of politics should be concerned by the implications of an administration running a long investigation involving spying into the activities of its opposing party. Many questions about Halper's activities need answering and the probes could well determine if there was a serious problem of abusive tactics.

Establishing the exact date when Halper's work targeting Trump officials was ordered and by whom will prove key to the ongoing criminal investigations. Former FBI Director James Comey has asserted many times that the probe into the Trump campaign did not start until the end of July 2016. That claim is in tatters. My testimony and numerous news accounts continue to push the date earlier and earlier. Even the Deep State plot denier the *Washington Post* reported the conundrum:

> The professor's interactions with Trump advisers began a few weeks before the opening of the investigation, when [campaign foreign policy adviser Carter Page] met the professor at the British symposium.[53]

As John Solomon wrote in *The Hill* in June 2018,

---

[53] Tom Hamburger Robert Costa and Ellen Nakajima. The *Washington Post* "*Cambridge University perch gave FBI source access to top intelligence figures — and a cover as he reached out to Trump associates.*" June 5, 2018.

It [the investigation] originated earlier, 1,700 miles away in London, where foreign figures contacted Trump campaign advisers and provided the FBI with hearsay allegations of Trump-Russia collusion, bureau documents and interviews of government insiders reveal. These contacts in spring 2016—some from trusted intelligence sources, others from Hillary Clinton supporters—occurred well before FBI headquarters authorized an official counterintelligence investigation on July 31, 2016.

My experience with Halper in early 2016 shows that the July 31 date is dead as an official start date of the investigation. Moreover Halper's "interactions" with his next target Carter Page began in June. There must be clarity as to when and why the operation or investigation "opened." Rep. Devin Nunes, ranking member of the House Intelligence Committee, amongst many others, is very clear that the spying began much earlier, at the end of 2015 or at the beginning of 2016. The importance of my story is that by uncovering the true start and extent of Halper's work, which included a false report to the FBI about General Flynn), I do not just contradict James Comey's prior statements but raise new questions as to why the FBI moved so quickly and intrusively against the Trump campaign.

Certainly, a lot of government money was paid to Stefan Halper. The Pentagon Office of Net Assessment alone paid Halper more than $1 million, ostensibly for "research and development in the social sciences and humanities".[54] It was so much money, some of the biggest contracts in its history, it caught the attention of Senator Chuck Grassley. The Senator and now the Defense Department Inspector

---

[54] Office of Net Assessments Contract.

General have been asking questions, and so far, the answers are raising fresh concerns. Halper is apparently "too ill"[55] to answer questions, according to Senator Grassley. If, as perhaps seems likely, the ONA (Office of Net Assessments) contracts are a sham, Professor Jonathan Turley says this has legal implications, not just for Halper but those who paid him.

If Halper was paid hundreds of thousands of dollars as a spy or "informant", as the FBI laughably calls him, it would change how he is viewed. If he was paid as an asset and used to target Trump campaign figures, it reduces the legal justification of the FBI dramatically. There are other notable payments like Halper's payment of $3,000 to George Papadopoulos, a Trump foreign policy adviser. He gave the money and travel compensation to Papadopoulos for a paper on energy issues. However, when Papadopoulos met with Halper in London, he probed the Trump Campaign's political strategy and tried to place a conversation about collusion with Russians on tape. Papadopoulos was clearly viewed as an entry into the workings of the Trump campaign. As this money ultimately came from the FBI, Professor Turley argued this could constitute the use of federal funds to induce a Trump official to be an indirect or direct asset for the investigation.

The most serious legal allegation Professor Jonathan Turley identified is based on Stefan Halper's many efforts to advise the Trump campaign and secure a position in the new administration. If Halper was a longtime paid asset of the FBI and CIA, such a role would be "deeply troubling."[56] Had he been successful, the FBI and CIA would

[55] Sen. Grassley, *Fox News,* December 2019.

[56] Jonathan Turley, *The Hill* (May 22, 2018), https://thehill.com/opinion/judiciary/388785-FBI-source-in-Russia-probe-raises-alarms-over-political-surveillance.

have had a person working with the campaign or even in the administration who was on its covert budget. Even if they stopped paying Halper, it is doubtful he would disclose his prior relationship. Trump officials were unaware of the connection. Professor Turley goes on to say:

> in his meetings, Halper was clearly trying to influence or possibly join the campaign while working with the FBI. At a minimum, Halper met with Trump campaign advisers, including Papadopoulos, Page and former national campaign co-chairman Sam Clovis. Trump economic adviser Peter Navarro reportedly submitted Halper's name for a post during the presidential transition. If the FBI knew Halper was actively seeking a role in either the campaign or the administration, this could be every bit as serious as Trump alleged.[57]

In conclusion, Turley points out that while the liberal media has tended to downplay allegations about Stefan Halper, they are "manifestly serious." The use of a paid FBI asset to target a national campaign in this way would be unprecedented. The closest we have come historically was the allegation in 1980 that aides to Ronald Reagan spied on Jimmy Carter's campaign and obtained confidential documents Carter used to prepare for a debate. As we shall see, while he has denied involvement, one of the aides identified in that operation was Stefan Halper.

Since the publication of Turley's May 22, 2018 article, much more evidence has emerged. Could it be that long before the official start of the 2016 Trump Campaign, Halper began working with others,

---

[57] Ibid.

schemed, lied, and ensnared members of the campaign team in his dark web? Halper might well have sought to trap the eventual winner of the election—the next president—in his web of damaging fables.

Could Halper have played a pivotal role in fabricating and sustaining the fantastical narrative of the Russian hoax? According to several journalists he was their source for stories [58] In 2017, the timing of his leaks about me and Gen. Flynn to journalists could suggest he might have collaborated with the intelligence establishment to take the "kill shot on Flynn,"[59] leaking classified information to his associates in the press to destroy the General's reputation.

Halper's shadowy role is slowly being exposed to the public eye. Could his Achilles' heel be the money trail of outsized payments from US taxpayers? Sen. Grassley is probing these contracts in his efforts to curtail government waste. On November 21, 2019, investigative journalist Sara Carter revealed to Sean Hannity on Fox News that these taxpayer-funded contracts are the focus of the criminal investigation led by United States Attorney for the District of Connecticut, John Durham.

It is vital to get to the bottom of this murky matter as it is possible that CIA Director John Brennan fed Halper's work up the chain of command to President Obama's desk. As former White House officials leaked in 2017, President Obama spoke to Donald Trump in November as follows:

---

[58] Matthew Rosenberg *New York Times* and Rob Barrie in the *Wall Street Journal.*

[59] Filings by Sydney Powell in the Flynn case

Mr. Flynn's name came up during a broader discussion about personnel issues, the former administration officials said. Mr. Obama's concerns about Mr. Flynn, ..But one of the former administration officials said that Mr. Obama was also aware of Mr. Flynn's well-publicized trip in 2015 to Moscow and *other contacts with Russia*.[60] (Emphasis mine)

Jim Acosta of CNN added more spice by reporting:

Obama's concerns were not related to the firing of Flynn from the Defense Intelligence Agency but rather in the course of the investigation into Russian interference into the 2016 election. "Flynn's name kept popping up," according to a senior Obama administration source.[61]

Could it be that the stream of fake "intelligence" from Halper started the FBI investigation that fed into the Mueller inquiry, which found no Russian collusion in the Trump campaign or administration—wasting a further $40 million tax dollars on what turned out to be a hoax? As the president's tweets suggest, Stefan Halper is President Trump's enemy number one.

[60] Michael D. Shear "Obama Warned Trump About Hiring Flynn, Officials Say" New York Times May, 8 2017.

[61] https://www.cnn.com/2017/05/08/politics/obama-trump-michael-flynn/index.html

Chapter Three: Your Liberty under Threat

In this country we have one great privilege which they don't have in other countries. When a thing gets to be absolutely unbearable, the people can rise up and throw it off. That's the finest asset we've got — the ballot box.

—Mark Twain

King Charles: A democracy, Mr. Cromwell, was a Greek drollery based on the foolish notion that there are extraordinary possibilities in very ordinary people.

—Ken Hughes, *Cromwell*

D emocracy is an ancient system of government based on the assumption that power is transferred peacefully following a popular election. In America's constitutional republic, though not a pure democracy, the peaceful transfer of power and voting are still critically important. Today American elections are big business. Officially, Hillary Clinton's unsuccessful 2016 presidential campaign spent $768 million. The Democratic National Convention and other supporters spent further billions to fail. That is an awful lot of promises made and money handed over for no return. For the Washington political aristocracy—the Deep State—the election of an outsider to be their president is a catastrophe. Over generations, they have gathered power to themselves and will not loosen their grip willingly.

"Democracy" first appeared in the ancient Greek city-state of Athens in 508–507 BC. The word derives from the Greek *demos*, meaning "common people" and *kratos*, "strength." The day after democracy was established in a succession of small ancient Greek city-states, the first election fixers appeared. There was a need. The elite fear the decision of ordinary people. Politicians are small in number, derive outsized benefits from governing, and develop a belief over time that they alone have a right to rule others. Election fixers will push a candidate over the winning line. They buy, steal, or cheat elections. The elite embrace them, use them, pay them extravagantly, and when necessary cover for them.

Electoral corruption posed significant problems for the late Roman republic and contributed to its collapse. The benefits of high office were so lucrative, greed led to fierce, competitive, rigged elections. Electoral crimes were known as *ambitus*, and laws were passed trying to eliminate them. But candidates frequently broke the laws restricting spending, even bribing voters directly.

The heyday of election skullduggery was in nineteenth-century England. Many parliamentary constituencies became termed "Rotten Boroughs." Formerly prosperous towns now in decline retained an ancient right to return a Member of Parliament. The few qualifying electors were paid cash or plied with drink to return the "right" man to Parliament. Today we call countries who allow election fixers to stuff the ballot box with false votes "banana republics".

US elections are choreographed following a formal timetable of key events leading up to the crucial November election night results. Elections are about building popular momentum to get the vote out for your candidate and suppress the turnout of your opponent. With only a few swing and battleground states a small proportion of overall voters are key. Politics success requires setting the media agenda and keeping your opponent wrong-footed. Crucial to these efforts are the election fixers. These shadowy figures carry an innocuous title such as "crisis manager" or "communications director" while practicing their dark arts of smears and news manipulation.

Is such a man Stefan Halper in this category? He is an affluent Washington "Swamp dweller," his life has been seemingly steeped for decades in the dirty tricks of politics, espionage, money, and journalism. Based on numerous accounts that have emerged he has long been a go-to man on both sides of the aisle if your campaign required a boost.[62] In 1972 Carl Bernstein, the investigative journalist and author of *All the President's Men*, asked his source "Deep Throat" about President Nixon's election interference, or what he termed "Ratf*cking." "Deep Throat" was puzzled: "Ratf*cking? in my day. . . it meant double-cross…it means "infiltration of the Democrats."[63] In 2016 was Halper the infiltrator, a "double agent" in intelligence speak, targeting the Republican campaign? When he presented himself as a supporter keen to help the campaign and Donald Trump was his true goal working to undermine both?

Stefan ("Stef") Allan Halper was born on June 4, 1944, in Glen Ridge, Essex County, New Jersey. Glen Ridge is and was an affluent, sleepy commuter community outside Newark. His parents were first-generation Russian Jewish immigrants: Stefan, their only child graduated with a Bachelor of Arts from prestigious Stanford University in 1967.

---

62 https://theintercept.com/2018/05/19/the-fbi-informant-who-monitored-the-trump-campaign-stefan-halper-oversaw-a-cia-spying-operation-in-the-1980-presidential-election/

63 Carl Bernstein and Bob Woodward, *All the President's Men* (New York: Simon & Schuster, 1974), 135.

Halper paints and robustly defends, as I know to my considerable cost, a thoroughly respectable picture of himself. There is the veneer of a highly experienced senior White House foreign policy expert, successful businessman, and academic. But a simple internet search brings up plenty of results suggesting that Halper is perhaps not all he seems. Stefan Halper is reported, by a number of first hand accounts, to be a Swamp blowhard.

According to an old interview, the future FBI informer very early on developed his uncanny ability to be in all the right places at just the right time. Or so he claims. Let's look at one example. Following graduation from Stanford, Halper obtained a Doctorate of Philosophy in 1971 from prestigious Oxford University, England. By fortuitous happenstance, Halper was a contemporary with one William Jefferson Clinton. The future President was a Rhodes Scholar at Oxford. The charismatic, party-loving young Bill Clinton was an anti-Vietnam war activist.

Given Clinton and Stefan Halper's widely different political philosophies, it would seem unlikely their paths crossed at Oxford. But apparently, they did. The then left-wing rebel, Clinton, a party animal, was unlikely to remember the watching presence of Halper. But Halper seemingly squirreled away damning observations of Bill Clinton for future use.

In an interview on August 14, 2004, with R. Emmett Tyrrell for his book *The Clinton Crack-Up: The Boy President's Life after the White House,* Halper came out of the shadows and put his name to a piece of gratuitous Bill Clinton poison. Clinton was no longer president; there was no point in the attack. Halper positioned himself as an eyewitness of Bill Clinton's student activities in England some thirty-five years earlier. Stefan Halper's trademark style in these attacks is to provide no actual evidence to support his accusations.

> One sees the pattern beginning at Oxford in the 1960s where he [Clinton] partied, "networked," traveled to foreign parts [behind the Iron Curtain to Czechoslovakia and the Soviet Union], squandered time in bull sessions, and wasted Rhodes scholarship money in politicking. His last year was spent mainly in London organizing demonstrations against American foreign policy, a favored tactic being to scatter marbles beneath the hooves of police horses and enjoy the equine mayhem. Then it was back to Oxford and a feverish round of negotiations with professors for his degree and pulling every available string with the administrators. All failed, and he became the rare Rhodes Scholar to leave without a degree.[64]

In the interview, Halper claims to have been on the spot as a fellow student to witness and years later talk about ex-President Bill Clinton's doings. Stefan Halper uses his trademark long, clunky sentences to level layers of increasingly serious accusations against the former president. Did Bill Clinton maim British police horses? I doubt it. Stefan Halper's account is long on hyperbole and short of any actual evidence. But when he later deployed similar political dirty tricks against the Trump campaign using the same tone and approach, we will see the gambit was devastatingly effective not least the false "eyewitness" account Halper gave the FBI about General Flynn and me!

---

[64] R. Emmett Tyrrell, *The Clinton Crack-Up: The Boy President's Life after the White House* (Nashville: Thomas Nelson, 2007)

Was Stefan Halper studying at Oxford University by accident or design? Could Halper have begun his career as an intelligence agency informer at Oxford? (He would not be the first. John le Carré worked for British counterintelligence in 1952 and was sent to Lincoln College, Oxford, to spy on left-wing groups.) In June 1969, President Nixon directed the CIA to report on the growing anti–Vietnam War movement. Suspicious Nixon wanted to know what foreign communist support the demonstrators might be receiving.

The CIA launched an operation codenamed CHAOS, which remained in effect until 1974. The spying directly violated the Agency's charter. The charter, created in 1947, reflects the constitutional principle that American citizens are entitled to a high degree of personal privacy. The CIA mandate is to focus its counterintelligence efforts on overseas targets only. The goal of "Operation CHAOS" was to establish proof of foreign influence on American protest movements at Universities. Initially, the CIA deployed agents to universities across the United States, including Stanford, where   Stefan Halper was enrolled.

The agents infiltrated the "New Left," learning the culture and lingo of the movement. Once successfully infiltrated in the US, the agents deployed to foreign universities. In their work, the agents collected the names of more than 300,000 American citizens, including Bill Clinton. The operation was an expensive failure. The CIA reported to the White House there was "very little evidence of communist funding and training of such [protest] movements and no evidence of communist direction and control."[65]

_____

[65] https://www.history.com/news/cia-surveillance-operation-chaos-60s-protest

In a planned operation toward the tail end of the 1992 presidential election, the media was suddenly full of negative stories about Bill Clinton's Oxford days. In particular, the story focused on "the strange case of Mr. Clinton's trip to Moscow." The origin of the stories were the usual vague "intelligence sources" we are so familiar with today. The timing of the "intelligence"coved in media reports just three weeks before the election -was an "October surprise."

The intelligence operation had a significant impact on the first presidential television debate. The polite, patrician Mr. Bush first raised his concerns in an attack on the *Larry King Show*. Mr. Clinton should "level with the American people on the draft, on whether he went to Moscow, how many demonstrations he led against his own country from foreign soil. I don't have the facts, but to go to Moscow one year after Russia crushed Czechoslovakia, and not remember who you saw—I think the answer is, level with the American people."[66]

Mr. Bush repeated the attack in a live debate rattling candidate Bill Clinton. But Bush lacked the political instinct to go in for the kill. Clinton dodged the bullet that night. But for the first time in the contest, the Clinton campaign team was wrong-footed by an attack from the Bush campaign. "It's a pathetic ploy by a desperate politician,"[67] Mr. Clinton's spokesman said which translates as *That really hurt.*

According to the *Los Angeles Times* it was James Baker III, Bush's Chief of Staff, who was instrumental in organizing the attack on Bill

---

[66] "Patriotism Attack Was Hatched in Oval Office: Campaign: Congressmen urged Bush to raise questions on Clinton war protests and a visit to Moscow." by Jack Nelson Los Angeles Times October 9, 1992

[67] https://www.theguardian.com/world/1992/oct/09/usa.martinwalker

Clinton. Baker ran the unsuccessful Bush 1980 campaign that Halper worked on. Bush was told he could "kill Clinton, politically"[68] if he would hammer him on the issue of the Arkansas governor's efforts to avoid the draft and his visit to Moscow as a twenty-three-year-old Rhodes scholar. I hypothesize that in 1992 Halper was unlikely to keep silent about his Clinton yarns. Politics can be a dirty business as Halper later told Carter Page.

---

[68] ibid

Chapter Four: Blowhard

And every one that heareth these sayings of mine, and doeth them not,
shall be likened unto a foolish man, which built his house upon the
sand;
and the rain descended, and the floods came, and the winds blew, and
beat upon that house; and it fell; and great was the fall of it.

—Matthew 7:26-27

"You could be the perfect spy. All you need is a cause."

—John le Carré, A Perfect Spy

I n reconstructing Stefan Halper's life, there are problems in getting
to the truth: Stefan Halper appears to lie, bully, and blackmail.
Journalists researching his background after his exposure in May 2018
published revealing portraits of Halper. On August 7, 2018, the
American Spectator who used to commission Halper to write for them
gave this description of Halper:

> TAS [the American Spectator] has spoken to old colleagues of
> Halper and they describe him as "bumptious," a "blowhard,"
> and "an avaricious fraud" who entered the Deep State through
> a door opened by his father-in-law at the CIA, Ray Cline. After
> Halper behaved foolishly during the 1980 Reagan campaign,
> he tried to get a job in the new administration. But initially he
> couldn't; Reagan aides had sized him up as a jackass. Halper

persisted and eventually nabbed a phony-baloney position in the State Department. But say this for Halper: he knows how to wedge his finger into DC's pies. The Walrus scented a final meal in the 2016 campaign. He assumed Hillary (whom he endorsed in press reports while simultaneously spying for the Obama administration against her opponent!) would win and reward him with a new gusher of Deep State cash.[69]

If you challenge what appear to be Halper's lies as I have, he attacks. Stefan Halper appears based on the reported evidence to have based his whole life on a foundation of embellishments, half-truths, and whoppers. Halper is fuzzy about dates and appears to inflate his job titles. As the *American Spectator,* who know him well, reported, Stefan Halper is a known professional deceiver working the Swamp money-go-round.

In his intelligence career the legendary spy writer le Carré encountered such deceivers.—One such rogue was the model for his character Magnus Pym, in his novel *The Perfect Spy*. There is much of the fictional deceiver Magnus Pym in the real-life character of Stefan Halper:

> The portraits reveal Pym as a man who for so long has manipulated his appearance to those closest to him that, in the end, he was unable to hold together the conflicting personae

---

[69] George Neumayr, "Who Hired Stefan Halper?" *American Spectator* (August 7, 2018).

within him. Magnus Pym has been a perfect spy but at the cost of his soul.[70]

I have found time and again in my research that spies and informers are not the glamorous figures depicted in movies; they are squalid professional deceivers. Sometimes they betray their own country, but mostly they betray their friends and acquaintances for money. The intelligence community embraces such dubious characters. In return these informers describe themselves as "patriots" forgetting to say they did it for money.

In the 1930s, Stalin's Secret Service fell victim to a fraudster named Ludwig Lore. Just like Halper, Ludwig Lore was an American newspaper writer, lecturer, and politician. Both Lore and Halper wrote columns on foreign affairs. Lore wrote "Behind the Cables" for the *New York Post.* For the Soviets, accurate political intelligence proved harder to acquire than science and technology. Without reliable sources, the information they acquired was either biased or in some cases downright false. An early large-scale NKVD operation in the 1930s, based in New York and Washington, turned out after many years and a detailed investigation to have relied on a completely fake source. The enterprising *New York Post* journalist, Ludwig Lore, created a family industry producing political information for the NKVD by employing his son and wife in the enterprise. The NKVD were entirely taken in.

Lore claimed his intelligence reports came directly from a network of well-placed agents in the State Department in Washington, even insisting the State Department's head of research, David A. Salmon,

---

[70] https://www.amazon.com/-/es/JOHN-CARRE/dp/B001VAW8PI

was his principal agent. In reality, none of Lore's agents existed. He plucked names from the internal phone directory of the State Department.

Lore was nevertheless able to charge the NKVD exorbitantly for several years for the information he provided, which consisted either of old news stories reheated or pure invention. Without checking, the NKVD had already put some of the fake material on Stalin's desk, describing it as "must read." Stalin believed he was reading the very words of America's ambassador to Tokyo, Joseph Grew, in private meetings with the emperor's top officials. It was nothing of the sort; Lore made up the entire conversation.

Stefan Halper never seems to correct the false impressions others may have formed about him from the information he has provided. A straightforward example is, despite all the press scrutiny, no one has spotted that Stefan Halper is not and has never been a professor of the University of Cambridge. Observers form that impression and it has become, through his artifice, his cover.

Like the fictional Baron Munchausen, perhaps tale-telling comes naturally to Stefan Halper but he appears to get angry and aggressive when challenged. According to video evidence, his response to close questioning is bluster, anger, and spin. Halper claims a charmed life, an impressive pedigree moving from glittering academic success at Oxford University to a series of vitally essential jobs with rapid promotions to senior positions at the White House. Next, a highly successful business career followed by success as a top academic. But the results of research suggest that he perhaps embellished and exaggerated it all.

If one starts scratching the surface of Halper's life, it is clear wherever Halper goes, he seemingly collects scandals like some people collect sports cars or postage stamps. I believe there has never been an academic at the University of Cambridge, whose resume includes such accomplishments as an arrest for possession of crack cocaine[71] or being sued for bank fraud.[72] Halper and his first wife were rescued from the middle of the Mozambique civil war in the late 80s by soldier of fortune Robert MacKenzie[73].

Halper has even already appeared in front of a Special Counsel[74] investigating election interference. And that's all before you get into the exciting stuff. Halper claims in a government document, "he has served four American presidents in the White House and Department of State and is an expert on US foreign policy, national security policy."[75] The statement sounds impressive. But it seems at best an exaggeration. In an age before Google made internet searches easy and archives were digitalized, inconsistencies in his CVs[76] might have gone unnoticed. But not now, not today.

What is true is Halper, although he denies it, apparently boasts an extraordinary pedigree in the world of political dirty tricks. Political dirty tricks and intelligence disinformation operations are two sides of the same coin. Halper joined Nixon's White House in 1971, having

---

[71] Virginia Court Records, July 11, 1994.

[72] Virginia Court Records, January 19, 1990.

[73] https://en.wikipedia.org/wiki/Robert_C._MacKenzie.

[74] Martin Tolchin, "House Votes to Investigate 'October Surprise,'" *New York Times* (February 6, 1992).

[75] Office of Net Assessment; "China: Three-Warfare Study" (May 2013), https://cryptome.org/2014/06/prc-three-wars.pdf

[76] *Curriculum vitae* ("course of life")

obtained a doctorate from Oxford University, England.[77] He claims to have arrived at the White House just in time to observe firsthand the whole Watergate fiasco unwind.

Halper claims his first job was as a member of the White House Domestic Council. Later in 2013, Stefan Halper needed to boost the book sales of his deep credentials as a China commentator. He claimed, and it is recorded on video at a book promotion at Wellesley College[78], he first traveled to China in 1971 to set up Nixon's groundbreaking trip the next year. In his book *The Beijing Consensus*, Halper makes no mention of this extraordinary claim. Why did he forget to put his contribution to the historic moment in his book? I hypothesize that perhaps it didn't happen.

Instead, in his book, he says that as a junior staff member, he was excited *by hearing the news* of the trip. In the same video Halper claims to have visited China thirty-one times, but in his book he makes a more modest claim of twenty visits.[79] This might all seem minor but remember whoever hired Halper to investigate the Russia hoax might have or should have known they were recruiting someone with a potentially criminal past,—a braggart who exaggerates, certainly distorts, and maybe outright lies.

The entry-level position Stefan Halper describes in the White House was an ideal platform for an aspiring, ambitious conservative politician. He was undoubtedly in the right place to learn the ugly, dirty side of politics, the pursuit of power at any cost. In 1971 going

---

[77] CV of Stefan Halper, Department of Politics and International Studies University of Cambridge

[78] "Legitimating Authoritarianism in Our Time," (October 23, 2013), https://www.youtube.com/watch?v=2ljks9Mat_M.

[79] Stefan Halper, *The Beijing Consensus: How China's Authoritarian Model Will Dominate the Twenty-First Century* (New York: Basic Books, 2010).

into the presidential election, Richard Nixon was popular with the broader population despite the war in Vietnam.

Stefan Halper's CVs he published later online claims he served in the White House Domestic Council under President Nixon and then-President Gerald Ford from 1971 to 1973. If this is true, his first boss would have been John Ehrlichman, Assistant to the President for Domestic Affairs. Ehrlichman was a key figure in events leading to the Watergate break-in and the ensuing Watergate scandal. He was convicted of conspiracy, obstruction of justice, and perjury, and served a year and a half in prison.

Nixon won a landslide victory in the 1972 presidential election. But later, it emerged that during the campaign, the president's operatives conducted illegal and, as it transpired, unnecessary clandestine missions designed to infiltrate and undermine the Democratic Party. Nixon recruited his own personal "dirty ops" team to his campaign payroll. "Tricky Dickie" used the team obsessively to surveil his political opponents from both the Democrat and Republican parties.

His operatives were mostly ex-CIA men who gathered scandalous information on opponents, distributed black propaganda to the press, bugged offices, and even staged break-ins.[80] One such operation was the bungled break-in of the Democratic National Committee Headquarters at the iconic Watergate Building. One of five burglars arrested was E. Howard Hunt, an old China days colleague of Dr. Ray S. Cline, Stefan Halper's father-in-law and ex-Deputy Director of the CIA.

The failed break-in gave rise to a congressional investigation. Nixon denied any involvement in the operation. A tape emerged, revealing the president knew about the White House connection to the Watergate

---

[80] Bob Woodward and Carl Bernstein, *All the President's Men* (New York: Simon & Schuster, 1974).

burglaries shortly after they occurred. The House of Representatives initiated impeachment proceedings and upon the urgings of Vice President Ford, Nixon resigned.

Nixon was a devious political operator and staged the original and best "October surprise" in the 1972 contest with Democrat George McGovern. The United States was in the fourth year of protracted negotiations with its Communist opponents to end the very long and domestically divisive Vietnam War. On October 26, 1972, twelve days before the election on November 7, the United States' chief negotiator, the then-presidential National Security Advisor Henry Kissinger, appeared at a press conference held at the White House. He announced, "We believe that peace is at hand."

Nixon vowed to end the unpopular war during his presidential election campaign four years earlier but failed to cease hostilities. Kissinger's "peace is at hand" declaration was an "October surprise," a spectacular news event to increase the incumbent Nixon's already high standing with the electorate. The timing is crucial. The news has to be delivered close to polling day for maximum impact. In the event, Richard Nixon triumphed, outpolling his opponent McGovern in every state except Massachusetts and achieved a twenty-point lead in the nationwide popular vote. Nixon laid down a challenge for future political operators to emulate.

After President Richard Nixon's resounding election triumph, Stefan Halper claims to have transferred internally into the White House Office of Management and Budget. He claims between 1973 to 1974 he was an assistant director, Management, and Evaluation Division. The title is maybe an exaggeration based on later records.[81] From sometime in 1974 to January 20, 1977, he claims he served in the

---

[81] US government archives at https://www.archives.gov

White House Office of the Chief of Staff as Assistant to the Chief of Staff.

He describes his responsibilities as creating a "summary and analysis of foreign developments and security issues."[82] Stefan Halper next claims to have worked as an assistant to three Chiefs of Staff—Alexander Haig (until September 21, 1974), Donald Rumsfeld (from September 21, 1974, to November 20, 1975), and Dick Cheney (from November 20, 1975, to January 20, 1977).

Yet a host of documents dated in 1976 and readily available online in the US government archives at https://www.archives.gov apparently throw a good deal of shade on Stefan Halper's alleged prestigious White House career.[83] The records show Halper held only a very junior White House position for a very short time. A document prepared for the transition from the outgoing President Ford to President Carter records that Stefan Halper was appointed as a consultant to the Communications Department only on May 17, 1976, and given a permanent appointment on August 8, 1976.[84] He was eventually named a staff assistant in the White House Communications Department. Maybe there are mistakes in these documents but if they are true records Halper did not hold the glamorous role he claims as assistant to three White House Chiefs of Staff.

One document in the archive is the President's Diary is titled *"Photo Opportunity with Office of Communications Staff, The Oval Office December 16, 1976."* Demonstrating how junior he was in the pecking order in a long list of people listed by importance, Stefan Halper is in the last line but one from the bottom. His title is recorded as Staff

---

[82] https://www.iwp.edu/faculty/stefan-halper/

[83] Ibid.

[84] Ibid.

Assistant which is certainly not a senior foreign policy advisor role.[85] It seems Halper's position was working as one of the editors of a 500-page eulogy of the first two years of the Gerald Ford presidency published in August 1976. The official records seem to suggest his entire White House career lasted just a few months as a consultant and then six months as a staff assistant. Stefan Halper was scathingly critical of the patterns of Bill Clinton's behavior, so maybe we should be too of Halper's lying.

---

[85] https://www.fordlibrarymuseum.gov/library/document/0036/pdd761216.pdf

Chapter Five: Dr. Ray S. Cline

"Verily, verily, I say unto you, The servant is not greater than his lord; neither he that is sent greater than he that sent him."

—John 13:16

"You don't buy photographs from Otto Leipzig, you don't buy Degas from Signor Benati, follow me?"

—John le Carré, *Smiley's People*

T he making of Stefan Halper's political and espionage career began in earnest in 1976 with his fortuitous marriage to the headstrong firebrand Sybil Cline, daughter of CIA legend and State Department Head of Intelligence Dr. Ray S. Cline. Halper has exploited Cline's intelligence connections to this day. Wherever Cline went, Halper always turned up like a bad penny. Halper seems to have wanted to emulate his father-in-law, to be a second Ray Cline, an intellectual super spy, but he has nowhere near the charisma or talent.

Cline's influence is still felt today. He was credited in 2018 by the New York Times with inventing the CIA's handbook of electoral interference in an article headlined "Russia Isn't the Only One Meddling in Elections. We Do It, Too."[86] According to the article the

---

[86] "Russia Isn't the Only One Meddling in Elections. We Do It, Too." New York Times Scott Shane February 17, 2018. Cline's name was removed from the original article in an update.

classic CIA methods include "breaking into party headquarters, recruiting secretaries, placing informants in a party, giving information or disinformation to newspapers." How many of these techniques, updated for technological innovation were employed in 2016?

Cline rewarded his son-in-law's devotion with jobs in politics,[87] positions in prestigious think-tanks and directorships of CIA-related organizations.[88] Halper performed various tasks in return. Long after Cline's death CIA loyalists continue the tradition of treating and protecting Halper as one of their own. Ray Cline is apparently the mastermind who helped invent the CIA manual of political dirty tricks and electoral interference.

The wedding of Halper with Cline's daughter took place on November 9, 1976, in glamorous St. Thomas, US Virgin Islands. The couple later divorced on January 6, 1989. The ceremony was just a week after the presidential election that saw the Democrat Governor Jimmy Carter sweep to power. With the defeat of President Ford in the 1976 election, Halper was out of a job and had to find work outside the White House. From 1977 to 1979, he was a Congressional aide to Senator William Roth and Special Counsel to the Joint Economic Committee. Thanks to his link to his new father-in-law, Halper was mixing socially and networking with the CIA nobility. Stefan Halper boasted throughout his life of this great connection to Ray Cline.

Ray S. Cline is a commanding, bordering on legendary figure in the US intelligence community. Cline joined the Office of Strategic Services in the middle of World War II and became Chief of Current

---

[87] *Washington Post; The American Spectator*

[88] www.CIA.gov

Intelligence in 1944. He worked in China with many of the most famous OSS officers, such as John K. Singlaub, Richard Helms, E. Howard Hunt, Paul Helliwell, Robert Emmett Johnson, and Lucien Conein.

Cline's career-long fascination with the strategic importance of China rubbed off on Stefan Halper, who has positioned himself as a China expert for a decade.[89] In 1946, Ray Cline was assigned to the Operations Division of the General Staff of the United States Department of War, tasked with writing the history of the Operations Division.

Ray Cline joined the newly created Central Intelligence Agency in 1949. He was responsible for developing intelligence on the situation in Korea, but he failed to predict North Korea's 1950 invasion of South Korea. From 1953 to 1957, Cline was the CIA desk officer charged with monitoring the Soviet Union and the People's Republic of China. He correctly predicted the Sino-Soviet split. In 1958 he became chief of the CIA station in Taiwan, with his official title being Chief of the United States Naval Auxiliary Communications Center.

In 1962, Cline moved to CIA headquarters in Washington, DC, as head of the CIA's Directorate of Intelligence, the Agency's analytical branch. Cline played a crucial role in the Cuban Missile Crisis. Under Cline's leadership, the Directorate of Intelligence concluded that the Soviet Union shipped nuclear warheads to Cuba. Cline was among those who informed President John F. Kennedy of this development. Cline remained head of the Directorate of Intelligence until 1966 when

---

[89] Halper neither reads or speaks Chinese.

President Lyndon B. Johnson passed him over to appoint an outside director of the CIA.

Cline was furious at the snub and determined to leave the CIA. His old friend Richard Helms intervened to have him posted as Special Coordinator and Adviser to the United States Ambassador to Germany in Bonn. In 1969, Cline returned to the United States when President Richard Nixon nominated him to the State Department as Director of the Bureau of Intelligence and Research and he subsequently held this office from October 26, 1969, until November 24, 1973. In this capacity, he oversaw US intelligence in the build-up to the Yom Kippur War.

On leaving government in 1973, Dr. Ray S. Cline, an Oxford University graduate, set out successfully to make a fortune in the private intelligence sector by being among the first to integrate business with espionage. Cline was among the first to realize there was big money to be made in scaring American business about communist threats and offering commercial presidential-style intelligence briefings to boardrooms. His consultancy model has grown to be a huge industry that surrounds, advises, and consults the US intelligence community to this day.

Cline is criticized in *Rollback!: Right-wing Power in US Foreign Policy* by Thomas Bodenheimer and Robert Gould for developing extreme right-wing connections at home and abroad. He built a network of ex-Agency professionals many from the cowboy early days of the Agency whom he employed in various enterprises. Cline founded the highly successful "think tank" model with the creation of the Center for Strategic and International Studies (CSIS) at Georgetown University, Washington. CSIS's purpose is to define the future of national security and is the number one think tank in the US Advice from ex-intelligence professionals to companies soon crossed into political lobbying, blurring the lines, if they ever existed between intelligence and politics.

Edward S. Herman wrote in his book *The "Terrorism" Industry* that Cline was an outspoken proponent of the use of disinformation and even the direct manipulation of the US press by the CIA. Press communication is Halper's skill-set. In testimony before the House Select Committee on Intelligence, Cline defended the Agency's extensive use of such covert devices as "black propaganda" and saw nothing wrong in the funding and control of friendly journalists by government spy agencies to get its message to the American people. Most famously he argued, "the First Amendment is only an amendment"[90] and as the end justifies the means, it is fine for the intelligence community to work around constitutional protections.

 Despite his known CIA background, extensive connections with the extreme right at home and abroad, his open disregard for free speech and the rules of evidence, and the heavily propagandistic character of his writings, Cline was a frequent guest on liberal TV channels such as ABC's *Nightline*, speaking on the subject of terrorism and defending the US government's use of Nazi war criminals as missile scientists.[91]

Until Spygate, many had forgotten how historically, agencies work hand-in-glove with the press. We are shocked to see how the intelligence services manipulated the public to promote the Russian hoax. The campaign was sophisticated, prolonged, and effective.

---

[90] Obituary for Ray S. Cline, *New York Times* (March 16, 1996).

[91] Cline's October 18, 1984 appearance on *Nightline* as noted in Edward S. Herman's *The "Terrorism" Industry* (New York: Pantheon Books, 1989), 151.

Above all it was brazen. Once one understands the big picture that the press was selling a narrative, it becomes easier to join the dots in the open source material. The media stories poisoned the minds of a broad section of American public opinion.

Into this fog of war, the apparent coup plotters John Brennan, James Clapper and James Comey gave extensive interviews feeding information and disinformation into the public arena. The spikes in this media activity correspond with key moments in the evolving plot against Donald Trump. Track the plotters and their interviews with the chronology and the whole plot is revealed.

Switch on your cable news and you see an array of ex-professional intelligence people employed as contributors. The Fourth Estate has wholeheartedly embraced spooks. It is one of the stranger alliances formed during Spygate between liberal journalists and some in the security services who are more naturally opponents. After the Watergate scandal, the manipulation of the press by elements of the security services was exposed to the public eye through the work of the Church Commission. It was supposed to stop.

The Bush Connection
Dr. Ray Cline's, ex-CIA Deputy Director and Stefan Halper's strongest connection was to the future vice president and later President George H. Bush. The pair shared a deep passion for the CIA. In 1979 George H. Bush ran as a Republican presidential candidate. Dr. Cline immediately joined the Bush campaign as a top foreign policy and defense adviser. The campaign team had a strongly, almost alarming spooky feel.

"Simply put, no presidential campaign in recent memory—perhaps ever—has attracted as much support from the intelligence community as the campaign of former CIA director Bush."[92] The intelligence community's support for George Bush's campaign has only been eclipsed by the support for Hillary Clinton in 2016. There were so many ex-CIA and intelligence community notables attached to the Bush campaign one supporter commented: "It's sure as hell not a CIA coup or anything like that."[93]

George H.W. Bush had a deep passion for the CIA describing it as "part of my heartbeat."[94] He is the only president who ever ran the Agency. The CIA headquarters at Langley, Virginia bears his name. He believed in the CIA Cold War code: "Admit nothing, deny everything."[95]

Prior to Bush, a politician, the Agency was headed by intelligence professionals or military men. In January 1976 the CIA was under attack and "a quarter-century of dirty secrets were spilling out as Congress combed through its secret files following the Watergate scandal and the revelation the CIA spied on Americans in violation of its charter." [96]

It was a terrible time for the nation's spies. The *Washington Post* goes on to say, "Bush spent much of his energies during his 11 months as

---

[92] Bill Peterson and Ronald White, "Coming in From the Cold, Going Out to the Bush Campaign," *Washington Post* (March 1, 1980).

[93] Ibid.

[94] Tim Weiner, "Bush practiced a CIA omerta that may have died with him," *Washington Post* (December 3, 2018).

[95] Ibid.

[96] Ibid.

Director battling senators. They uncovered the existence of assassination plots, secret wars, antidemocratic coups, and mind-control experiments using LSD on unwitting human guinea pigs."[97] Bush decried these revelations saying, "they devastated the morale of perhaps the finest group of public servants this country has." After Jimmy Carter was elected president in November 1976, Bush was sacked.

Only the ex-CIA Deputy Director Dr. Ray Cline, now a Washington think tank dweller, a resident of the Swamp, was a stauncher defender of the CIA than Bush. Cline founded and became the first director of the Center for Strategic and International Studies at Georgetown University. Today CSIS is still the Washington "think tank" of choice for the CIA. Cline's career was the prototype for all ex-spies now teaching at leading universities. There are a surprisingly large number.

I can only hypothesize that Stefan Halper seemingly sought to emulate Cline throughout his life. With apparently far less talent, Stefan Halper plodded along the path Cline blazed. Cline was delivering pro-CIA lectures on college campuses around the country and elsewhere since 1973 when he left the government in disgust "over what they were doing to the intelligence agencies."[98]

For years post-Watergate he was heckled at almost every stop. "I don't get any heckling now. I'm quite popular," he says. "I found there was a tremendous constituency for the CIA in the sticks when everyone in Washington was still urinating all over it."[99] Bush turned to his old

---

[97] https://www.history.com/topics/us-government/history-of-mk-ultra
https://www.cia.gov/library/readingroom/document/cia-rdp81-00261r000300050003-5

[98] Peterson and White, "Coming in From the Cold, Going Out to the Bush Campaign."

[99] Ibid.

CIA pals when he began pulling his team together for his presidential run:

> Cline, Wilson, Aaron, and Gen. Richard Stillwell, once the CIA's chief of covert operations for the Far East, are considered top-level advisers on foreign policy and defense matters. Cline's role is probably the most important here. He organized groups of experts for Bush to meet with and frequently talks with the candidate. Cline recommended his son-in-law, Stefan A. Halper, a former Nixon White House aide, be hired as Bush's director of policy development and research.[100]

The appointment to the Bush campaign was apparently Stefan Halper's great opportunity. Thanks to his family connection to Ray Cline, he was launched firmly into the Bush dynasty's political orbit, and he was determined to stay there.

Halper's role in the George H. Bush campaign was according to contemporary accounts ostensibly policy communications with the press. Once on the campaign trail, George Bush's star was eclipsed by that of the eventual winner—the Californian populist Ronald Reagan. George H. Bush eventually conceded when Ronald Reagan won sufficient Republican delegates to clinch the nomination.

According to one source, it was Halper who fielded the first late evening call from the Reagan team at the Republican convention inviting George H. Bush to join the Reagan ticket as Vice President.[101]

---

[100] Ibid.

[101] Richard V. Allen, "George Herbert Walker Bush; The Accidental Vice President," *NYT* (July 30, 2000). Halper was one of two Bush people Allen contacted to leave a message.

Halper was appointed the National Director, Policy Coordination for the Reagan-Bush 1980 presidential campaign.

George H. Bush was not Reagan's first pick as a running mate. Ronald Reagan went through many rounds of negotiation with ex-president Gerald Ford before selecting the Bush option. But coming out of the convention, Reagan trailed the incumbent President Jimmy Carter by a considerable margin in opinion polls and added a moderate to the ticket. Reagan overturned the most significant poll deficit since Gallup polling began in 1936 and went on to win. It was his impressive performance at the debate that turned the election in his favor.

Russiagate Rehearsal?

"Debategate" which broke in 1983 is the first of the political scandals to expose Stefan Halper as a "political dirty tricks" operator. The investigation forced Halper out of the shadows where he operates into the limelight to face congressional, press, and public attention. Before it fizzled, Debategate caused a severe political stink. The crisis Stefan Halper triggered had the potential at the time to escalate and perhaps end the Reagan presidency prematurely.

It was revealed that when Ronald Reagan was rehearsing for the presidential debate with President Jimmy Carter, unknown to the candidate his staff gave him the very briefing book being used by Carter to prepare for the encounter. The briefing book was delivered by an unidentified "mole" who had access to the Carter White House. The press pack led by the *New York Times* concluded Halper controlled the "mole." The resulting furor ended Stefan Halper's political career.

It was widely reported at the time that the mole was none other than his wife Sibyl who worked in President Carter's White House.[102]

The key aides involved in Reagan's debate preparation were James Baker III, David Gergen, and Rep. David Stockman. Stockman played the role of President Carter in four days of rehearsals and was the source for the news story. He spoke at a Michigan Optimist Club lunch on the day of the debate. Stockman said in assisting with Reagan's preparations, he had access to a "pilfered" copy of President Carter's briefing book. The legendary British American journalist Alastair Cooke explained what happened when the scandal broke in his iconic radio show *Letter from America* on the BBC:

> You may recall the famous stand-up debate between Carter and Reagan one evening in the 1980 presidential campaign. Earlier that day, one David Stockman, now a Cabinet officer but then an unknown Michigan congressman, was addressing a small audience of buddies at lunch in the inconsiderable town of Cassopolis, Michigan. He'd just spent four days pretending to be Jimmy Carter in a sort of private, mock debate with Mr. Reagan, a rehearsal for the actual event.
> Every candidate, if he's on the ball, does this, of course. His staff fish out the opponent's well-known positions on issues, domestic and foreign and they try them out on the candidate, but young 33-year-old Mr. Stockman boasted to his audience that the rehearsal had been a specially whopping success because he'd had access to what he called "a pilfered copy" of the briefing book that Mr. Carter's aides had prepared for him.
> Next day, a neighboring newspaper, the Elkhart Truth, covered the actual Carter-Reagan debate and noted that several times the two candidates said almost word for word what Stockman had predicted. The files of the Elkhart Truth lay untouched, unprobed, for three

[102] Associate Press reporting in *Public Opinion* Chambersburg, Pennsylvania July 8, 1983.www.newspapers.com

years till, a couple of weeks ago, the paper itself resurrected and reprinted its story.

The boys in the White House said at first, in effect, "No big deal, we have stacks of Carter papers on file." The president was challenged at a press conference. He said he'd never heard of the Carter briefing papers, but Stockman had spoken, and he couldn't go back on his story. Who purloined the papers? Were they stolen? Or did some disaffected mole on the Carter staff slip them to the Reagan campaign team?

At the moment, Mr. James Baker, who is the top Reagan aide, says he got a copy of Carter's briefing book from Mr. Casey, who is now the head of the CIA. Mr. Casey says he has no recollection. Mr. Casey says, "Nonsense!" Mr. Casey says he wouldn't have touched any such material with a ten-foot pole. Somebody is lying. Some White House aides say the papers were useful, very useful, in alerting Mr. Reagan to the sort of questions President Carter would put to him and the president, after brushing the whole thing off as trivial, almost funny, dropped his chuckle and ordered the Justice Department to begin a criminal investigation.

The FBI, as the department's investigating arm, has moved in, and Briefing-gate already has a nostalgic creepiness of its own. It is not going away. A culprit or a team of culprits will be found. Somebody could go to jail. The White House is haunted by a hollow voice intoning, "I have been here before." Two weeks ago, Briefing-gate seemed facetious and pointless, and it may turn out to be so. Maybe not.[103]

The First Congressional Investigation into Halper

In the summer of 1983, Democrats in Congress seized on Debategate. President Reagan was forced to ask the Justice Department to "monitor" the issue. Ex-president Jimmy Carter complained the

---

[103] Alastair Cooke on *Letter from America* radio show on the BBC (July 10, 1983), https://www.bbc.co.uk/programmes/articles/2T4dkXX5Cc36nQxPs0XbRcx/briefing-gate-to-be-investigated.

pilfered documents revealed the "essence" of his campaign, and his reelection bid suffered great harm. In retirement Jimmy Carter long believed this covert action cost him the election.

In 1983 the affair became a severe scandal as key Republicans accused each other of being responsible. The ridiculously-titled US House Committee on Post Office and Civil Service's Subcommittee on Human Resources launched an investigation under the chairmanship of Democratic attack dog Donald J. Albosta. The investigation's goal was to force the appointment of a Special Prosecutor, an echo of the Watergate Affair.

The committee findings were published in a snappily titled report "Unauthorized Transfers of Nonpublic Information During the 1980 Presidential Election" published in May 1984. The report confirmed the Reagan campaign received, copied, and used "a pilfered copy" of President Carter's debate briefing book. The campaign also acquired materials from the National Security Council. The investigation turned up hundreds of pages of documents from the President Jimmy Carter's campaign in Stockman's files as well as in the Reagan campaign archives stored at Stanford University's Hoover Institute. One paper, an itinerary for President Carter's travels during the week before election day, had "report from White House mole"[104] written on it. The wording seemed to confirm the material was stolen.

The Committee reported some witness statements were not entirely candid, to put it mildly. United States District Court Judge Harold Green found the Reagan Administration was required by law to appoint an independent counsel or special prosecutor to conduct an

---

[104] https://babel.hathitrust.org/cgi/pt?id=uc1.aa0005421789&view=1up&seq=219, page 163.

investigation. The Special Counsel would determine whether to seek indictments against any of the high-level presidential appointees who knowingly received and used the stolen White House briefing book. Attorney General Ed Meese declined to appoint an independent counsel.

Stefan Halper features heavily in the investigation, even swearing an affidavit that he had not organized the acquisition of opposition documents. He admitted to handling the debate file but conveniently could not remember how it came to him or what he did with it.

The *New York Times* reported that Stefan Halper was the "person in charge" of running a "highly secretive" operation.[105] The mission was to get "inside information" about the Carter Administration's foreign policy and pass it to the Reagan campaign. Halper was running his operation out of Reagan's campaign headquarters in Arlington, Virginia, according to reports from other Reagan administrative officials.

Several retired Central Intelligence Agency officials were alleged to be involved in his activity. Halper was supposed to be a campaign aide responsible for providing twenty-four-hour news updates and policy ideas and officially worked under Robert Garrick, the director of campaign operations. Leslie H. Gelb, the *NYT* journalist, described Halper's role in his article "Reagan Aides Describe Operation to Gather Inside Data on Carter" on July 7, 1983. He quotes Garrick who said to the newspaper about Stefan Halper, "I kind of thought he had

---

[105] Leslie H. Gelb, "Reagan Aides Describe Operation to Gather Inside Data on Carter," *NYT* (July 7, 1983).

another agenda going—he was always on the phone with the door closed, and he never called me in and discussed it with me."[106]

David Prosperi, another Reagan campaign aide, said, "He provided us with wire stories and Carter speeches, but people talked about his having a network that was keeping track of things inside the Government, mostly in relation to the October surprise."[107] Another official who wished to remain anonymous told Gelb "There was some C.I.A. stuff coming from Halper, and some agency guys were hired."[108]

Gelb believed Halper was working for David Gergen during the election who became the Reagan White House Communications Director. Gergen was highly instrumental with Cline in getting Halper a job in the State Department after the election. Once exposed in the newspapers, Halper fled town. It was Ray Cline, his father-in-law, and former senior Central Intelligence official, who stepped forward to dismiss the Reagan aides' disclosures. He called Gelb to say:

> "There was definitely no reporting relationship to either [David] Gergen or [James] Baker during the campaign effort." Mr. Cline said Mr. Halper, his son-in-law, was on a "special staff to analyze campaign issues, just as he did in the Bush campaign, and that he was responsible for looking for booby traps and studying what Carter people were saying to look for vulnerabilities. I think this is all a romantic fallacy about an old C.I.A. network. I believe I have been close enough to the intelligence community for the last 40 years that I would have discovered it. Such an effort would not have been worthwhile and I believe it was not executed.'" He added, "That does

---

[106] Ibid.

[107] Ibid.

[108] Ibid.

not mean that some individual or individuals didn't do something, but there was not a deliberate effort to penetrate" the Government.

The *NYT* revealed Halper's *modus operandi*. Halper involves himself in shady political operations and when he gets caught he relies on his intelligence connections to bail him out. Debategate was never resolved as both the FBI and a congressional subcommittee failed to determine how or through whom the briefing book came to the Reagan campaign. The reason the Justice Department cited was "the professed lack of memory or knowledge on the part of those in possession of the documents."[109]

Halper told ABC World News Tonight on July 7, 1983 rather unconvincingly (for reasons that are not clear, this interview was monitored by the CIA and stored in their classified files) "It's flatly untrue. I mean, there is absolutely no basis to that allegation. There was not such a formal network of, of, as you say a spook network that I know of."[110]

The Congressional investigation revealed the Reagan campaign formed three committees devoted to monitoring and addressing the Iran hostage issue during the period preceding the 1980 presidential election. The committees collectively referred to the potential release of the hostages before the November election as the "October surprise." A second much later investigation looked into the "October surprise." The allegation was the Reagan campaign colluded with the Iranian regime by delaying the release of US hostages held by Iran

---

[109] Congressional Records, "Report of the Department of Justice Regarding the Carter Debate Briefing Materials," (February 23, 1984).

[110] www.cia.com/thevault

until after the election. Again, the Committee interviewed Halper but reached no conclusions.

The press speculated and campaign documents showed the Reagan election team was concerned that President Carter would pull an "October surprise" during the final days of the campaign. They feared the administration was cutting a deal with Ayatollah Khomeini for the release of the fifty-two hostages held in Iran. The campaign felt this diplomatic bombshell might be enough to persuade voters to send President Carter back to the White House for four more years. *Newsweek* wondered whether a clandestine operation involving ex-CIA agents was been undertaken by the Reagan team to keep close tabs on the Carter campaign.

Time confirmed in its July 25, 1983, issue that William Casey brought in former agents of both the CIA and the FBI to gather information from colleagues who were still with that agency. Once again Stefan Halper's name popped up time and again as the man in charge of the freelance intelligence operation. The CIA helpfully collated all the articles. In "A Question of Treason," an article by Daniel Freed published in *The Rebel* on November 22, 1983, he describes the unproven allegations about Halper's role:

> Sensitive material from the NSC [National Security Council] began to flow to Allen. Secret information from CIA and ex-CIA sources reached [William] Casey. A top "control" or "agent- handler" in Casey's ring was Stephan [sic] Halper, a "researcher" from the Bush campaign. Halper's father-in-law was Dr. Ray Cline, former Deputy Director of the CIA and a high Reagan adviser. Halper, through Cline, had far-reaching access to the most sensitive sources.[111]

---

[111] https://www.cia.gov/library/readingroom/docs/CIA-RDP90-00965R000302110004-4.pdf

The hypothesis might be that the experience of working on a political campaign hand in hand with the security services was a formative experience for Halper and no doubt became invaluable during the Spygate operation. Halper had a long background in both using and procuring opposition political research dating back decades to prior administrations. Was Halper's experience in deploying such dirty tricks one of the key reasons for his involvement in the operation?

Chapter Six: Foreign Affairs

And Moses sent them to spy out the land of Canaan, and said unto them, Get you up this way southward, and go up into the mountain: And see the land, what it is, and the people that dwelleth therein, whether they be strong or weak, few or many; And what the land is that they dwell in, whether it be good or bad; and what cities they be that they dwell in, whether in tents, or in strong holds; And what the land is, whether it be fat or lean, whether there be wood therein, or not. And be ye of good courage, and bring of the fruit of the land. Now the time was the time of the firstripe grapes.

—Numbers 13:17-20

Sometimes we do a thing in order to find out the reason for it. Sometimes our actions are questions not answers.

—John Le Carré, *A Perfect Spy*

As a reward for services rendered during the successful election campaign, along with his brother-in-law Roger Fontaine, Stefan Halper was apparently appointed to a plum State Department position. He was Deputy Assistant Secretary of State for Politico-Military Affairs. Halper's portfolio apparently included China-US relations, Taiwan, non-proliferation, technology transfer, unconventional warfare. It was his only official foreign policy role. Halper claims to have served at the State Department from 1981–1984. But this again may be an exaggeration. He seemingly left the State Department in June 1983. Halper must have begun planning to leave the State Department from the moment he arrived as he submitted an application for his new banking business in 1982.

The way he told it to the Cambridge Intelligence Seminar when he was at the State Department, Halper had a ball. He cannot contain his delight even now, describing how he was at the center of world events. For once, the archives back him up. The records show him attending all sorts of high-level foreign policy meetings on behalf of the State Department.

Years later, Halper recounted one tale at the University of Cambridge Intelligence Seminar about how he was once at a meeting with President Reagan. Halper believed his story to be highly amusing. At this gathering, the CIA presented President Reagan with a grim assessment of the overwhelming military capabilities of the Soviet Union. The report dramatically exaggerated the military power at the disposal of the Communist bloc.

According to the report, the Soviet Union had far more missiles than the United States. Ironically, Professor Christopher Andrew taught on his "Secret World" course that this report is known as "Missilegate," one of the most significant intelligence failures of the CIA. Ignorant of Andrew's scathing assessment, Halper recounted that President Reagan had grown tired of listening to the list of US deficiencies and asked: "What do we have more of ?" The answer was money. Reagan ordered an arms race. Halper was the only attendee of the Cambridge seminar to find his own story amusing.

Stefan Halper had a timely exit from the Reagan Administration before the scandal broke. It was pretty damn quick just as the "Debategate" and "October surprise" scandals broke. The raging scandals Halper was a crucial part of threatened to engulf the Reagan presidency. Halper's departure perhaps stemmed from the expected revelations of his work on the 1980 election campaign. He abandoned the center stage of politics never to return.

A Very Political Bank

Halper left the State Department to start what became apparently a shady and scandal-plagued business career in finance according to contemporary accounts. He co-founded a bank in Washington, exploiting his Republican political connections. Despite having no previous banking experience, Halper became the chairman and later claimed to be the majority shareholder of three banks. Palmer Bank was founded on June 1, 1983, by Stefan Halper and Harvey McLean, Jr., a real estate developer from Dallas, Texas, who served as the southern finance chairman in the 1980 presidential campaign of George H. W. Bush. Palmer was the name of McLean's daughter.

Critics and press reports argue that Palmer Bank was a CIA front company initially funded with supposed Mafia money. The start-up capital was channeled from notorious Louisiana businessman Herman K. Beebe, a suspected organized crime family associate with strong intelligence connections. Beebe is described as the "godfather of dirty savings and loans" and of "having more connections to the intelligence services than a switchboard."[112] In 1985 the OCC listed Palmer Bank as one of a dozen banks under the control of Beebe. The new bank

---

[112] Alan Alkan "American Civilian Counter-terrorist Manual: a fictional autobiography."

opened in a sleek new downtown building on K Street, Washington. Beebe's banking empire later collapsed, costing the taxpayer millions.

Between 1983 and 1990, Halper claims he worked in banking—first at the Palmer National Bank, Washington, DC, then The National Bank of Northern Virginia, Leesburg, and The George Washington National Bank of Alexandria, Virginia. Halper talked to the *Washington Post* about his new business in 1984. The venture he claimed was about reaching high-technology customers, entrepreneurs, and an "upscale market."[113] The bank attracted more than $25 million in deposits from conservatives in its first year of operation. Palmer National became the place to bank for a wide range of conservative groups, thanks to the Republican credentials of the bank's organizers.[114]

Halper told the *New York Times*, despite the paper's evidence to the contrary, the bank's politically related lending is insignificant. "We're really uninvolved in politics," he said. "Our business is business." Loans to political committees and campaigns are permissible under Federal banking and election regulations, "provided that the credit is extended in the ordinary course of business and the terms are substantially similar to extensions of credit to nonpolitical debtors which are of similar risk and size of obligation."[115]

The *New York Times* uncovered that the National Conservative Political Action Committee borrowed on very favorable terms from Palmer. The Palmer loan was at prime, the rate banks charge their best

---

[113] Jeff Gerth, "A Bank That Banks on Conservative Dollars," *NYT* (November 1, 1984).

[114] Ibid.

[115] Ibid.

customers, while another bank charged the same customer two percentage points more.

A Palmer Bank executive, Mr. Hayes, told the *NYT* the customers are professionals, companies involved in technology, the military and exporting, and a generally "upscale marketplace." He wasn't kidding about the military and exporting. Palmer National Bank, it transpired, was heavily involved in the Iran Contra affair.

In 1985, when a new non-profit organization called the National Endowment for the Preservation of Liberty (NEPL) needed a bank, Palmer National was its choice. NEPL, headed by Carl R. "Spitz" Channell, was used to funnel money for weapons to the Nicaraguan contras, in direct violation of the Boland Amendment. Channell was one of the few private citizens who were convicted of crimes relating to the Iran Contra scandal. Later Halper's business partner in various schemes including another bank and the World Freedom Foundation was Channell's attorney J Curtis Herve.[116] An internet search quickly reveals just how connected Halper is to many of the figures in this shadowy affair.

As if the Iran Contra affair was not enough scandal, Halper was sued in 1990 for bank fraud, perjury, RICO (Racketeer Influenced and Corrupt Organizations), and other offenses.[117] The case settled out of court, but Halper left banking soon after. Bank president Hayes claimed in a 1990 newspaper interview that Halper left Palmer Bank in 1986. Another of many striking cases of inconsistency in his life is that it seems McLean, not Halper, was the majority shareholder.

---

[116] https://militarist-monitor.org/world_freedom_foundation/

[117] Virginia Court Records, Civil Action No 90-00071-A, filed 01-19-1990

Running what appears a deeply political bank neck-deep in the international scandal was not enough to keep Halper busy. He was still moving in elite CIA circles building contacts. In 1981 the journalist and heavily-rumored CIA asset David Ignatius, now at the *Washington Post*, was awarded a cash prize by Halper and Cline for his supportive articles about the CIA.[118] Ignatius would later admit to me that Halper was his long-term source. In May 1986 he attended the Bill Donovan memorial dinner with guests of honor, the Reagans.[119] He became a director of Ray S. Cline's influential National Intelligence Study Centre with the great and the good of Washington.[120]

From 1986 onward, the hardly busy financier began his media career writing a weekly nationally syndicated column appearing in thirty regional newspapers. The column focused on "foreign policy and national security matters." Halper also found time to write in his busy schedule a weekly script and host *World Wise,* a wholly forgotten nationally televised program on foreign and national security affairs. Later in 1998 he did the same for *This Week from Washington,* a national radio program from conservative Radio America heard on 130 radio stations around the country. His future wife was the producer. Halper claims he found time to squeeze in being a senior advisor to the Department of Defense and apparently a senior advisor to the Department of Justice.[121] Halper is silent on his C.V. regarding his work with his ex father in law such as his position as program director for Ray Cline's United States Global Strategy Council, a group

---

[118] https://www.cia.gov/library/readingroom/docs/CIA-RDP84B00890R000700020059-7.pdf

[119] https://www.cia.gov/library/readingroom/docs/CIA-RDP88G01332R000700810018-7.pdf

[120] Ibid.

[121] Halper's online CV at https://www.iwp.edu/faculty/stefan-halper/.

"dedicated to the improvement of strategic planning and decision-making by the Executive Branch and the Congress of the United States " and "economic strategist" for World Strategy Network.

In 1989 Sibyl Cline Halper published an extraordinary book about the Mozambique RENAMO movement for the US Global Strategy Council[122], a Washington-based organization, which was under the chairmanship of its founder, her father, Ray Cline. The US State Department denounced RENAMO which was co-sponsored by the Rhodesian Central Intelligence Organization and the South African apartheid regime for its scorched-earth terror tactics and murder of more than 100,000 Mozambicans.

According to its Amazon entry, Sibyl held a very different view: her book "about the anti-communist guerrilla forces in Mozambique describes the efforts of Renamo to oppose Frelimo's one-party rule. For more than a decade Renamo has fought to bring a pluralist political system, with free and fair elections, to its nation. The author details how Renamo's leader, Afonso Dhlakama, has attempted to develop, within his ranks, a democratic society with education, health, and human rights standards."[123]

The anti-communist RENAMO was also sponsored by Cline who attracted funding and support in Washington for the movement.[124] Alarming reports of massacres in the US press eroded the movement's "white hat" anti-Communist credentials. Private proxy wars were a

---

[122] One of Ray Cline's lobbying organizations.

[123] https://www.amazon.com/Renamo-Sibyl-W-Cline/dp/0943057027/ref=sr_1_fkmr0_2? dchild=1&keywords=sibyl+cline+halper&qid=1586630506&s=books&sr=1-2-fkmr0

[124] Apartheid's Contras: An Inquiry Into the Roots of War in Angola and Mozambique William Minter

part of the great game in the 1980s. Communist and anti-Communist movements faced off against each other around the globe, armed and financed by one or another superpower. Halper and his wife visited the war zone.

The trip to Mozambique was Stefan Halper's only known "live-in-the-field" intelligence operation and it was a disaster. He and his wife got trapped. The party needed a rescue. Cline turned to the dashing soldier of fortune and famed international mercenary Robert C. MacKenzie. MacKenzie organized a raid into Mozambique and freed Halper and his wife.

In a twist, MacKenzie ended up marrying Sibyl soon after in November 1989.[125] Despite his divorce in January 1989, Halper remained close to ex-father-in-law Ray S. Cline. Years later, at the University of Cambridge, Halper was spending big money, I heard paying a fellow academic for a fresh history of the CIA eulogizing Ray S Cline. Halper was a contributor of anecdotes, reminiscences, and provided access to his private papers.

Lobbying and Freelance Spy?
From 1990 until 2000, Stefan Halper claims in his CV he was chairman and chief executive officer of a shadowy PR and lobbying company named Halper, Roosevelt, & Brown. Halper employed Cline's other son-in-law, Roger Fontaine, in the firm.

Roger Fontaine is a Latin American expert a contemporary of Halper at the State Department. Fontaine was deeply involved in supporting and controlling the Nicaraguan Contra movement. By coincidence,

---

[125] https://en.wikipedia.org/wiki/Robert_C._MacKenzie; Bernard Leeman, (*Lesotho and the Struggle for Azania, 2nd Edition* (1999).

Fontaine is now working in academia at the Institute of World Politics with Halper (see below). The activities of the shadowy lobbying group are unclear. Records show the firm involved itself in political lobbying on behalf of foreign governments[126] and attacking a CIA chief with a poison pen newspaper article.

Halper used one of his syndicated newspaper columns to attack the reputation of President Bill Clinton's first CIA Director, James Woolsey, with thinly veiled allegations. The article appeared in many papers on February 21, 1994, including the *Tampa Bay Times*.[127] Halper was agitated that the Director of the CIA refused to take a polygraph test. He used the article to blow the issue into a huge test of character of Woolsey. Halper argued, "the polygraph forms a bond among those who have taken it. In a way, it defines an elite community that is entrusted with the nation's most sensitive information."[128]

Halper widened his attack to taint CIA Director Woolsey as unfit for office as he has access to sensitive information and must be hiding something. The director must "have sensitive information that bears on national security or an individual's safety, and the government must know if these employees are stable and discreet." Further Woolsey's action "impose [s] additional risks upon those who rely upon the absolute security of sensitive information—information that, if used improperly, could harm them." Halper concludes Woolsey "potentially endangers the lives of loyal employees and the success of vital initiatives."[129]

---

[126] https://www.justice.gov/nsd-fara/page/file/991746/download

[127] *Tampa Bay Times*, St. Petersburg, Florida (February 21, 1994)

[128] https://www.newspapers.com/clip/35160127/tampa-bay-times/

[129] Ibid.

Eerily reminiscent of his later attacks on Gen. Flynn, Halper knows his way around security clearances and pushes the buttons to cause alarm and disgrace. When he raises the specter of "national security," Halper knows what he is doing—causing the maximum amount of harm simply by innuendo. Interestingly, Halper and Woolsey's paths would cross again at the Institute of World Politics. Halper honed his extensive press contacts, think tank appointments, and devious media skills in a decade of such venomous work.

Scandal continued in Halper's life. At age fifty, on July 11, 1994, a criminal case was filed in the Eastern District of Virginia court against a Stefan Halper. He was charged with counts of possession of crack cocaine, failure to comply with a traffic control device, and for operating after suspension. The case was terminated on February 17, 1995, and the case file record then destroyed. It would appear he took a plea deal, admitted the offense, and paid a $400 fine.[130] Between 1995 and 1997, Halper tried his hand at lobbying, representing the government of Romania and registered under FARA with a company called Brown Communications.

Prior to his recruitment as an informer for the FBI Halper demonstrated some unusual credentials. He certainly knew his way around the the murkier parts of politics. Crucially and unusually for an informer he understood the machinations of the intelligence world. Were the FBI team aware, or should they have been aware of Halper's background before making him a pivotal part of the most sensitive investigation in their history?

---

[130] https://bigleaguepolitics.com/court-docs-trump-campaign-spy-stefan-halper-busted-for-crack-cocaine-possession/

Chapter Seven: The "Cambridge Club"

Ye are the salt of the earth: but if the salt have lost his savour,
wherewith shall it be salted? it is thenceforth good for nothing, but to
be cast out, and to be trodden under foot of men.

—Matthew: 5:13

I won't belong to a club that accepts me as a member.

—Oscar Wilde

Despite making a very large personal donation of around $85,000 to George W. Bush's successful 2000 presidential election campaign, Halper was not invited to join the new administration in a doubtless much-longed-for foreign policy role.[131] The snub was maybe the final straw for the long-term Bush Republican. He began a journey from being a right-wing conservative diehard supporting causes around the world to one of the party's fiercest critics and a fan of Hillary Clinton. The targets of years of Halper's ire were what he described as the "Neo cons" who came to dominate American foreign policy post the 9/11 attack. Strangely for a man so close to Sir Richard Dearlove, Halper became a harsh critic of the Bush doctrine and the

---

[131] https://www.washingtonpost.com/politics/who-is-stefan-a-halper-the-fbi-source-who-assisted-the-russia-investigation/
2018/05/21/22c46caa-5d42-11e8-9ee3-49d6d4814c4c_story.html

second Gulf War after the event. Halper published two books attacking his former political friends and allies.[132]

Stefan Halper, then aged fifty-eight, created his "I am an academic" cover story of which he is so proud of later in life and used to such devastating effect. As le Carré says "The more identities a man has, the more they express the person they conceal."[133] While at the distinguished University of Cambridge, he apparently continued his nefarious activities, and possibly expanded them while all the time posing as a respectable professor. The *Washington Post* headlined their apology for Halper: "Cambridge University perch gave FBI source access to top intelligence figures—and a cover as he reached out to Trump associates."[134]

Stefan Halper developed, according to newspaper accounts a deserved reputation around the Washington swamp for liking the sound of his own voice and tirelessly telling everyone how clever he was. My hypothesis is that he set out to buy all the trappings of academic respectability so everyone would know he was smart and an expert in foreign policy. Yet his actual foreign policy experience at the State Department was short and out of date. At Cambridge according to the *Post* "he was known as a foreign policy expert with a network of intelligence sources cultivated over decades." It also gave "a valuable cover to assist the FBI in a secret operation."[135] Could it be that Halper is simply a spy posing as an academic?

---

[132] Stefan Halper, Jonathan Clarke *The Silence of the Rational Center*. Stefan Halper *America Alone: The Neo-Conservatives and the Global Order.*

[133] John le Carré, *Tinker, Tailor, Soldier, Spy* (New York: Penguin Books, 1974), 269.

[134] Tom Hamburger, *Washington Post* (June 5, 2018)

[135] Ibid.

Halper's CV states he was appointed senior fellow at the Centre of International Studies and director of the American Studies Program in 2001 at the University of Cambridge. This is quite a plum appointment for someone who on the face of it never taught before and seemingly did not possess any previous academic experience. He last attended a university in 1971, some thirty years before.

In fact, Halper apparently had an easy route into academia. He was sponsored by his great friend and business partner, the philanthropist William D. Roosevelt, a grandson of President Franklin D. Roosevelt and more usefully part of the William H. Donner Foundation. In 2001, this philanthropic trust was dominated by conservatives and they supported an overseas expansion of their foundation's charitable largesse. Halper brought to the University of Cambridge his own large, and more importantly the Donner Foundation's inexhaustible checkbook.

The University of Cambridge loves money: rich benefactors, generous donors, and big fee-paying international students are all welcome. Money makes a big splash and buys a lot of influence in impoverished academic circles. Halper did not endure the usual annual desperate hunt for sponsorship money bedeviling real academics. He was giving out money. Universities do not pay researchers salaries, and teaching undergrads is minimum wage work with no guaranteed hours, if you can get it. Most academics have to build a portfolio of jobs and sponsored research is a huge boon. Halper was an employer. He apparently paid financially stretched students to research for him. He used others' research for his books and to bulk up his now infamous studies.

Halper's academic position as Director of Studies of a course in international relations was sponsored by his long-time friend's Donner Foundation, not apparently earned on teaching credentials. Halper established a Stefan Halper Family Foundation and together with the Donner Foundation both sponsor generous scholarships at Magdalene College.[136] Could endowing scholarships be seemingly one way to get you an unpaid fellowship at the University of Cambridge?

Magdalene College is one of Cambridge's smallest colleges with just a few hundred undergraduates. The college's most famous alumnus is the seventeenth-century diarist Samuel Pepys. His papers and books, including six original bound manuscripts of his famous diaries, are housed in the beautiful Pepys Library. Learning from the master Dr. Ray Cline, Halper seemingly pedaled influence by offering cash prizes for essays by British experts on national security. It worked. Despite not being a world leading academic, he wheedled his way inside the inner sanctum of the University of Cambridge.

Bizarrely, as he had one already, Halper completed a second and utterly unnecessary Doctorate in 2004. Halper seemingly published no credible academic body of work. He did put his name on the cover of several books—two were savage attacks on Neo-Conservatives; one on the history of Tibet; and one a book on China.[137] Halper employed a veritable industry of Cambridge academics on his string of lucrative contracts for the Department of Defense and his books. He had a couple of graduate students full-time doing the heavy lifting on his studies. Several senior academics got used to receiving a regular

---

[136] https://www.magd.cam.ac.uk/

[137] Lezlee Brown Halper, Stefan Halper *Tibet: An Unfinished Story* Stefan Halper *The Beijing Consensus: How China's Authoritarian Model Will Dominate the Twenty-First Century.*

payday from him. Otherwise he ghosted around the world giving leaden speeches at the taxpayers' expense.[138]

Professor Stefan Halper is not a University of Cambridge professor. You would be forgiven for thinking he was, given the press coverage. A peculiarity of the British education system is there are very few academics who can call themselves professors. The title is rightly highly regarded around the world.

America has a different approach to the academic title. Halper's "Professorship" is American and specifically a research one. He obtained it from a small US school he never mentions. He is listed as a research professor at the Institute of World Politics (IWP), an independent graduate school specializing in national security. American "research professors" do not teach or receive a salary; instead, they must fund themselves entirely through research grants.

IWP was founded in 1990 by John Lenczowski, the former Director of European and Soviet Affairs at the United States National Security Council during the Reagan administration. The Institute holds the private library of former CIA Director William Casey and the American Security Council Foundation Library. The ASCF created the "National Strategy for Peace through Strength" and has been cited numerous times with providing the overall foreign affairs theme for the administration of former president Ronald Reagan.

In 2005, "at the request" of the US Secretary of Defense, Halper started his apparently lucrative relationship with the Pentagon. He

---

[138] www.Grassley.senate.gov *Grassley Receives Corrective Action Plan from DoD Regarding the Office of Net Assessment*
Aug 12, 2019

prepared his first study on the Iraq War. He claims the report drew upon the British Ministry of Defense, the US Department of Defense, and academic, diplomatic, and intelligence analysts from both countries.[139]

This study likely brought Halper into the orbit of Sir Richard Dearlove's "Cambridge Club." On his retirement from MI6, Dearlove took up his position as Master of Pembroke College in August 2004 facilitated by Professor Christopher Andrew. Dearlove and Halper are today steadfast if unlikely friends and business partners. Dearlove defends Halper implausibly in the circumstances as a "good academic and patriot."[140] The former British spy chief is close to being Halper's only public defender. No American has come forward to offer a sympathetic picture of Halper. As le Carré says, "The trouble is, when professional spies go out of their way to make a definitive statement about one of their own, the public tends to believe the opposite."[141]

Is it solely because of Halper that Cambridge became the front line in the fight against Russian collusion? There seems no other reason.

---

[139] www.iwp.edu

[140] Tom Hamburger, Robert Costa, Ellen Nakashima, *The Washington Post* (June 6, 2018), https://www.washingtonpost.com/politics/cambridge-university-perch-gave-fbi-source-access-to-top-intelligence-figures--and-a-cover-as-he-reached-out-to-trump-associates/2018/06/05/c6764dc2-641e-11e8-99d2-0d678ec08c2f_story.html

[141] John le Carré, *The Guardian* (April 12, 2013), https://www.theguardian.com/books/2013/apr/12/john-le-carre-spy-anniversary.

Chapter Eight: All's Quiet

*Beware of false prophets, which come to you in sheep's clothing, but
inwardly they are ravening wolves.
Ye shall know them by their fruits. Do men gather grapes of thorns, or figs of
thistles?
Even so every good tree bringeth forth good fruit; but a corrupt tree bringeth
forth evil fruit.
A good tree cannot bring forth evil fruit, neither can a corrupt tree bring
forth good fruit.*

—Matthew 7:15-18

*Thou and I are but the blind instruments of some irresistible fatality, that
hurries us along, like goodly vessels driving before the storm, which are
dashed against each other, and so perish.*

—Sir Walter Scott

The reaction following the February 28, 2014 dinner with General
Flynn was a small short-lived buzz of excitement around
Cambridge. The organizers sent each other congratulatory emails
about just how well the evening went and I was tasked with staying in
occasional touch with Gen. Flynn as part of my informal role as
Professor Christopher Andrew's social secretary. As such, I sent
around the photographs I took of the dinner.

Over the next few months, I was asked to send occasional pieces of
research in emails to Gen. Flynn to ensure the proposed Cambridge
Security Initiative conference remained on his agenda. Andrew
reviewed each email I sent and he reviewed, if any, the answers.
Contrary to press reports, Gen.Flynn never signed off his emails as

"General Misha." In fact, he would send his regards to Sir Richard Dearlove and the group.

It was over this email exchange that I was betrayed years later, and falsely reported to US intelligence as a possible Russian spy, for performing the very tasks the group asked me to do. The people who knew me so well for years, Andrew and Dearlove, later threw me under a bus by failing to support me. They could and should have come forward to refute the accusations made against me by Halper. The "Cambridge Club" should be judged harshly as they acted in highly duplicitous ways. Of course, the US authorities would have poured over the few emails I sent and received and concluded the content was completely innocuous. One of the intercepts was leaked to the press in an article in *The Guardian* in March 2018–and that was my history book proposal (later published as "The Spy who Changed History.")

The events all started innocuously enough years earlier on the morning of March 1, 2014, long before the start of the Trump campaign, Michael Flynn's role in the new administration or Spygate. I received an unexpected invitation from Christopher Andrew, the founder of the discipline of intelligence history, to co-write a book with him. At the time, I thought I had made it. With his name on the cover alongside mine, the book would be a best seller and catapult me to the front rank of Cambridge historians.

Andrew is the doyen of intelligence history lauded by senior intelligence figures on both sides of the Atlantic. He has authored fifteen books on intelligence history including the official history of the British counterintelligence agency MI5. He has lectured at Langley, the headquarters of the CIA, as well as the FBI. There is no more trusted figure in the intelligence establishment. Andrew holds one of the highest levels of security clearances in the UK. Annually he has to report all his contacts to the authorities. As Andrew told me, there has never been one question or "whisper" about me. The recent release of the Crossfire Hurricane team's closing file on their bogus counter intelligence investigation into Gen. Flynn confirms there are no adverse reports about me in either the U.S or UK intelligence databases.

The reason Andrew wanted to help with the book was due to how impressed he was by the reaction of Gen. Flynn to my research. He was willing to put all his other projects aside. He saw the opportunity to be part of an exciting project and he sensed success in the offing. Andrew hoped for a very significant advance from a publisher to supplement his pension. He got his influential literary agent to secure a lucrative contract from his US and UK publishers. His proposal felt at the time like a winning combination of my extraordinary research discoveries endorsed by the leading figure in espionage history and best-selling author. I agreed to his proposal, we collaborated for the next two years, and Andrew reviewed every piece of research I discovered in the Moscow archive. Years later, Halper over-reached himself by making the outrageous and false claim that the research I shared each day with the official historian of MI5, Britain's counterintelligence agency, and leading expert on intelligence was somehow given to me by the Russian president Putin. Halper said my research was supposed to be the definitive proof I was a Russian spy.[142]

---

[142] Luke Harding et al The Guardian "*Michael Flynn: New evidence spy chiefs had concerns about Russian ties.*" March 31, 2017.

I would have to be the only spy in history to bring secret documents from Russia to expose Soviet operations. Generally Russian spies based in the United Kingdom are supposed to exfiltrate secret British documents to Moscow, not Russian documents to London. In my case, Halper seemingly reversed the basics of espionage. Could it be that Halper had developed a business over decades of selling trickery in the worlds of black propaganda and political dirty tricks?

Kept from the general public is the fact some elements of intelligence agencies have long moved on from the task of simply gathering and reporting information on enemies or friends. An important role of some elements of intelligence services is the distribution of propaganda and disinformation. My Professor and one-time book collaborator Andrew is the tip of this spear; himself an ace storyteller. He polishes with equal aplomb the successes of Western intelligence and lampoons the failure of their opponents.

Andrew's greatest achievement is to bring intellectual rigor to the chaotic world of intelligence. He is so admired in security circles because he has achieved the remarkable feat of both promoting the history of the Secret World—that is his term for espionage—while glossing over the failures of intelligence services except, of course, Russia. Espionage history is the only discipline where the primary source material remains secret, allowing for the peddling of certain myths. Andrew is the master. He has identified that intelligence practitioners never learn from the past, as they don't study their own history. The maniacal obsession with maintaining secrecy has hamstrung the intelligence community's own evolution.

Could it be that starting in 2015 and continuing throughout 2016 the "Cambridge Club" with their various public and private interventions acted as if Donald Trump and Gen. Flynn were enemies of US and UK "national security?" It was perhaps no coincidence that the status quo, the Establishment, paid the club members a steady stream of money. Often the group would talk in grandiose alarmist terms at the seminar about the threat a Trump presidency represented to the security structures that had preserved the security of post-War Europe. Was it just talk? The failure to come forward and deal with the scandals created by Halper and Steele's press leaks creates dark suspicions. All the characters in the Cambridge club are pillars of society and as such their continuing silence does them little credit.

It boiled down to this: Donald Trump was an unpredictable force. He was not a career politician but in Halper's words "a maverick candidate."[143] A maverick is someone unorthodox, independently minded. Donald Trump could not be relied on or be controlled to operate within the established rules of the globalist game. Could it be that to counter this threat the "Cambridge Club" seemingly fed a stream of disinformation via a backchannel to the US intelligence community to undermine his candidacy and later presidency? If so, they soon overreached themselves. Seemingly, their wafer-thin stories about the compromise of General Flynn by a Russian intelligence asset would not survive under scrutiny.

In a few weeks in 2014, the buzz in Cambridge about Flynn's visit completely dissipated. A new Cold War broke out over Ukraine. Dearlove in particular was frustrated. He awaited a call from Whitehall, the center of the British government that never came. He was confidently expecting to be asked for his counsel in how to deal

---

[143] Stefan Halper, speaking at lecture series at Pembroke-King's Programme (July 9, 2016), https://pembrokekings.wordpress.com/2016/07/09/the-p-stands-for-plenary/

with Russia. Dearlove told me how annoyed he was that he had contacts with Kremlin figures but no one in the UK wanted his help.

Dearlove found out in 2014 he was an irrelevancy. No one wanted his counsel. In the past, intelligence figures used such back channels to their opposite numbers to diffuse international crises, such as the Cuban Missile Affair, that politicians could not be relied on to handle. On a day-to-day basis the fiercest opponents maintain communication away from the public eye.

In April 2014, Director of National Intelligence James Clapper dismissed Gen. Flynn during the Ukraine crisis from his top post at the Defense Intelligence Agency. According to various accounts and in particular from Representative Devin Nunes, Gen. Flynn was railroaded out of office. In Nunes's opinion, Flynn was the most exceptional military intelligence officer the United States had produced since the Vietnam War. But his vocal opposition to President Obama cost him his career.

When he stood smiling on the stage in Cambridge on February 28, 2014 thousands of miles away from the Washington Swamp, no one in the audience guessed General Flynn was in the midst of a war of words with the other heads of US intelligence agencies. The rancor may have started in 2010 when the combat hero Gen. Flynn broke all established protocol by publishing a paper titled *"Fixing Intel"* based on the experiences of the long war in Afghanistan. The analysis was deeply critical of the CIA's role in Afghanistan and its Washington leadership.

President Obama spotted the opportunity ahead of his re-election in 2012 to bring the combat hero and vocal critic inside his tent. He promoted General Flynn to be the Head of the Defense Intelligence Agency for a three-year appointment. His new boss, the Director of National Intelligence James Clapper, told Gen. Flynn his mandate was to make radical reform. It was not.

Over his two-year tenure, Flynn made no secret of his views about the CIA and made a sworn enemy of its leader John Brennan. Clapper fired him over disagreements, especially it seems about Obama's flagship Iran policy.

Back in Cambridge, Christopher Andrew's conversations were suddenly full of stories about what a disaster the general was for the Defense Intelligence Agency. It was unclear to me how he was getting this information. The very man he publicly praised to the heavens on stage weeks before was now a pariah. The lesson was apparent; when Gen. Flynn could no longer provide money to the group through the DIA, no one was interested in him. Andrew's interest in Flynn dropped to the point where he periodically asked me to invite the recently retired General Flynn to the seminar to speak, unpaid, when he was stuck for a speaker.

The University returned to being a quiet backwater. The exception to the calm being explosive bickering between seminar members which were the only blots on an otherwise peaceful time. In the years following, there was never the slightest hint the group had any issues with me. I was invited by Sir Richard Dearlove to become a fellow of his new business venture, the Cambridge Security Initiative at its launch. I was invited to join the group to meet with General Flynn's successor as head of the Defense Intelligence Agency, General Vincent Stewart, when he was planning a visit to Cambridge in May 2015. My other advisory projects involved working with NATO and the British government on Russia-related subjects.

The Department of Defense Conference in Cambridge for NATO, discussed back in February 2014 but now cohosted by John McLaughlin, ex-Deputy Director of the CIA, took place eventually in September 2015. Gen. Flynn's departure did not derail the plan. I spoke on the ongoing Ukraine Crisis to a crowd of intelligence specialists. After my talk I was introduced to former CIA Deputy Director John McLaughlin and we chatted for far longer than I ever spoke to General Flynn. McLaughlin stressed the importance of keeping the dialog open with the Russians saying that he had just had lunch with figures from the ex KGB, one of the former Soviet Union's security services. Clearly my participation demonstrated that I was certainly not considered a danger to US security chiefs in the fall of 2015. In September 2015, at the same time back in Washington Halper was being awarded his first of his Pentagon contracts coinciding with Spygate.

I learned through the conversation that ex-Director of the CIA John McLaughlin is a friend of the "Cambridge Club" and later discovered he might know Halper. The pair sat on the advisory board of John Hopkins University in Washington D.C. School of Advanced International Studies. McLaughlin has a long connection to the ex-SVR head Vyacheslav Trubnikov. The SVR is Russia's CIA. When both were deputy directors of their respective spy agencies, they collaborated on intelligence sharing following the collapse of the Soviet Union. Trubnikov was the KGB's expert on America in the days of the Soviet Union—the perfect choice to work with Russia's new friend.

General Trubnikov joined the KGB in 1967 and worked undercover in India. After the collapse of the Soviet Union he became the first deputy Director of Foreign Intelligence Service of Russia (SVR). General Trubnikov later ran the SVR from June 2000 to July 2004. On retirement from the intelligence services he became a Deputy Foreign Minister and later the Russian ambassador to India.

McLaughlin is not the only connection with the retired head of Russian foreign intelligence. It remains unclear how Halper and Trubnikov first came to be acquainted, it may be through CIA connections. In May 2015, Halper arranged Gen. Trubnikov's visit to speak at the Cambridge Intelligence Seminar. The retired intelligence general was supposed to come earlier in February 2015, but that visit was delayed. I was copied on some of the email correspondence involving Halper about the logistical arrangements because I was the emergency substitute speaker. The discussions about the visit all started back in October 2014.

I think it is safe to assume that the urgency to get Gen.Trubnikov to Cambridge may well have been to gain an update on the Ukrainian peace process which formed part of the pre-Minsk agreement discussions. Gen. Trubnikov was a key part of a joint non-governmental Russian/American team known as the Boisto Group which worked on a twenty-four-point plan with the Carnegie Peace Foundation to find common ground for a peace deal in Ukraine.[144] In October 2014 there was a great issue with UK visa for Trubnikov which Halper requested Dearlove to resolve with the British government.

In the summer of 2015, General Flynn decided, fatefully, to enter the bear pit of politics. He became a TV pundit criticizing Hillary Clinton

---

[144] Uri Freidman, "A 24-Step Plan to Resolve the Ukraine Crisis Meeting in Finland, a group of Americans and Russians develops an agenda for peace," *The Atlantic* (August 26, 2014).

over her growing email scandal. A lifelong Democrat, Gen. Flynn emerged on the public stage as a savage critic of President Obama and, in particular, his Middle Eastern policies.

The retired General was working on the book *The Field of Fight.* Promoting his book, Gen. Flynn began appearing regularly on US television. He became a fixture on conservative news networks such as Fox News. He also appeared on Al Jazeera, British Sky News, and Russia's RT (Russia Today).

Discreetly, Gen. Flynn began consulting with several putative Republican presidential candidates. The discussions with Ted Cruz, Carly Fiorina, and Ben Carson were fruitful, but General Flynn chose to work with the businessman and soon front-runner Donald Trump. The initial deal between the pair was that Gen. Flynn was going to be Donald Trump's vice president.

The pair bonded following a meeting in August 2015 as two "patriotic disrupters."[145] Tough, uncompromising talkers, the pair hit on an election strategy to "Drain the Swamp." Gen. Flynn had as the target in his sights the multi-billion-dollar bloated government-funded intelligence industry. He wanted to unleash a military-led takeover of the CIA. From his days in the field in Afghanistan and Iraq, Flynn decided on a plan to empty the desks in Washington and put more agents into the field to gather intelligence. Gen. Flynn wanted to dispense with the thousands of private contractors to the intelligence community leaching off the federal budget.

---

[145] Rep. Matt Gaetz, *Fox News* (October 2019).

In October 2015, General Flynn was approached by the CIA-linked *New York Times* reporter Matt Rosenberg to give an interview. Rosenberg has claimed that he received information from an ex CIA director. No doubt, the notes of this interview were soon shared with the Agency.

Gen. Flynn perhaps didn't realize this when talking so openly to Rosenberg in 2015. Telling Rosenberg the CIA did not serve the interest of the US people was deeply provocative:

"They've lost sight of who they actually work for," Mr. Flynn said in an interview with *The New York Times* in October 2015. "They work for the American people. They don't work for the president of the United States." He added, speaking of the agency's leadership: "Frankly, it's become a very political organization."[146]

Gen. Flynn argued the CIA was the political arm of the Obama Administration, a view Donald Trump allegedly shared, which became a problem after November 2016: "Mr. Flynn's assessment that the C.I.A. is a political arm of the Obama administration is not widely shared by Republicans or Democrats in Washington. But it has appeared to have been internalized by the one person who matters most right now: Mr. Trump."[147] Gen. Flynn was expanding on his 2010 published paper *Fixing Intel* which stated the CIA was only marginally relevant to the overall strategy as they had no comprehension of the cultural complexity of Afghanistan. The CIA was furious about the criticism. According to Rosenberg, "Mr. Flynn's

---

[146] Matt Rosenberg, "Michael Flynn Is Harsh Judge of C.I.A.'s Role," *NYT* (December 12, 2016).

[147] Ibid., https://www.nytimes.com/2016/12/12/us/politics/donald-trump-cia-michael-flynn.html?login=smartlock&auth=login-smartlock.

searing critique was seen at the agency as the height of insensitivity."[148]

My hypothesis is that deep in the Washington Swamp, the beast stirred. The legion of Gen. Flynn's enemies in the intelligence community hoped they had seen the last of him following his ignominious sacking from the DIA in 2014. They began to hatch an elaborate plan to end the nuisance and political partnership of General Flynn and Donald Trump. The establishment wanted a plan to destroy the reputation of the retired three-star general and decorated war hero once and for all.

---

[148] Ibid.

Chapter Nine: Motive

But he answered and said, Every plant, which my heavenly Father hath not planted, shall be rooted up.
Let them alone: they be blind leaders of the blind. And if the blind lead the blind, both shall fall into the ditch.

—Matthew 15:13-14

"In every operation there is an above the line and a below the line. Above the line is what you do by the book. Below the line is how you do the job."

—John le Carré, *A Perfect Spy*

Every election day makes or breaks thousands of Washington Swamp careers, including the likes of Stefan Halper. The cunning operative planned ahead. After what he no doubt saw as a lifetime of unfair and unjustified rejection, the fiercely determined Halper wanted a well-paid legacy. As Randolph Churchill, father of Sir Winston, warned in June 13, 1886, "beware the ambition of an old man in a hurry." Halper burned with a desire to crown his career as "a foreign affairs expert" with a senior diplomatic post and didn't care who gave it to him. He always was a commentator, never a player.

Halper was a founding member of the club of old men at Cambridge who fought against the tide of time. By June 2015, Halper's role was for all intents and purposes over at Cambridge. All his connections were retiring and stepping back from the University; in particular, Sir Richard Dearlove stepped down as Master of Pembroke in 2015. Halper, now aged seventy-two, was perhaps looking at a future of irrelevancy and a sharp drop in income. Seemingly this type of future did not feature in Halper's plans. Nothing if not ambitious, Halper believed he had something very special to offer and was entitled to a top role, perhaps as the United States ambassador to China. If Hillary Clinton won the election, perhaps he hoped to be rewarded for his service. Halper began heaping very public praise on Hillary Clinton, such as in March 1, 2013, when he made an unintentionally hilarious comment "an elegant Secretary of State, Hillary Clinton, who was loved by everyone" to Reuters[149]

He kept up his public support for Hillary right up until the eve of the election. On November 3, 2016, just five days before Americans went to the polls, Halper gave an interview to the Russian news agency *Sputnik* voicing support for Clinton. Halper told the Russian news service "the victory of Hillary Clinton, who is more experienced and predictable than her Republican rival Donald Trump, in the US presidential elections will be more beneficial for the US-UK relations and for relations with the European Union."[150] If in the unlikely event Donald Trump triumphed, Halper was also working on a Plan B.

The 2016 election was supposed to be a no-contest, a smooth procession leading up to the coronation of Swamp Queen Hillary Clinton as the 45th President of the United States. It was her turn. With Hillary's accession to the seat in the Oval Office, the Democrats, self-styled natural party of US government, would cement their grip on the lucrative and most influential positions in Washington. The establishment had kept their hands on the levers of power and budget and grown fat pocketing the cashflow. At the gift of the president are

---

[149] Arshad Mohammed, *"Cosmopolitan Kerry courts Europe, his old stomping ground,"* *Reuters* (March 1, 2013).

[150] *Sputnik* (November 3, 2016), https://sputniknews.com/politics/201611031047032702-clinton-us-uk-cooperation/.

over 9,500 Federal executive positions with fancy salaries located in the Washington area alone.

Since the days of Ronald Reagan back in the 1980s, no president acted as a change agent to shake up the cozy Washington status quo. Donald Trump threatened to be that disruptive force. The Washington elite is all about smooth continuity, despite the occasional heated political rhetoric. Whether it is the Reds or the Blues in power, the federal government inexorably grows each year in size, budget, and power. If the 2016 election went to plan, the Clinton money machine would seamlessly absorb outgoing President Obama's incumbent team for the next eight years of business as usual before anointing a successor.

In mid-2015, the Deep State became collectively concerned about the then unlikely possibility of President Donald Trump. In response, they created the "Russia collusion" ruse. Did some of the chief players of federal law enforcement and the national intelligence agencies become the prime movers? Most assumed Hillary Clinton would be the next president and some that their extralegal efforts to "ensure" her victory would be rewarded, regardless of the potential illegality and unethical behavior required.

Hillary Clinton was the chosen continuity candidate of the Swamp and everyone in the Washington bubble invested heavily in her. It was the surest bet in political history. The polls the Swamp dwellers saw pointed to a landslide. The liberal newspapers they read were full of pro-Hillary stories. They lived in an echo chamber. If you wanted to continue your lucrative career post-election in Washington, you had to support her.

Hillary raised millions of dollars in donations from those hoping for advancement or access. It is the familiar Clinton way: pay to play. At stake in November 2016 was control of the world's cup of largesse. For the fiscal year 2018, the US federal government spent a staggering $4.11 trillion. Government spending was the equivalent of 20.3 percent of the nation's gross domestic product. Government agencies have taxpayer-funded budgets equivalent to entire industries.

Each agency has a political appointee at their head. The intelligence community leads this trend with billions of unaudited dollars of secret money and unaudited budget funding. Believe it or not, the last audit of the intelligence community took place after the Watergate scandal in the 1970s. Gen. Michael Flynn proposed to change all this with an unprecedented audit. He talked about having the senior leadership reapply for their positions and slashing jobs in Washington. Donald Trump endorsed Gen. Flynn's plan to drain the intelligence community Swamp.

Since resigning as President Obama's Secretary of State in 2013, Hillary was preparing for her anointment and busy planning every step of her succession. Clinton passed millions of dollars from her campaign to the heavily indebted Democratic National Committee. Donna Brazile, the DNC Chair, commented: "that in exchange for bailing out the party, which was broke, the Clinton campaign would get control over certain decisions and aspects of the DNC."[151] By 2015, Hillary owned the DNC, so her nomination as their candidate was assured. But despite seemingly holding all the cards, she could not "kill off" the pesky Senator Bernie Sanders's challenge in the primaries.

---

[151] Lulu Garcia-Navarro, "Donna Brazile Criticizes Clinton Camp in Campaign Memoir," *NPR* (November 12, 2017).

Her message to the American electorate was simple enough. Hillary Clinton was the most qualified candidate. She had the experience as First Lady and Secretary of State. Her campaign decided the issue the election would be fought on was her turf of foreign affairs. What could go wrong? The answer was simple: Hillary. A sizable part of America knew what the Clinton experience meant for them: corruption, bigger government, more laws, higher taxes, and no solutions to their problems.

When Hillary realized she turned off swathes of voters, she decided the problem lay not with her, but with the electorate. She dismissed the malcontents, arrogantly turning her back on the American voters she desperately needed to become president, terming them "a basket of deplorables." She insulted Trump supporters, calling them "racist, sexist, homophobic, xenophobic."[152]

The most explosive issue of the 2016 election was Hillary Clinton's email scandal. Hillary's travails with her missing emails and the chronology of "Spygate" closely intertwine. The email controversy began back in March 2015 and ran throughout the campaign season. On July 10, 2015, the FBI opened a criminal investigation codenamed "Midyear Exam" into Hillary Clinton's handling of classified information while Secretary of State.

Many of the same FBI team who conducted the "Midyear Exam" serendipitously also conducted the later "Crossfire Hurricane" investigation. Secretary Clinton had exclusively used a personal email account on a non-government, privately maintained server when

---

[152] Hillary Clinton at a campaign fundraising event in New York City (September 9, 2016).

conducting official business. Despite all Clinton's denials of wrongdoing, experts, officials, members of Congress, and political opponents,—especially General Mike Flynn—contended her use of her own messaging system software and a private server violated federal laws and regulations. She left her confidential, perhaps even highly classified communications vulnerable to potential hacking by anyone, including hostile foreign powers.

Hillary Clinton's carefully cultivated image as the competent president-in-waiting was tarnished and then further damaged when in a joint statement released on July 15, 2015, the Inspector General of the State Department and the Inspector General of the Intelligence Community said their review of her emails contained classified information when sent, remained so at the time of their inspection and "never should have been transmitted via an unclassified personal system."[153]

The dream candidate of the establishment was in deep trouble if just one email reappeared. Hillary Clinton's candidacy was a hostage if her emails resurfaced during the campaign. The problem was not the FBI investigation, as the Swamp could and would ensure a benign outcome. After all, what FBI senior office holder was going to deliberately upset the next president, especially one with a reputation for taking revenge?

From the outset, it was unlikely the investigation was going to lead anywhere, probably because too many influential people would be caught up and exposed. The real concern was that if a hostile foreign

---

[153] https://www.nytimes.com/2015/07/25/us/politics/hillary-clinton-email-classified-information-inspector-general-intelligence-community.html

power released one classified email, Hillary would be finished as a credible candidate.

Hillary's enduring nightmare throughout the campaign was that her missing emails fell into the hands of one or more of her many opponents and would reappear at a decisive moment as a dreaded "October surprise." As much as she might like to, Hillary could not control if and when those missing emails appeared. She could not change what was written in them. Hillary needed a plan. If she could not change the message, she could change the messenger. So the goal of her operation was to deflect their damaging effect by creating in advance a storm of indignation about who the hostile actors were who might release them.

The containment strategy was to have the national security scandal twisted and deflected into a problem for the rival Trump campaign. By re-characterizing the crime from Hillary's handling of classified material into the method of releasing the Clinton's emails, she removed the perception that she compromised America's interests by her actions. The tactic was so effective, it was used a second time in 2019 to shield the White House "whistleblower." It became a "crime" to investigate or name the "whistleblower" to distract from what he said and did.

The Swamp always assumed that the Republican campaign would search for, find and then exploit Hillary's email scandal. Democrats pushed the story that Russian intelligence had accessed her server. The FBI informer Stefan Halper, put to his target Carter Page that in past campaigns he was involved in, "we would have used it in a heartbeat."[154] The Democrats suggested that the nominee for the GOP campaign would have the most to gain from the release of Hillary's emails into the public domain. Donald Trump by default became the "prime suspect." Having formed these assumptions, the establishment planned an insurance policy surveillance and disinformation operation. The plan was to find a way to arrange surveillance on the Trump campaign to monitor the non existent preparations for an "October surprise" that existed only in Democrat fantasies.

Simultaneously, the offensive strategy was to damage the Trump campaign's electoral prospects. Donald Trump and Gen. Flynn were hard at work creating a potent populist patriot movement—"Make America Great Again"—as a base for the election. What better way to undermine the nascent patriotic movement than expose its leaders as traitors, Russia's puppets? The disinformation operation painted the pair's work related trips to Russia as sinister. The plotters apparently mined the rich old seam of Soviet-era suspicion and the fear of Russian espionage to resonate with the American people. My hypothesis is that their covert plan hearkened back to the age that Halper and his employers were all happier living in, channeling the sordid games of the Cold War. Director of National Intelligence James Clapper, for one, frequently and easily slips back into the rhetoric calling Russians "Soviets." The Soviet Union collapsed at the end of 1991.

---

[154] FBI transcript from IG Report, 318; https://apps.npr.org/documents/document.html?id=6571534-OIG-Russia-Investigation-Report. https://thefederalist.com/2020/01/28/ig-report-proves-obama-administration-spied-on-trump-campaign-big-time/

Chapter Ten: Means and Opportunity

Ye are of your father the devil, and the lusts of your father ye will do. He was a murderer from the beginning, and abode not in the truth, because there is no truth in him. When he speaketh a lie, he speaketh of his own: for he is a liar, and the father of it.

—John 8:44

We will set fires, we will launch legends, the unrest will begin and rolling will be of such magnitude that the world has not seen before.

—Fyodor Dostoevsky *"Demons"*

"Will you walk into my parlor?" said a spider to a fly;

"t'is the prettiest little parlor that ever you did spy."

—Mary Howitt *"The Spider and the Fly"*

Means

Planning for Spygate seems to have begun around July 2015 by a small group within the intelligence community. My hypothesis is that the most likely catalyst was Halper—his report from Cambridge about the Russian president supposed loathing of Hillary Clinton and speculation of what Putin might do in 2016. July is the most likely month when Halper would have submitted his proposal to the

Pentagon's Office of Net Assessment which was approved in September 2015.[155]

At the very top echelon of the intelligence community, sat President Obama loyalists and political maneuverers CIA Director John Brennan and Director of National Intelligence James Clapper. Both men were apparently keen to curry favor with Hillary Clinton. Each wanted to stay in their positions post-election and were eager to demonstrate their loyalty to the candidate they expected to win.

The old chess game of state versus state espionage was meat and drink to the bureaucratic old-fashioned CIA with its deeply entrenched anti-Russia house views. The then-Director was among the fiercest Russia haters. As we see throughout Spygate, John Brennan is "more of an ideologue than he is an intelligence officer. He sees the world a certain way, and he tries to comport the facts to fit his vision," said CIA Station Chief Daniel Hoffman, a critic in a recent interview.[156]

Brennan claims in his own words that because he made a close study of the methods of long-dead KGB Soviet-era chief Yuri Andropov. The then CIA Director just *knew* without any current evidence that Russia was interfering in the 2016 US presidential election by working with the Trump campaign long before anyone else. His "radar just went up."[157] Brennan famously does not do evidence; he does intelligence.

---

[155] Senator Chuck Grassley's audit, of the Office of Net Assessments https://www.grassley.senate.gov/sites/default/files/constituents/DoD%20OIG%20Memo%20on%20ONA%20Contracts%20with%20Professor%20Halper%20%20-%20D2019-D000AX-0104.pdf

[156] Edwin Mora, "Former CIA Station Chief: DNI Richard Grenell Bringing 'Much Needed Efficiency' to 'Bloated' Intel Community," Breitbart (April 4, 2020).

[157] Congressional Hearing (May 23, 2017).

The fact is, Russia, China, any number of nations try to use cyber espionage techniques to monitor the American elections to gain insight into candidate's thinking. During a speech in September 2016, at the Intelligence and National Security Summit in Washington, then Director of National Intelligence Clapper, lacking evidence declined to directly place blame on the Kremlin for the DNC hack. Clapper simply said what is widely acknowledged that the cyber attacks highlight the fact that "people all around the world, not just opposing parties, want to know what the candidates are thinking."[158]

The supporting act to John Brennan was the Director of National Intelligence James Clapper. He is quoted in September 2016 telling David Ignatius of the *Washington Post*, "Russia has tried to influence US elections since the 1960s."[159] Clapper is referring to reports of Soviet ambassadors allegedly offering financial support to two Democratic presidential candidates in the 1960s, which were rebuffed. Clapper knows, however, the Soviets didn't take political sides in US elections, but tried and mostly failed to cultivate both parties and all candidates. Backing just one candidate is a desperate and shortsighted strategy. Clapper's disingenuous statement was used as solid evidence to support the first FISA application on Trump foreign policy advisor Carter Page a month later in October of 2016, a month before the earth-shattering Trump victory.[160]

John Brennan and James Clapper, the two most senior intelligence figures, who perhaps kickstarted the Russia hoax claiming they felt in

[158] https://www.politico.com/story/2016/09/russia-hacks-america-james-clapper-227831

[159] https://www.washingtonpost.com/video/postlive/clapper-russia-has-tried-to-influence-us-elections-before/2016/09/20/0c08d0c0-7f98-11e6-ad0e-ab0d12c779b1_video.html

[160] Carter Page FISA warrant application, https://assets.documentcloud.org/documents/4614708/Carter-Page-FISA-Application.pdf

their guts the Russians and the Trump campaign were up to something. Did they order an operation in search of a crime predicated by still unknown "intelligence?" According to press reports, the US is blind to Russian intelligence activities and intentions. The report says that the CIA have no "high-level intelligence sources inside Moscow," according to the anonymous intelligence community members who regularly feed stories to Adam Goldman of the *New York Times*.[161] Think about this for a moment, the vaunted CIA with all its untold billions at its disposal may well have no "high level sources inside Moscow". It is for this reason Halper's "reports" from Moscow and the fabricated "Steele Dossier"—despite both clearly fake—became so vital in the Russiagate hoax. Brennan and Clapper had nothing else.

The CIA were exposed as recently as 2014 for spying on US politicians domestically, lying about it, and getting away with it. None other than John Brennan of all people was taken to task by the Democrats who called for his resignation for CIA spying on an inquiry into the rendition, detention and interrogation network. The Director first denied the charge. "Nothing could be further from the truth," he said. "We wouldn't do that. That's just beyond the scope of reason in terms of what we'd do."[162]

Months later his denial to Congress was publicly proved false. The CIA internal investigation found its officers penetrated a computer network used by the Senate Intelligence Committee to report on the CIA's detention and interrogation program. *The New York Times* reported: "The report by the agency's inspector general also found that

---

[161] Adam Goldman and Julian Barnes, "Russia Trying to Stoke US Racial Tensions Before Election, Officials Say," *NYT* (March 10, 2020).

[162] Alex Emmons, "Five Questions for https://theintercept.com/2016/02/19/5-questions-for-cia-director-john-brennan/

C.I.A. officers read the emails of the Senate investigators and sent a criminal referral to the Justice Department based on false information."[163] Despite the exposure of manifest wrongdoing within the Washington establishment elite and the Intelligence community, there was no accountability and no price to pay for lying and spying.

The Operation

The hypothesis is that the first stage of what was originally a small-scale CIA operation ran through to July 2016. Despite the later depiction of an enormous threat to the United States from Russian intelligence, the counter operation started out as a one-man "investigation." Most likely Brennan's CIA hand-picked Stefan Halper, who was not a trained investigator but a septuagenarian, ham-fisted "off the books" contractor with a terrible reputation. The Deep State knew what they were going to get when they hired Halper, which is why they chose him. The "intelligence" was going to be wild accusations, and unprovable smears which could be widely disseminated like all opposition research with the added value they could never be objectively disproven. That's why using a spy is a win-win.

Spygate might have begun as a low-resource sideshow, but its intensity and significance certainly   increased as Donald Trump rose in the polls. The operation went into overdrive after the election result. Even my innocuous contact with Gen. Flynn had to be presented to Congress as proof of collusion between the Trump Campaign and Russian intelligence.[164]

---

[163] NYT "Inquiry by C.I.A. Affirms It Spied on Senate Panel" By Mark Mazzetti and Carl Hulse August 1, 2014

[164] John Brennan testimony before Congress (May 23, 2017)

Faced with the dire prospect of Gen. Flynn as National Security Advisor in a Trump presidency, the intelligence Swamp apparently launched a campaign of leaks to the press to undermine them. Could it be that rumors emanating from Halper's Cambridge Club were dressed up as gold-plated British intelligence product to bolster their worth and later leaked? Such press "reports" generated unprecedented fierce denials by the British government of any official involvement in Spygate by their snooping bureau GCHQ.[165]

According to Rep. Devin Nunes, the Ranking Member of the House Intelligence Committee, "the first Trump associate to be investigated was General Flynn."[166] Gen. Flynn was the initial target of the intelligence effort. Spying is not limited to gathering information; it is also dirty ops such as the creation and placement of a false narrative. Long before joining the Trump campaign, Gen. Flynn made himself a target by being extremely vocal in his criticism of Hillary Clinton. Through Halper's work for the Obama administration he had contacts with Russians and was at one stage very likely to become the vice president or some similar high position if Trump won.

The hypothesis is that the initial espionage by Halper was to provide enough rumor, masquerading as "intelligence," to trigger an official FBI counterintelligence investigation into the General. The predicate for the operation was my supposed "Russian intelligence" contact with Gen. Flynn in 2014. Once the FBI launched its inquiry, which it did in, the existence of the investigation would perhaps be leaked to the press

---

[165] Alastair Jamieson, "Britain's GCHQ Denies 'Ridiculous' Claim It Helped Wiretap Trump," NBC (March 17, 2017).

[166] Congressional Record of Special Counsel Robert Mueller (July 24, 2019), https://www.washingtonpost.com/politics/transcript-of-robert-s-mueller-iiis-testimony-before-the-house-intelligence-committee/2019/07/24/f424acf0-ad97-11e9-a0c9-6d2d7818f3da_story.html

as it was for explosive effect as close to the election as possible. There was no better way to diffuse a surging patriot movement than to reveal its leaders were in cahoots with the world's greatest foreign bogeyman: Russian president Vladimir Putin.

The CIA lacks investigative authority, only the FBI possesses both counterintelligence and law enforcement powers. The FBI can legally investigate, without evidence such crimes as terrorism and espionage if they merely suspect one may occur. This was the achievement of the then FBI Director Robert Mueller after 9/11, later the Special Counsel. It was Mueller who demanded that the FBI be given unprecedented law enforcement powers to be, in his words, "more forward-leaning, more predictive, a step ahead of the next germinating threat."[167]

The key to the FBI's new mandate was intelligence—the holy grail of national security work. Mueller got the legal authority for the FBI to collect intelligence on America's enemies before crimes are committed. The FBI used these same powers intended to combat terrorism in 2016 to target a domestic political campaign. John Brennan told the House Intelligence Committee that the CIA began uncovering from the start of 2016 and then he passed along enough intelligence that Russia was undermining Hillary Clinton's campaign and supporting her opponent Donald Trump to justify in his opinion opening the FBI investigation.[168] Throughout early 2016 he likely passed intelligence from his source Halper to James Comey's FBI to investigate.

---

[167] Mueller's comments after 9/11, https://www.fbi.gov/history/brief-history/a-new-era-of-national-security.

[168] https://www.justsecurity.org/wp-content/uploads/2019/08/Open-Hearing-On-Active-Measures-During-the-2016-Election-Campaign.pdf

The Intelligence Cycle

Intelligence does not appear from thin air; there is a process to create it. The process is known as the intelligence cycle. First, intelligence must be commissioned or directed by someone in a position of authority. The next stage is intelligence collection. The third stage is the analysis of the intelligence gathered, and the final step is the dissemination of the results. The cycle is complete when the instigator commissions more intelligence.

At each stage in the Spygate intelligence cycle then CIA Director John Brennan was intimately involved, which was highly unusual. For the intelligence cycle to work, the instigator has to allow the other stages to act independently. In Spygate, this did not happen. The instigator predetermined intelligence would be found linking Gen. Flynn to a Russian intelligence operation interfering in the US election involving Donald Trump.

The Instigator

Attorney General William Barr assigned the US Attorney in Connecticut to review the origins of Russia inquiry[169] to identify who the instigator of Spygate was and what, if any, was their predicate. Put simply, the instigator of Spygate could be the person or persons who commissioned "super-spy" Stefan Halper.

Retracing the trail of Halper, who seemingly produced much of the early intelligence could lead to identifying the instigator. Then CIA Director John Brennan's public statements and actions suggest he is

---

[169] Adam Goldman, Charlie Savage, Michael S. Schmidt, "Barr Assigns US Attorney in Connecticut to Review Origins of Russia Inquiry," *NYT* (May 13, 2019).

the likely chief suspect for the instigator. In May 2017, Brennan explained to Congress he directed the initial intelligence gathering in early 2016. It was his hunch, as he put it: "his radar went up." Brennan knew the Russians were up to something because, in his opinion, Russian president Vladimir Putin hated Secretary Hillary Clinton:

BRENNAN: I think that they, most of the time, believed that Secretary Clinton was going to win the election, and so their efforts to denigrate her were not just to try to diminish her chances of winning, but also to hurt her and—for her eventual presidency. But also it's my assessment that they clearly had a more favorable view toward Mr. Trump, and actions they were taking were trying to increase his prospects, even though I think that they probably felt as though they were not all that great.

ROONEY [REP. TOM ROONEY (R), FLORIDA]: Why? Why did they—why did they want her—why did they want him and not her?

BRENNAN: I think it's a variety of reasons. One is that there was a— had been a traditional, I think, animus, certainly, between Mr. Putin and Secretary Clinton, as well as that there has not been a good relationship between the Putins (sic) and—between Putin and the Clintons over the years: felt that Secretary Clinton, with some of her actions while she was secretary of state, led to some of the domestic disturbances inside of Russia. And I think he was more concerned that she was going to be more rigid on certain issues, particularly on human rights and other issues.[170]

On December 16, 2016, Hillary Clinton linked protests in Moscow in 2011 and supposed Russian intelligence intervention in her election campaign. "Putin publicly blamed me for the outpouring of outrage by

---

[170] http://edition.cnn.com/TRANSCRIPTS/1705/23/ath.01.html

his own people, and that is the direct line between what he said back then and what he did in this election,"[171] she claimed. Vladimir Putin was reported as having concerns about comments made by Hillary Clinton.[172] Brennan took a pre-packed theory from Hillary's long list of excuses for her defeat to explain the reason for the Russian collusion no-one found. This absurd claim is the foundation of the Trump Russia collusion narrative. Hillary via the New York Times foisted a delusion on a gullible and hostile segment of the electorate, media and DC elites, all too willing to believe anything that explained Trump's stunning victory, no matter how unlikely in the real world.

The Intelligence Collector

It appears that for the task of collector assigned to find the signs of Russian intelligence activity, CIA Director John Brennan decided not to use any of the vast resources of the CIA. He might have needed the services of an amoral, unscrupulous intelligence operative or a fantasist. Brennan had just the one right on hand. Was the collector Stefan Halper, who has performed this type of work before in political campaigns, and, more importantly despite later exposure got away with it? During Spygate, Halper also worked for, and was paid by, the FBI, Obama's Department of Defense, and had links to the Hillary campaign's dirty tricks operation.

Halper's motives may well include ambition, money, and political motivation. No doubt he would have loved being at the center of another election fix. According to his friends in the media, Halper was

---

[171] Amy Chozick, "Clinton Says 'Personal Beef' by Putin Led to Hacking Attacks," NYT (December 16, 2016).

[172] David M. Herszenhorn and Ellen Barry, "Putin Contends Clinton Incited Unrest Over Vote," *NYT* (December 8, 2011).

a CIA asset and informer for decades.[173] In 2008 he began double-dipping, perhaps being paid for the same work by the FBI.[174]

Helping Halper, there were known holes in FBI procedures ripe for exploitation. One example is if a confidential human source is trusted and has provided reliable information before, everything the source provides is considered verified.[175] A second loophole is the FBI has no ability, desire, or even space on its forms to verify non-US sub-sources.[176] Further, the FBI must have known, after all who didn't, about Halper's lurid past and his close connections to the CIA. Director Wray has introduced in December 2019 a reform to the procedures about handling Confidential Human Sources. It is now an imperative for the FBI to check with other agencies such as the CIA about possible relationships to their sources .[177]

Yet the US has in place a strict legal prohibition against the weaponization of intelligence for political purposes. At every turn, the plotters put in place workarounds to circumvent the law. Halper's orders appear to have been to gather (manufacture) evidence to transform a hero, General Michael Flynn, into a traitor. You would think inventing an entirely fake back story is a tough task in the internet age. Luckily, if the story remained as an intelligence report it did not have to be the slightest bit credible, as the intended audience was never going to ask questions.

---

[173] *New York Times* and *Washington Post*

[174] Horowitz Report https://www.justice.gov/storage/120919-examination.pdf

[175] Ibid.

[176] Ibid.

[177] https://www.nytimes.com/2018/07/12/us/politics/white-house-fbi-informant.html

The Deep State must hope that precisely what the spy Halper may have reported to John Brennan will remain forever concealed behind a cloak of secrecy. The CIA and FBI jealously guard their "sources and methods", one of their founding principles. In what would be an absolute perversion of justice, a rotten apple can be absolutely protected so every other past, present, and future CIA or FBI source will feel secure. Even President Trump cannot directly name Halper when asked, only referring to him as the Spy. In TV interviews, the President is forced by convention to avoid the question. This is the genius, and the most significant frustration to those unpicking the plot, of using politicized intelligence agencies to stage a coup.

Halper seemingly left us lots of clues as to what he reported to Brennan. A willing press pool was one of the weapons used in the attempted coup. In Congress in May 2017 to the Russian Investigation Taskforce, Rep. Mike Turner of Texas summarized the early "intelligence" Brennan passed on: "You said that you saw intelligence that indicated that there had been contacts with individuals—with—with Russians—that were of a nature that bore investigation." In response Brennan expounded a circular argument: "It is when it's in the context that there is something else going on—and so we knew, at the time, that the Russians were involved in this effort to try to interfere in our election. So with that backdrop, and increasing indications that they were involved in that, seeing these types of contacts and interactions during the same period of time raised my—my concern."[178] The duplicity is clear. Brennan states that his gut feel in early 2016, well before any hacking is even reported, is proof positive that the Russians were intervening in the election and

---

[178] Transcript from May 23, 2017 Congressional hearing, http://transcripts.cnn.com/TRANSCRIPTS/1705/23/ath.01.html.

therefore the "contacts" with Trump campaign officials form part of that operation.

We know from a declassified FBI report that Halper was identifying "suspicious" contacts between Gen. Flynn and Russian intelligence and uncovering the "evidence" Russia was colluding with the Trump campaign in the election. Luckily for Halper, it was all apparently happening on his doorstep in Cambridge, England involving people he knew.

Intelligence Analysis

Having apparently fixed the choice of a collector, John Brennan ensured his CIA analysts accepted Halper's nonsense as credible information. For information to be classed as intelligence, it has to pass a very low bar anyway. It does not even have to be true. "Human intelligence" is essentially gossip. The only difference between gossip and intelligence is who relays that information to the Agency. The key is the credibility of the human source, providing the intelligence. The CIA employs legions of analysts; supposed experts in the fields. These analysts assess how much reliance can be placed on the intelligence passing across their desks. Verification from a second source is ideal.

Halper may have been the sole source for all the CIA Spygate intelligence. But if you look at his past, Halper has no credibility. His unverifiable concoction must have seemed fantastical and incredible. Despite his long association with the CIA, his intelligence would have serious issues and problems. As John le Carré's greatest creation George Smiley points out in *Tinker, Tailor, Soldier, Spy*: "impressive topicality" makes intelligence "suspect" at once. "If it was genuine, it was gold-dust, but there was no earthy reason to suppose it was genuine."[179] Everything Halper delivered as "gold-dust" was easily proven untrue and far too topical.

All his intelligence should have failed at the analyst stage of the cycle. The fact is the normal process was not followed. This suspicion is confirmed by two facts. Firstly, it was reported that US Attorney Durham, as part of his criminal investigation, has interviewed the CIA analysts involved in Spygate after a monumental public fight.[180] Secondly, John Brennan bypassed normal channels by setting up a handpicked small working group. The main issue is Brennan, who directed intelligence gathering, was influencing the analysis with a positive confirmation bias before it could be verified.

The US Attorney in Connecticut John Durham is also reportedly investigating the analysts.[181] In turn, the analysts have lawyered up. CIA defenders are out in force in the press, explaining how these experts just guess. It is termed "best understanding." Leading the apologists is John McLaughlin, who served as deputy director of the CIA from 2000 to 2004 and acting director in 2004, wrote in the *Washington Post* that "Prosecutors investigating intelligence analysts is a dangerous idea":

> More often he or she is seeking to assess what an adversary is thinking, intending or doing based on incomplete information. But an intelligence analyst does not have a prosecutor's luxury to decline to proceed in the face of ambiguous information;

---

[179] John le Carré, *Tinker, Tailor, Soldier, Spy* (New York: Penguin, 1974), 178.

[180] John McLaughlin, who served as deputy director of the CIA from 2000 to 2004 and acting director in 2004, writing in the *Washington Post* hints at the scale of dispute.

[181] Daniel Chaitin, "Ex-top CIA official perturbed by John Durham's review of intelligence analysts," *Washington Examiner* (June 22, 2019).

even when information is incomplete and conclusions uncertain, policymakers need to make decisions. We will rarely if ever, have definitive proof of what Vladimir Putin is planning . . . but the president and his advisers still must decide what to do even in the absence of proof beyond a reasonable doubt. They need the intelligence community's best understanding—even when that understanding is incomplete or inferential.[182]

In 2016, the CIA heard all kinds of scuttlebutt that they put in their reports. Having gold-plated the gossip, they then disseminated and leaked it the press, leaving victims, such as myself to disprove the smear.

Dissemination of Intelligence

John Brennan took personal charge of the dissemination of the Spygate intelligence. His efforts are explored in a later chapter. After the intelligence failures identified after 9/11, the intelligence community was ordered to coordinate better. Brennan used this directive to form a small hand-picked working group. Through this route he would have been able to pass on to the FBI whatever Halper apparently fabricated as intelligence. Brennan stated to Congress:

> If there are Russian—known or suspected Russian intelligence officers who seem to be cultivating contacts with US persons, and there are reasons for CIA or others to be concerned about what's happening there, we would make sure that the Bureau is aware of it. . . . The CIA has very unique counterintelligence authorities as well, and we have a unique collection of authorities that make us the—I think, the closest partner with the Bureau in this matter, because we

---

[182] Robert S. Litt and John McLaughlin, "Prosecutors investigating intelligence analysts is a dangerous idea," *Washington Post* (January 16, 2020).

have the intelligence liaison relationships with our foreign service—sister services. We have covert action responsibilities; we have clandestine collection responsibilities and authorities, we have all sorts of analytic capabilities—the best analysts in the US government, bar none. And so that combination of talent and capabilities is able to give the Bureau what they need.[183]

As it has been reported, the CIA has no "high-level sources in Moscow", nor did they have Five Eyes foreign intelligence product.[184] Did Brennan make all this up? Further, Brennan apparently shared the explosive best bits with everyone from the White House down. Could it be that that the strategy was always for unverified fantastical false intelligence to be leaked to the media before election day?

Payment

Could it be that Halper's outsized contract with the Pentagon formally awarded in September 2015 is the clearest evidence of possible Spygate preparations? It is a fixed point in the saga. The criminal investigators and Congress are reportedly looking into them.[185] Halper would have needed paying. This is a big clue as to the genesis of Spygate. Halper needed paying a lot. The initial contract awarded to Halper under the Obama administration was for $244,000 of taxpayers' money in September 2015. Following normal practice Stefan Halper would have to submit his application to the Pentagon for rubber stamp approval a few months earlier, probably in July 2015.

---

[183] John Brennan testifying before Congress (May 23, 2017), http://transcripts.cnn.com/TRANSCRIPTS/1705/23/ath.01.html.

[184] The Five Eyes is an intelligence sharing agreement between the intelligence services of the US, UK, Canada, Australia and New Zealand.

[185] https://saraacarter.com/durham-probe-expands-to-pentagon-office-that-contracted-fbi-spy-stephan-halper/

Clandestine operations maintain plausible deniability by making their payments off the books. There can be no direct money link that can be traced back to the CIA or other agency. In the bloated federal budget, there are many places for the intelligence services to stash untraceable rainy-day cash. Could one of the CIA's slush funds for off-the-books contracts be Pentagon's tiny Office of Net Assessments?[186] The ONA's role would have remained hidden but for a whistleblower spotting a combination of huge payments and shoddy work that smelled of corruption. Luckily for the American people, Iowa Senator Chuck Grassley,[187] Republican Chairman of the Senate Finance Committee, has been continually probing the possible slush fund. Despite obfuscation and delay, Grassley's persistence is exposing one of the ways the Deep State paid Halper.[188]

The Office of Net Assessments

The United States Department of Defense Office of Net Assessment (ONA) was created in 1973 by Richard Nixon to serve as the Pentagon's "internal think tank" that "looks 20 to 30 years into the military's future, often with the assistance of outside contractors, and produces reports on the results of its research." According to Defense Directive 5111.11, the Director shall "develop and coordinate net assessments of the standing, trends, and future prospects of US military capabilities and military potential in comparison with those of

---

[186] https://www.realclearinvestigations.com/articles/2019/07/15/stefan_halpers_wages_of_spying.html

[187] https://saraacarter.com/durham-probe-expands-to-pentagon-office-that-contracted-fbi-spy-stephan-halper/

[188] https://saraacarter.com/sen-grassley-demands-answers-from-pentagon-on-fbi-spy-stefan-halpers-questionable-defense-contracts/

other countries or groups of countries in order to identify emerging or future threats or opportunities for the United States."[189]

However, interview transcripts confirm, under questioning, Office of Net Assessments officials have acknowledged the Office has not produced a net assessment, despite its core mission, since 2007; that means the ONA has not fulfilled its prime mission.[190] Vested interests in the Defense Department constrained what could and could not be written in the independent studies, which is one of the perennial problems with Washington politics. The Defense department decided what could and could not be addressed by the ONA. At some point in mid-2015, was the ONA's mission altered from "future predicting" to possibly playing a part of a black bag dirty tricks financing department?

Andrew Marshall was the ONA's first director, appointed by Nixon in 1973. "Yoda is the nom de guerre for Andrew W. Marshall, the ninety-two-year-old futurist who directs the Pentagon's obliquely described internal think tank. A fixture in national-security circles since the dawn of the Cold War, Marshall contemplates military strategy and apocalyptic scenarios that could emerge in the decades to come."[191] Marshall held his position under every administration since Nixon until he retired in January 2015 to be replaced by the apparent Swamp denizen Colonel Jim Baker in May 2015. The ONA is a tiny group of no more than a dozen employees with an annual budget of $20 million. So what is a net assessment exactly? It is a multidisciplinary strategic assessment process used to provide a comparative evaluation of the

---

189 https://www.esd.whs.mil/Portals/54/Documents/DD/issuances/dodd/511111p.pdf

190 Witness testimony in the Adam Lovinger case.

191 Craig Whitlock, "Yoda still standing: Office of Pentagon futurist Andrew Marshall, 92, survives budget ax," *Washington Post* (December 4, 2013).

balance of strengths and weaknesses. A key aspect of net assessment involves analyzing technological influences on the security environment. Net assessment involves the combined use of business principles, scenarios, crisis and path gaming, conflict situations, and other tools. Nothing in the description particularly fits dirty operative Halper's bag of tricks.

Halper had a long-term relationship with the Office of Net Assessment and the Department of Defense with known contracts dating back as far as 2005. In just the four years to 2016, Halper, described as a shadowy "academic," was paid more than $1 million for research papers of dubious, if any, value. As one reporter commented, observers, including Senator Grassley, are asking whether the ONA is actually a US government think-tank equivalent of the fictional "Universal Exports," used in James Bond's books for paying for British intelligence operatives.[192]

According to reports, Halper's contracts now form a part of the US Attorney in Connecticut John Durham's criminal investigation into the origins of Spygate.[193] The money came in 2015 and 2016 from somewhere during the Obama administration. There are reports that it might have come from the CIA.[194] The number of individuals authorized to make large payments is limited so following the money trail should not take long.

---

[192] https://www.realclearinvestigations.com/articles/2019/07/15/stefan_halpers_wages_of_spying.html

[193] https://saraacarter.com/durham-probe-expands-to-pentagon-office-that-contracted-fbi-spy-stephan-halper/

[194] Sidney Powell, Flynn's attorney, terms the ONA a CIA slush fund in her legal findings.

Halper's research projects for the ONA were barely supervised and of no apparent value. Senator Chuck Grassley concluded the audit of Stefan Halper's contracts "illustrates a systemic failure to manage and oversee" the spending of federal dollars.[195] So why not simply ask Halper a few questions? One roadblock to the truth is, according to Senator Grassley in a December 2016 Fox News TV interview, Halper is avoiding official scrutiny about his contracts by claiming he is too ill to answer any questions about where the taxpayer's money went.[196] He is, however well enough to direct an aggressive legal campaign against the victim of his fabulist intelligence assaults—this author!

"What is Halper doing, and why is he being paid astronomically more than others?" was reportedly a topic of conversation at the ONA.[197] The lack of controls helps explain how Halper was able to collect so much money from the Pentagon in what was described as a "sweetheart deal" in just four years. According to the ONA whistleblower Adam Lovinger's attorney Sean Bigley: "Nobody in the office seemed to know what Halper was doing for his money," Mr. Bigley said. "Adam said Jim Baker, the director, kept Halper's contracts very close to the vest. And nobody seemed to have any idea what he was doing at the time. He subcontracted out a good chunk of it to other academics. He would compile them all and then collect the balance as his fee as a middleman. That was very unusual."[198]

---

[195] https://www.grassley.senate.gov/news/news-releases/grassley-continues-press-dod-over-mismanagement-stefan-halper-contracts

[196] "Mornings with Maria," Fox News (December 29, 2019).

[197] Interview with Adam Lovinger's attorney, *The Washington Times* (August 15, 2018), https://www.washingtontimes.com/news/2018/aug/15/adam-lovinger-pentagon-analyst-lost-security-clear/

[198] Ibid.

Adam Lovinger blew the whistle and reported problems with Halper's contracts. The Office of Net Assessments in turn accused Lovinger of mishandling sensitive data, and he has been suspended without pay. Lovinger has since been cleared of that allegation, but his career has been destroyed.[199] There are no length the coup plotters apparently wouldn't go to secure their own efforts to derail a legitimate investigation and ruin anyone who questions their actions.

A good proportion of the contract money went on Halper's unmonitored travel. The Office of Net Assessments does ask for receipts. Halper made three trips to London and one to New York in 2016, the year of Spygate, while allegedly studying Russia and China. His original proposal had built-in costs of travel to Moscow and Beijing, but Halper never went to either.

The Office of Net Assessments cannot explain why Halper's actual travels had apparently nothing to do with studying Russia-China relations but everything to do with Spygate. Halper travelled to the United Kingdom three times in 2016 in a failed attempt to see me, and to entrap Carter Page and George Papadopoulos.

An important area of focus perhaps should be Halper's alleged sources. He pitched his contracts at such large amounts because he claimed he was contracting with so many illustrious advisors and sources. The *Washington Times* examined those listed in one of his reports—"The Russia-China Relationship: The Impact on the United States' Security Interests"— in detail. Halper stated: "Consultants and Advisors. The following consultants and advisors contributed to the analysis within this study."

---

[199] https://www.washingtontimes.com/news/2019/aug/14/investigation-clears-analyst-accused-of-leaking-da/

134

Halper went on to list over two pages of names—forty-three contributors, an impressive collection of college professors and former ambassadors, White House national security staffers, and senior individuals inside the intelligence community. Even former Federal Reserve Chairman Alan Greenspan features on Halper's list. The *Washington Times* points out "listing such esteemed individuals would convey a well-connected Pentagon contractor able to network with Washington's establishment." The ONA recommends paying $3,000 per consultant. Forty-three consultants at $3,000 a time is $129,000 of taxpayers' money that went somewhere; the question is where?

When the *Washington Times* checked with fifteen of those he listed, the response was universally negative. "No memory of project or person. Quick search of calendar and email shows nothing," said Michael V. Hayden, retired Air Force general and former CIA director to the *Times*. The academic Jonathan Haslam, who is very close to Halper from his Cambridge University days and is now a Princeton professor, said:

"I was never asked to participate in this study, and I would not have agreed to do so anyway. I find it troubling that I am listed in a study that I never participated in and that some kind of payment may have been allocated to my name that I never received. I was asked to participate in a study of Russia and Afghanistan, probably back in 2013/14, but Stef failed to agree to the remuneration I wished for, so I dropped out. The pay was far too low for my expertise. I knew from working in DC in the mid-eighties how much specialist academic researchers for Andrew Marshall at the OSD usually got."[200]

---

[200] https://www.washingtontimes.com/news/2018/oct/1/stefan-halpers-russia-china-pentagon-study-lists-c/

David Shambaugh, political science professor and director of the China Policy Program at George Washington University: "No, I was not an advisor to his study. Have never communicated with him in my life." Lee Edwards, a political biographer and historian based at The Heritage Foundation: "I have no recollection of the study which is outside my area at Heritage." Michael Pettis, a finance professor at Peking University in Beijing:

"Consult" is a very strong word for my contribution. Halper is generous to include me at the same level as the rest of the group. I submitted a chapter to a book related to a DoD project he was running called "China 2030" . . . and he may have used that chapter to help him understand China's economic prospects. Aside from that, I can't say I otherwise contributed to 'The Russia-China relationship' project, and in fact, until this email, was not even aware of it."[201]

The *Washington Times* article goes on to mention Hans van de Ven, a professor at Cambridge University, where Halper has taught: "I know Stefan, and I have had lunch with him several times here in Cambridge. But I don't recall this report." Richard N. Haass, president of the Council on Foreign Relations "remembers meeting with Mr. Halper in 2016 and having a conversation with him, but does not recall and has no record of officially advising him on the Russia-China relationship." Given the others firm denials did the notable "contributor" Vyacheslav Trubnikov, who is mentioned twice take part in the study? Halper includes him in the footnotes as V.I. Trubnikov and V.S. Trubnikov.[202]

Could the ONA studies be a crucial point in understanding Halper's methods? What is in plain sight is Halper's approach to "sources" and

---

[201] Ibid.

[202] Lee Smith "The Plot Against the President : The True Story of How Congressman Devin Nunes Uncovered the Biggest Political Scandal in U. S. History."

"information gathering." In some cases he appears to have simply made the sources up; in others he uses the established intelligence disinformation, "contact method."[203] Halper has either previously met or knows of a contact with a "source." Having established a fixed date or an event, he is then free to attribute whatever information or opinion he likes to that "source."

Le Carré describes the contact artifice method in the plot of his first masterpiece *The Spy Who Came in from the Cold*—le Carré's leading character Leamas has been unwittingly set up by British Secret Service in an operation to create the illusion of an affair. The operation establishes a contact then fabricates the supporting evidence.

"But how could they know about me; how could they know we would come together?" . . . "It didn't matter—it didn't depend on that. They only had to put you and me in contact, even for a day, it didn't matter."

---

[203] It is very reminiscent of Christopher Steele's dossier.

Chapter Eleven: Follow the Money

And said unto them, What will ye give me, and I will deliver him unto you?
And they covenanted with him for thirty pieces of silver.

—Matthew: 26 :15

He who is not contented with what he has, would not be contented with what
he would like to have.

—Socrates

J ust like his fellow confidential human source Christopher Steele,[204] does Halper's deception unwind when someone starts checking with his sub-sources? Halper perhaps hoped to get away with inventing sources and bolstering the gravitas of his study. ONA reports are secret, unverified, and the sources he quotes were unlikely to ever find out their names were being used in this way. Yet it seems it is because of Halper's blatant fabrications that his own methods came under Congressional scrutiny and were shown to be deceitful.

On January 16, 2019, Senator Grassley requested the Department of Defense Office of Inspector General review the contracts with Professor Stefan Halper to see whether they were "used to support as has been suspected, potential partisan political or other allegedly

---

[204] https://www.dailymail.co.uk/news/article-8189913/Ex-MI6-spy-dirty-dossier-Donald-Trump-sued-three-Russian-oligarchs.html

illegal purposes."[205] The Department of Defense Inspectors started asking questions when they suspected corruption. What they have uncovered is potentially something far more sinister than just defrauding the taxpayer. The ONA reports are used for planning US defense strategy. Potentially there is a much, much bigger issue.

Could it be that with this potential swindle at the taxpayers' expense Halper has demonstrated that he is a fraudster? Is he untrustworthy, unreliable, and does he fabricate important information? It is important because Halper is also a confidential human source on the front line of the nation's counterintelligence operation tackling a grave crisis. The FBI even told the FISA court many times he was a reliable source.[206] So did Halper invent sources and intelligence to promote and sustain the Spygate narrative in the same way he did with his studies? If there is an issue of the billing of advisors for government studies, why should we give him any credence on the graver issue of intelligence fabrication?

Legal Framework

The "small group" planning a covert intelligence operation to interfere in a US election faced several significant challenges, not least of which was designing a workaround for the strict legal prohibition against just such activities. Maintaining the facade of "plausible deniability" if exposed and investigated requires the most legal work; mounting an operation is the easy part. Some in intelligence believe rules are a constraint imposed only on the "good guys "which gives the "bad guys" an unfair advantage. Finding a way around inconvenient rules to

---

[205] https://www.grassley.senate.gov/news/news-releases/grassley-continues-press-dod-over-mismanagement-stefan-halper-contracts

[206] IG Horowitz report

achieve a successful mission is viewed as acceptable if the end justifies the means. Spygate amply demonstrates the need for rules.

The seditious coup plotters working against President Trump knew from the start the legal prohibitions on what they planned to do. They avoided getting a legal finding to approve their actions as they certainly did not want a piece of paper like that floating around Washington, DC. There had to be a better way to pull off the coup. Does the evidence of these machinations date to December 2015 when the lawyer Lisa Page was sent text messages by her boyfriend, the now infamous FBI Special Agent Peter Strzok, "You get all our OCONUS lures approved? ;)?"[207] (OCONUS means outside continental United States and a lure is jargon for a double agent.) When the president learned of the message, Donald Trump tweeted on June 5, 2018, "Wow, Strzok-Page, the incompetent & corrupt FBI lovers, have texts referring to a counter-intelligence operation into the Trump Campaign dating way back to December, 2015. . . SPYGATE is in full force!"

The plotters worked hard on the design of an operation to get around the ban. The workaround was to create a foreign counterintelligence "threat" that could then be "imported" to the United States as a legal FBI investigation of Americans working for the Trump campaign.[208] The trigger event to import the investigation had to be a verified contact between a Trump campaign official and Russian intelligence. There were likely two attempts to manufacture a trigger events by Halper in February and in August 2016 when he reported on Gen. Flynn and this author.

---

[207] https://www.redstate.com/elizabeth-vaughn/2019/12/04/lisa-page-text-peter-strzok-get-oconus-lures-approved/

[208] https://www.gatestoneinstitute.org/15219/durham-indictments

The legal cover works if the illegal CIA political operation against an election campaign was framed as a genuine counterintelligence operation mounted against a Russian intelligence threat. The Russians had to be depicted as the first movers approaching campaign officials and the American's action a response.

Was Halper--who was already on the books as an FBI confidential human source (CHS) as well as a long-term CIA asset--readied in December 2015 as an "OCONUS lure? If so, he was to fabricate and report an evidence trail of Russian intelligence activity with campaign officials to the CIA. The agency would then pass on his "intelligence" about those US individuals he implicated to the FBI to investigate. Designating an informer a Confidential Human Source grants them a special legal status that prevents their name being officially released. As the invoices submitted to the Pentagon Office of Net Assessments suggest, Halper set to spying just before December 2015. My hypothesis based on his behavior is that his objective was to create false Russian intelligence contacts with General Mike Flynn, the key Trump campaign advisor. Conveniently the threshold to trigger an FBI national security investigation is set at an incredibly low level because of the serious nature of the threat.

However, defending the operation as a legitimate enterprise became impossible when it was revealed the intelligence community deliberately selected the known dirty operative Halper to lie, leak, and then investigate. His reputation is such that hiding Halper's involvement was crucial, hence the huge fight at the start of May 2018 to prevent his exposure.

The *Washington Post* reporter Tom Hamburger tried to defend the use of Halper on June 5, 2018 saying, "Former Justice Department and intelligence officials said Halper's work appeared to be routine—occasionally supplying limited information for a broad FBI inquiry into Russian efforts to intervene in US politics."[209]

However, as FBI Director Christopher Wray now admits: "Yes, surveillance of Carter Page was illegal."[210] Tom Hamburger of the *Washington Post* gained access to Sir Richard Dearlove who according to the journalist knew what Halper was up to in Cambridge. Hamburger wrote, "To colleagues and friends, Halper's participation in the case was appropriate for an experienced former White House official with access to individuals already of interest to investigators."[211] The question is who were the persons of interest to "investigators" when Halper was activated in December 2015 and what access did he have to them in Cambridge? The answer is crystal clear, General Flynn and myself.

Obtaining Surveillance

Forget the elaborate FISA process; US authorities possess other powers to snoop on its citizens. James Clapper, Gen. Flynn's mortal enemy, explained how it worked to CNN on April 12, 2019, saying "to the extent that there was surveillance of anyone, it had—it was occasioned by contacts with Russians who were targets, validated foreign intelligence targets."[212] If an American, in this case, Gen.

---

[209] https://www.washingtonpost.com/politics/cambridge-university-perch-gave-fbi-source-access-to-top-intelligence-figures--and-a-cover-as-he-reached-out-to-trump-associates/2018/06/05/c6764dc2-641e-11e8-99d2-0d678ec08c2f_story.html

[210] https://www.washingtonexaminer.com/news/fbi-director-carter-page-was-surveilled-illegally

[211] Tom Hamburger, Robert Costa, and Ellen Nakashima, "Cambridge University Perch," *Washington Post* (June 5 2018).

[212] https://www.realclearpolitics.com/video/2019/04/12/clapper_on_trump_spying_i_cant_speak_specifically_to_what_the_fbi_did.html

Flynn, has contact with a verified Russian intelligence target, that is enough to start surveillance on the campaign—without a court warrant.

Halper had to find a Russian who met Gen. Flynn even once and paint them as an intelligence asset to be the predicate for spying on one of Donald Trump's main advisors. Lazy Halper found this Russian on his doorstep in Cambridge, England: I was the one, he targeted an academic and a historian with no connection to Russian intelligence whatsoever. I became a victim whose life Halper turned upside down when he falsely depicted me as a "validated Russian intelligence target." The only "validator" was Halper.

Establishing Russian intelligence contacts with campaign officials was a necessary precondition to a mission in search of a crime involving surveillance on a US citizen; especially a senior one working at the top of the Trump campaign. It was hoped that through such surveillance not only could they keep tabs on the campaign, but perhaps a crime would be revealed that could be used to derail Donald Trump. An intercepted phone call or electronic communication would be far better than any of Halper's human intelligence.

As the intelligence on General Flynn and myself was entirely fabricated, the surveillance that followed was illegal. Ex-Director of National Intelligence James Clapper keeps saying the surveillance was spying on Russian activity—that is, on myself—and that the reports lead to an American, that is Gen. Flynn. Yet Clapper knows it was the other way around. The plotters wanted surveillance on Gen. Flynn, an American in the Trump campaign and so invented a Russian intelligence contact. Halper's claimed specialty is sourcing information on Russian involvement in US politics.[213] The obvious conundrum solved by my account is why Halper was activated in 2015, long before he met Carter Page for the first time in July 2016 and before any reports of hacking.

Russian Disinformation the False Motive

CIA Director John Brennan and Director of National Intelligence James Clapper told the world Russians have always interfered in US elections. But the history of Soviet operations is not quite what they claim. They were deliberately peddling a myth. Brennan and Clapper are both willing broadcasters of disinformation, unverifiable Soviet KGB tales distributed by MI6 the CIA had at one time concluded was fake. Brennan is quite clear he is referring to but not naming Vasili Mitrokhin.[214]

Legend has it that in 1991 a scruffily dressed old Russian approached the American embassy in one of the newly minted Baltic republics, some accounts say Latvia. He asked at the door to speak to the CIA representative. The former Soviet Union's economy collapsed, and such requests were commonplace at the time. The KGB made themselves the elite in the Communist workers' state, enjoying a privileged lifestyle. They had access to cars, the best flats, and unique shops. After the economic collapse, their pensions, political standing and reputation were worthless as Russia endured a crash course in capitalism.

---

213 Tom Hamburger et al, "Cambridge University Perch," *Washington Post* (June 5, 2018).

214 Intelligence Community Assessment and Congressional testimony. www.dni.gov › files › documents › ICA_2017_01

The CIA rep met with the man who revealed himself to be a long-retired KGB Major. He had a story and something to sell. The man was Vasili Mitrokhin and what he was carrying was a sample from his alleged list of US traitors: Western assets of his former employer, the KGB. Mitrokhin claimed to be the long-serving archivist of the KGB with access to every secret. Before retiring in 1984, he allegedly supervised moving the records of the spy agency from its old HQ Lubyanka in Dzershisnky Square, central Moscow to its new building at Yasenevo. Along the way, he said he copied nuggets from the thousands of files that crossed his desk and smuggled it out of the KGB building on scraps of paper. He claimed he hid these papers for years in milk churns in the garden of his dacha (country house). Mitrokhin planned an affluent retirement in the West on the proceeds of selling his stolen treasures.

The problem was the CIA found Mitrokhin not credible and his material false. The least of the issues was the "intelligence" was old. Mitrokhin always possessed a rarified exaggerated view on the value of his archive to the West. He believed that when he published his book, exposing the evils of the KGB, a copy would be bought by everyone in the West. But the CIA turned him away.

Mitrokhin was nothing if not determined. He tried his luck with the Brits. He apparently went to the British embassy, and MI6 saw his potential. An operation retrieved the 25,000 pages of files hidden in his house.[215] Mitrokhin and his family were then exfiltrated to Britain, and he set to work with MI6 decoding and translating his scraps of paper into some useful order.

---

[215] https://www.theguardian.com/news/2004/feb/04/guardianobituaries.russia

Mitrokhin Is Not a Reliable Source

The problem MI6 soon discovered was it was not just the material that was a mess, but Mitrokhin was eccentric. His political views were radical, sometime anti-Semitic, and occasionally off the chart. He called the Soviet Union the "accursed regime" and his archive "on the trail of filth." Mitrokhin was a difficult sell, especially as his material was not the actual KGB files, only his notes. But the British persevered using an ingenious route. The big prize was America. Rather than work with the CIA who had no interest in Mitrokhin's old dirty laundry, the Brits went instead to the FBI in 1992. The FBI loved the idea of arresting an array of traitors and waited each week anxiously for more names from the British.

But how were the cash-strapped British to pay Mitrokhin for his revelations? He was greedy. The US press got wind of the existence of this defector and started leaking stories. In August 1993, Ronald Kessler published his best-selling book, *The FBI: Inside the World's Most Powerful Law Enforcement Agency*. He reported that the FBI had been interviewing a former KGB employee who had access to top secret files. "According to his account, the KGB had many hundreds of Americans and possibly more than a thousand spying for them in recent years. So specific was the information the FBI was quickly able to establish the source's credibility."[216] Everyone loves a good spy story, so other journalists followed up on the explosive revelations.

MI6 decided that to end all the speculation, they would allow the publication of some of the Mitrokhin Archive. Profits from the book would pay Mitrokhin. In late 1995 Mitrokhin was introduced to

---

[216] Ronald Kessler, *The FBI* (New York: Simon & Schuster, 1993), 520.

Professor Christopher Andrew of the University of Cambridge—a "safe pair of hands" and the official historian of MI5. The Mitrokhin Archive was published in 1999. Andrew is skilled in selling a story. Who wouldn't buy a book with this preamble:

> The facts are far more sensational even than the story dismissed as impossible by the SVR. The KGB defector brought with him to Britain details not of a few hundred but thousands of Soviet agents and intelligence officers in all parts of the globe, some of them "illegals" under deep cover abroad, disguised as foreign citizens.[217]

Soviet Attempts to Interfere in US Politics Were Hopeless

For the ex-CIA Director John Brennan and ex-Director of National Intelligence James Clapper who embarked on selling the myth to a new generation that the Russians always intervene in US elections there is a big problem. The man who knew Mitrokhin best—the world authority Professor Christopher Andrew—is quite clear in his book that the alleged previous KGB efforts to meddle in US politics were a total failure. Mitrokhin found no evidence in the files of any significant recruitment of even minor US political figures by the KGB. Oops!

Mitrokhin alleged the intention of KGB head Yuri Andropov in the 1970s was to improve political intelligence on the Main Adversary, "Glavny Protivnik" (the United States), but his plans were never realized. In fact, according to Cambridge Professor Andrew, the world expert on Mitrokhin, throughout the Cold War, the main weakness of the KGB was its inability to recruit agents able to provide high-level political intelligence. Andrew's stunning conclusion is, *the general*

---

[217] http://movies2.nytimes.com/books/first/a/andrew-sword.html

effect of KGB political intelligence gathering in the United States was probably benign."[218]

The Cyrus Vance and Zbigniew Brzezinski Myths
Could two stories ending in abject failure about political recruitment from the "Mitrokhin Archive" perhaps be the genus of Spygate? One story is that an alleged KGB talent spotter, the Soviet journalist Aleksey Arbatov, had a series of innocuous contacts during the 1970s with former Under-Secretary of Defense Cyrus Vance. According to Mitrokhin, Vance unwittingly was even given a KGB codename VIZIR. During a visit to Moscow in the spring of 1973, Vance unsurprisingly agreed in questioning with the journalist Aleksey Arbatov on the need to "increase the level of mutual trust" in US-Soviet relations.

In 1976, Aleksey Arbatov was allegedly sent on a mission by the KGB to the United States. While there, he claimed an additional 200 dollars for "operational expenses" for entertaining Vance and others. From such inconsequential meetings, Mitrokhin claims Moscow Centre briefly formed absurdly optimistic hopes of penetrating the new American administration after Jimmy Carter's victory in the presidential election of November 1976 and his appointment of Cyrus Vance as Secretary of State.

Mitrokhin claims that on December 19, 1976, the KGB leader Yuri Andropov personally approved an operation against Vance, which was intended to make him a "trusted contact" of the KGB. The action was

---

[218] Christopher Andrew, "The Mitrokhin Archive," https://archive.org/stream/
TheSwordAndTheShield-TheMitrokhinArchiveAndTheSecretHistoryOfTheKGB/
The+Sword+and+the+Shield+-
+The+Mitrokhin+Archive+and+the+Secret+History+of+the+KGB_djvu.txt

doomed to failure. Mitrokhin claimed that in Vance's KGB file records once he entered the Carter administration, any possibility of unauthorized access to Vance and his family dried up.

According to Mitrokhin, the failure to cultivate Vance led the KGB to launch an even more unrealistic scheme to target President Carter's anti-Soviet National Security Advisor, Zbigniew Brzezinski. Mitrokhin claims in 1977 Andropov approved an operation that again failed to collect "compromising information" on Brzezinski as a means of putting pressure on him.

Here you have the model for the fake Gen. Flynn plot laid out in the "Mitrokhin Archive"—the alleged Soviet scheme to blackmail a national security advisor into treason using compromising material. Brennan may have simply recycled worthless 1970s Mitrokhin ideas in his plot to take out President Trump.

How can we be sure John Brennan knows about Mitrokhin? In addition to the references quoted on page five of the Intelligence Community Assessment which Brennan oversaw, this exchange from his Congressional testimony is illuminating:

> ROS-LEHTITEN: And as a young analyst, you probably had a lot of dealings with Andropov, the head of the KGB, in the early 80's, and he was very focused on—on this active measure campaign.
> BRENNAN: Well yes, I—as a young analyst, I wouldn't have had direct interaction with Andropov, but I have studied Russian intelligence activities over the years, and have seen it—again, manifest in many different of our counterintelligence cases, and—and how they have been able to get people, including inside of CIA, to become treasonous.. And frequently, individuals who go along that treasonous path do not even realize they're along that path until it gets to be a bit too late. And that's why, again, my—my radar goes

up early when I see certain things that—I know what the Russians are trying to do, and I don't know whether or not the targets of their efforts are as mindful of the Russian intentions as they need to be.[219]

The ex-CIA director in a grandstanding moment in front of Congress is accusing Gen. Flynn of sleepwalking into Putin's trap which Brennan could see a mile away. Brennan got the genus of his big idea he tries to sell to Congress of the "recruitment" of Gen. Flynn by Russian intelligence from Mitrokhin?

Target Gen. Flynn

The plotters used a version of history to establish an exaggerated backdrop idea of continual Russian intelligence recruiting individuals in the minds of Congress, media, and the American people. From December 2015, Halper's job was to move to the specific, to fabricate stories about individuals linked to Trump to fit the fake backstory to achieve present day ends.

The first target was to dirty up senior Trump campaign advisor General Mike Flynn. Why December 2015? The trigger was likely the photograph of Gen. Flynn sitting at a dinner table with Russian President Vladimir Putin on December 10, 2015. His appearance in Moscow unleashed wave after wave of Democratic political attacks on the Trump campaign. It was a monumental stroke of luck. Within days of Gen. Flynn's return, the FBI and Department of Justice were seeking approval for OCONUS lures which were approved on December 28, 2015.

---

[219] https://docs.house.gov/meetings/IG/IG00/20170523/105992/HHRG-115-IG00-Transcript-20170523.pdf

Halper had his work cut out to explain how a decorated war hero such as General Flynn might have been transformed by Russian intelligence into President Putin's personal asset. The overarching plot was lifted from the dusty pages of the Mitrokhin archive. Was it Halper who identified each stage of a fantastical "Russian intelligence operation," a long-drawn-out multi-year operation? According to the fantasy, General Flynn was first talent-spotted by Russian intelligence in 2013 on a work trip to Russia. Halper next submitted a false report that Gen. Flynn was "compromised" in 2014 by the author and finally recruited in 2015 whilst in Moscow. In addition to reporting I compromised Gen. Flynn in Cambridge on behalf of Russian intelligence, Halper apparently added that I might have been involved in the organization of Gen. Flynn's trip to Moscow to attend the RT[220] gala dinner.[221] All lies!

The likely key co-conspirator, former CIA Director John Brennan, described this nonexistent Russian intelligence operation as Gen. Flynn's "treasonous path" in his May 23, 2017 Congressional testimony. "I am not going to identify the individuals because this is information that, again, is based on classified sources and intelligence," said Brennan despite dropping broad hints throughout his Congressional testimony as to General Flynn's identity without naming him.

It was the CIA's unofficial mouthpiece *Washington Post's* Gregg Miller who immediately named General Flynn as the compromised Trump campaign official. In his *Washington Post* article "CIA director alerted FBI to pattern of contacts between Russian officials and Trump

---

[220] RT (formerly Russia Today) is a Russian government funded broadcaster. Flynn was a paid speaker at an event in Moscow in December 2015.

[221] Conversation with Matt Rosenberg NYT and the author in May 2017.

campaign associates" Miller quoted Brennan "Russian agencies routinely seek to gather compromising information, or 'kompromat,' to coerce treason from US officials who 'do not even realize they are on that path until it gets too late.'" Miller went on to say "The remark appeared to be in reference to Flynn."[222]

The "treasonous path" of the "compromised" General Mike Flynn is a thread running the length of the Spygate hoax. The tale keeps cropping up time and time again. The FBI used it to structure the questioning of Gen. Flynn in their infamous January 2017 interview and then appears in every newspaper story about him. Brennan is the architect of the story as he revealed in his Congressional testimony. The tale was the basis of the coup attempts against the President.

The hysterical aspects of the Halper/Brennan spy thriller are the glaring holes in the chronology and the assumption Russian intelligence possess almost supernatural predictive powers. The Russians are at least twenty moves ahead of the plodding Americans. The US would be facing an unequal struggle if they are indeed fighting such super humans. The only hope is the one-man counterintelligence task force Halper in his base in Cambridge, England; a seventy-two-year-old obese spy with his own super-power of being in the right place at the right time to observe what no one else can see.

According to the fantastical plot the Russian intelligence operation began sometime before 2011 when they talent-spotted the American businessman Donald Trump as a future politician and successful presidential candidate. The Russians began backing him knowing one day he would run for the Oval office. In 1998 the Russians placed an

222 https://www.washingtonpost.com/world/national-security/cia-director-warned-russian-security-service-chief-about-interference-in-election/2017/05/23/ebff2a7e-3fbb-11e7-adba-394ee67a7582_story.html

intelligence asset in the University of Cambridge because they knew that General Flynn was going to visit years later. In 2013 Russian intelligence identified the same General as someone who would work for them. Gen. Flynn was then a registered Democrat and President Obama's US intelligence leader; but according to the false narrative the Russians saw him as a future Republican political star in this crazy story.

The fantasy continues; the author, a Russian intelligence asset at Cambridge compromised Gen. Flynn in a very public setting on the orders of Vladimir Putin in February 2014. By 2015 having entered politics and become the right-hand man of Donald Trump, the General found he was under the control of Russians and it was too late to escape doing their bidding.

The Brennan/Halper plot is a sad stitch-up, a reverse-engineered joke with the conclusion established first and the "intelligence" added later to bolster the narrative. How did John Brennan keep a straight face telling this tale to Congress? Well, spies are professional deceivers. The invented story laid out to Congress has all the critical elements of many classic spy novels. It runs as follows. Russian military intelligence known commonly as the GRU identified Gen. Flynn as a "very influential" figure or a "rising star" on his official visit to Moscow in July 2013. The fake story goes on. In February 2014, President Putin dispatched an operative, Svetlana Lokhova, to seduce the General very publicly on the one occasion they met at the University of Cambridge. Lokhova was acting on the orders of Russian intelligence in a false flag operation; she was posing as a British citizen, and Gen. Flynn did not know she was Russian. Later the pair continued a personal relationship. It was "kompromat" or compromising material. This "kompromat" was to be used by Russian intelligence "to coerce treason" like the infamous and fake Donald Trump "pee tape."

Later in 2015, according to this false tale Gen. Flynn started taking money from the Russian government in payments disguised as fees for speaking engagements. The payments were alleged to culminate in the infamous RT dinner in Moscow also arranged by Lokhova. Gen. Flynn was photographed at the elbow of his new master President Vladimir Putin. There you have it—from hero to traitor.

But it is all untrue! Gen. Flynn was the Obama appointed head of the Defense Intelligence Agency in 2014 when I met him at a work dinner on just one occasion. I was never alone with him, let alone had an affair with him. I am British and have no connections with Russian intelligence.

In truth, the start of Spygate is in the late summer of 2015 when Gen. Flynn first started meeting Republican presidential hopefuls, including Donald Trump. In response, it is likely based on the Congressional testimony that the then CIA Director John Brennan activated Halper in late 2015.

Halper began drawing down Pentagon expenses in December 2015 as he started spying. He set to work spying on me in January 2016. Congressman Nunes is on record saying on TV and in Congress this was indeed the date the spying began. Halper's first act was to send an email to my mentor and then-friend Professor Christopher Andrew to organize a dinner with me to discuss our book. Andrew sold it to me as a brilliant opportunity as Halper would promote our book in the United States, so I had to bring examples of my research. Halper had never previously spoken to me nor showed the slightest interest in my work and the book was not even written.

Undeterred by my rebuff of his invitation, Halper set about "investigating" me around the campus. I was told his techniques by a fellow academic and once friend Dr. William Foster. Halper recruited Foster as an unwitting spy. Foster was encouraged by Halper to meet with me and, under cover of being interested in my work, ask about my background. Foster apologized to me saying he thought at the time he was passing on harmless gossip. Foster described the methods of the FBI informer as a collector. Halper drove the process by interrogating my colleagues intensely. He initiated aggressive, leading lines of questions such as "What do you really know about Svetlana's background?" or "Why is her research so good . . . are you sure she was not given special access by the Russians?" Halper built a web of lies to sell as intelligence. Foster told me Halper would put an outrageous assertion to him and if he disagreed he became aggressive. He no doubt reported that sub-sources, not Halper, held those suspicions in his reports. Rumor added to lie becomes a valuable currency for Halper.

By early 2016, Halper must have completed and submitted a dossier on Gen. Flynn and suspected links to the GRU. It is likely this is the information Brennan shared with the FBI. At some point early in 2016 the Trump campaign was placed under electronic surveillance. The surveillance scandal perhaps involving my emails to and from General Flynn broke slowly in the press starting first in January 2017. The *New York Times* team of Adam Goldman and Matt Rosenberg reported American law enforcement and intelligence agencies are examining "intercepted communications" as part of a broad investigation into possible links between Russian officials and associates of President-elect Donald J. Trump. One official said intelligence reports based on some of the wiretapped communications were *"provided to the White House."*[223]

Luke Harding of the Guardian newspaper in the UK, alleged recipient of CIA leaks[224] and mouthpiece for Christopher Steele, reported in mid-April 2017 that Britain's spy agencies played a crucial role in alerting their counterparts in Washington to contacts between members of Donald Trump's campaign team and Russian intelligence operatives. Harding claims, denied by the British government, that GCHQ "first became aware in late 2015 of suspicious 'interactions' between figures connected to Trump and known or suspected Russian agents"[225] from a source close to UK intelligence (perhaps Christopher Steele). Harding provides an enormous amount of detail for something that has been officially denied. He claims:

> In late 2015 GCHQ was carrying out standard "collection" against Moscow targets. These were known Kremlin operatives already on the grid. Nothing unusual here. Except that the Russians were talking to people associated with Trump. The precise nature of these exchanges has not been made public. According to sources in the United States and the United Kingdom, these interactions formed a suspicious pattern. They continued through the first half of 2016.[226]

It is likely the article is a cover story to add some official gravitas or gloss to the rumors dressed up as intelligence that were the real origins

[223] https://www.nytimes.com/2017/01/19/us/politics/trump-russia-associates-investigation.html

[224] Described by Peter Strzok as "weird and incorrect Agency leaks"

[225] Luke Harding, "British spies were first to spot Trump team's links with Russia," *The Guardian* (April 13, 2017).

[226] Luke Harding, *The Guardian* (November 15, 2017), https://www.theguardian.com/news/2017/nov/15/how-trump-walked-into-putins-web-luke

of Spygate and not official intelligence intercepts. Harding is describing the monitoring of my communications starting in December 2015 when Halper was activated. The Guardian article was read into the Senate Judiciary Committee Sub-committee on Crime and Terrorism transcript by Sen. Diane Feinstein on May 8, 2017 and the former Director of National Intelligence James Clapper confirmed the article was true but "sensitive".

Chapter Twelve: Treasonous Path

Blessed is the man that walketh not in the counsel of the ungodly, nor standeth in the way of sinners, nor sitteth in the seat of the scornful.

—Psalm: 1:1

A nation can survive its fools, and even the ambitious. But it cannot survive treason from within. An enemy at the gates is less formidable, for he is known and carries his banner openly. But the traitor moves amongst those within the gate freely, his sly whispers rustling through all the alleys, heard in the very halls of government itself.

—Marcus Tullius Cicero

In his fantastical, thoroughly discredited and debunked book *Collusion*,[227] Luke Harding—"journalist" from the *Guardian*—and his close collaborator Christopher Steele produced a chapter titled "General Misha: Moscow-Cambridge-London." In May 2020 we learned from the declassified David Kramer testimony given to Congress in December 2017, Christopher Steele was spreading Halper's "Flynn Lokhova affair" lie from November 2016. Kramer was Senator John McCain's emissary sent to meet Steele in London in November 2016. The plan was for Kramer and McCain to re-introduce Halper's debunked intelligence to the then Head of the FBI James Comey as intelligence from a fresh source. The lie was used to restart FBI surveillance on Gen. Flynn in early December 2016.

---

[227] Harding is a noted fantasist responsible for the fake story that Paul Manafort visited Julian Assange in the Ecuadorian Embassy.

Harding's nonsense book was described by the *New York Times* on publication as "an explosive exposé that lays out the story behind the Steele Dossier, including Russia's decades-in-the-making political game to upend American democracy and the Trump administration's ties to Moscow."[228]

Harding and Steele with the help of fellow *Guardian* journalist Nick Hopkins, started work on this crock in December 2016. It was eventually published in November 2017, ten months after General Flynn was unconditionally cleared of being a Russian agent by the FBI and Department of Justice. January 2017 was also the month when the Steele Dossier was debunked by the FBI.[229]

Throughout his tortuous book Harding expands on the Steele Dossier allegations to depict Gen. Flynn as the prime mover and number one villain in the nonexistent Russian collusion plot. Christopher Steele began feeding Harding news stories laced with supposed intelligence bombshells from December 2016. But where did Christopher Steele get his information about the parts of the investigation he was not involved in?

It transpires Steele was paid US taxpayers' money by the FBI to fly to Italy to be briefed on their investigation into Gen. Flynn and the three other suspects on October 3, 2016.[230] At that meeting the now discredited Steele was also offered a significant incentive by the FBI to find "intelligence" i.e. "dig dirt" on Gen. Flynn.[231] If some in the

---

[228] https://www.amazon.com/Collusion-Secret-Meetings-Russia-Helped-ebook/dp/B0776YZF4P

[229] The FBI interviewed Steele's principal sub-source.

[230]https://www.realclearinvestigations.com/articles/2020/02/13/buried_in_ig_report_fbi_gave_steele_highly_protected_secrets_122394.html

[231] Horowitz IG Report and Chuck Ross "FBI Offered To Pay Christopher Steele 'Significantly' To Dig Up Dirt On Flynn" *The Daily Caller* May 20, 2020

FBI hoped Steele would leak to the press (and the State Department), they were not disappointed. Just days later Steele admitted to the FBI on October 11, 2016, that he leaked to the press and was given a first official warning.[232]

The chapter featuring Gen. Flynn and myself in Harding's book opens with quotes attributed to a Russian-born novelist and Soviet-era GRU defector Victor Suvorov. Suvorov now lives in the United Kingdom since defecting from the Soviet Union in 1978. Suvorov is a pseudonym, a nod to the great Czarist Russian general Alexander Suvorov of the French Revolutionary Wars.[233] His real name is Vladimir Rezun. Once a bit of a celebrity in the exile circuit, he is now all but forgotten.

Even Luke Harding believes some of Rezun's tales are too much. With no sense of irony, Harding the self-described "storyteller"[234] describes Rezun's account of the GRU, Russian Military intelligence as a "novel." Rezun's account opens with a "chilling scene of a man, still alive and bound to a stretcher with metal wire, being fed into the Aquarium's crematorium."

Despite a few doubts, the Russia-hater Harding is a devoted fan of Rezun. He promotes the defector's tales in his news articles citing him as the leading authority on the GRU. It is no wonder the pair co-operate as they share the same anti-Russian views. It does not seem to bother the conspiracy theorist Harding a jot in using this out-of-date source: Rezun has not been in Russia since 1978, which is over forty years ago.

---

[232] John Solomon, *The Hill* (May 9, 2019), https://thehill.com/opinion/white-house/442944-fbis-steele-story-falls-apart-false-intel-and-media-contacts-were-flagged.

[233] Generalissimo Suvorov is one of the greatest commanders in Russian and world history. He never lost a single major battle where he had command.

[234] Harding interview with Aaron Maté, *The Real News Network* (December 23, 2017).

Despite serving only eight years in the Soviet-era GRU, Rezun is quoted in a Harding *Guardian* article on December 29, 2018, titled "Will they forgive me? No: ex-Soviet spy Viktor Suvorov speaks out" as the authoritative source on how today's Russian GRU interacts with Russian President Vladimir Putin. Of course, according to the pair it is Putin who micro-manages every botched operation and sinister plot. Harding does not stop to ask himself how Rezun would even know this? In this behavior Harding shares a cavalier attitude to sources just like his collaborator Christopher Steele in promoting a false narrative.

Doing what Harding does best, spinning conspiracy theories uncritically, he channels Rezun in *Collusion*. While providing no evidence for his assertions, we learn in the book, "of the three Russian spy agencies involved in espionage, the GRU was the biggest and the most powerful."[235] This is completely untrue because it is well known the SVR dwarfs the GRU. It is the equivalent of saying with a straight face the US Defense Intelligence Agency outguns the CIA in its foreign intelligence capability. Harding claims without any evidence to back it up, "the GRU is believed to have a larger network of agents abroad than the SVR, its foreign intelligence counterpart."[236]

In common with every intelligence organization in the world (but only sinister in the case of the GRU), "very little is known about its organizational structure. Since there's no press office, there isn't anybody to ask. Its activities are a state secret."[237] By way of comparison, imagine calling the CIA press office to ask questions about its organizational structure and for a comment on all of their

---

[235] When it suits Harding, he tells Aaron Maté the exact opposite that Russian intelligence is "pretty low budget and opportunistic."

[236] Luke Harding, *Collusion* (New York: Vintage Books, 2017), 116.

[237] Ibid., 116–17.

secrets, their foreign undercover operations, and overseas networks—
see how far you get.

The chronology of the General Flynn conspiracy myth is explained in
this whole painful chapter. The author seemingly follows the path of
Halper's "intelligence" fabricated to smear General Flynn. It begins
with a reinterpretation of the General's official visit to Moscow on the
orders of President Obama. Of course, the fanciful story is
unsupported by any official accounts or eyewitnesses. Harding is even
able to imagine the inner motivation of Gen. Flynn in becoming a
traitor despite never having spoken to the General:

> Flynn claimed to be the first American to be allowed inside the
> Kremlin's most secret espionage facility. It was a rare honor. At this
> point, he was the head of the Defense Intelligence Agency (DIA) and
> the Senior Military Intelligence Officer in the Department of
> Defense. He was also a self-styled maverick, "an atypical square peg
> in a round hole," as he put it.
>
> Obama appointed Flynn in April 2012. By the time of his Moscow
> visit, Flynn was disillusioned with the Obama administration. It had,
> he felt, succumbed to enfeebling political correctness. It failed to
> appreciate that the United States was losing in a world war, a war
> being waged by radical Islamists and "evil people." The White
> House didn't even recognize its principal enemy—the Islamic
> Republic of Iran.[238]

The passage from *Collusion* perhaps reveals some of the verification
used to support the RUMINT (Rumor Intelligence) fabricated at the
origins of Spygate. According to his Office of Net Assessments
proposal in 2015, Halper was paid to interview ex-Russian intelligence
officers (GRU). Halper only traveled to London so that is likely where
these Russians are based. According to Harding there is only one,
Rezun.

---

[238] Ibid., 117–18.

Yet where did Harding get his information? Well as we now know, in early October 2016 just a month before the presidential election, the FBI invited and paid Christopher Steele $15,000 taxpayer dollars to travel to Italy. The FBI wanted to tell their source everything about their investigation; why they did this is open to speculation. Despite or perhaps because they knew he leaked like a sieve to the press, the FBI told him every detail of the case they were building against General Flynn and others.

When Steele and Harding met a month later, Steele dutifully passed on all this information. Harding is London-based but now knows all about the FBI investigation. Even if Steele and Halper did not directly collaborate in fabricating intelligence, which I believe highly unlikely, the FBI provided a leaker with all their "evidence" gathered from Confidential Human Source 2, Halper. The book *Collusion* is an example of the false "treasonous path" thread running through Spygate. Its plot follows uncannily the line of questioning recorded in Gen. Flynn's FBI 302 notes from his interview with agents Peter Strzok and Joe Pientka.

By the time Halper came to the United Kingdom to "investigate" Gen. Flynn in mid-February 2016, the outline story of the General's treachery was already fabricated. Halper had already reported via the "Cambridge Club back channel" the outline Russian plan to interfere in the election he ascribed to the ex-Head of the SVR Vyacheslav Trubnikov his guest in the summer of 2015.

Halper was busy putting flesh on the bare bones of the knock off le Carré-based plot by adding details of the devious long-term but nonexistent Russian operation that lived only in his head. He has a particularly fertile imagination as we know, but Halper added a few "Russian experts" to stand up and verify his spook-based Cold War fantasy. During early 2016 the Spygate conspiracy narrative about Gen. Flynn was created and promoted by the "Cambridge Club" geriatrics no doubt in some oak-paneled room in an ancient Cambridge College. "I can see them working it out, they're so damned academic; I can see them sitting round a fire in one of their smart bloody clubs."[239] They are past masters of just this type of operation. The Cold War relics and highly experienced disinformation experts created a patently untrue plot line but enough to be investigated especially when they put their names to it with suitable caveats. That is their art.

The "Cambridge Club," which includes Halper and Steele, is a money-making machine that creates "intelligence", not evidence; there is a huge difference. They cast aspersions, hint at wrongdoing but never provide anything concrete by way of actual evidence. The plan was similar to the plot of le Carré's *Smiley's People*. It involved possible blackmail, a sinister espionage organization, killers, sex as blackmail, and sleeper agents. Halper and Steele's trick is to ascribe their views to others, preferably "Russians" who could never be interviewed. The best bit was their customers, the CIA, the FBI and the Hillary campaign were desperate for this conspiracy theory because it fitted their own plans.

Steele's last job at MI6, the British equivalent of the CIA, was Head of the Russia Desk. It sounds like an impressive title but following the end of the Cold War and no threat it called for minimal resources. Intelligence was simply no longer the high stakes game it was between superpowers; it was reduced to chasing organized crime and money launderers. In reality, Steele babysat a network of financially stretched, washed-up Soviet-era defectors living in the UK.

---

[239] John le Carré, *The Spy Who Came in from the Cold* (New York: Penguin, 1963), 213.

Did Steele employ these defectors as contractors for his company: the private contractor Orbis? Sir Richard Dearlove laughingly told the BBC he "will not confirm or deny that he knows Christopher [Steele]"[240] on the flagship *Newsnight* program in December 2017. Steele previously worked for him so of course he knows him. Dearlove went on to reveal in the interview he believes Steele's dossier contains "some truth" which makes him amongst the last people on the planet to think this.

Dearlove is Halper's only friend and defender.[241] In the Fusion GPS book *Crime in Progress*, the authors[242] reported Steele met Dearlove, the former head of MI6 and Steele's old boss, at the Garrick Club in December 2016 for a second time. Simpson and Fritsch write that Steele "walked" Dearlove through the dossier's explosive contents.[243] Dearlove reportedly found the reporting "credible." Steele's dossier on Donald Trump included claims the Kremlin obtained potential blackmail material from a Moscow hotel room. The Fusion book claims:

> Dearlove then surprised Steele by indicating that he was already aware that the British government had suspicions about links between Russia and members of the Trump campaign. It seemed that the British government had made a political decision not to push the matter further.[244]

---

[240] BBC *Newsnight* December 2017.

[241] *Washington Post* articles by Tom Hamburger and David Ignatius May and June 2018
https://www.washingtonpost.com/opinions/global-opinions/stefan-halper-is-just-another-middleman/2018/05/22/b9c3b1b2-5df9-11e8-9ee3-49d6d4814c4c_story.html
https://www.washingtonpost.com/politics/cambridge-university-perch-gave-fbi-source-access-to-top-intelligence-figures--and-a-cover-as-he-reached-out-to-trump-associates/2018/06/05/c6764dc2-641e-11e8-99d2-0d678ec08c2f_story.html

[242] Given that the source for this information is Fusion GPS the reader is advised to exercise caution.

[243] Glenn Simpson and Peter Fritsch, *Crime in Progress* (New York: Random House, 2019).

[244] Ibid., 133.

The British government and MI6 have been openly critical of the Steele dossier calling it opposition research, not verified intelligence. Sir John Scarlett, former MI6 chief was asked what he thought of the dossier and if he believed what was written in it. "Well, no," Scarlett said.

In addition to Dearlove, whose name and reputation, wittingly or unwittingly, helped Halper, Steele and Fusion GPS add credibility to their bogus claims, were others used in a similar way? The farcical allegations about how the modern day GRU viewed General Flynn's official visit to Moscow from Rezun, the 1970s Soviet defector probably recharacterized as a trusted current GRU source, was likely music to Brennan's ears. According to Harding, Rezun mused:

> The GRU staff officers who witnessed Flynn's arrival must have experienced a moment of cognitive wonder. For decades, they had worked to undermine what the KGB referred to as the *glavny protivnik* — the main adversary, the chief enemy—the United States. The pause in the Cold War hadn't changed this. Most of them had never seen an American spy. Now here was one made flesh, an object of intense professional interest. Flynn had come to Moscow to deliver a lecture on leadership.[245]

As we can see, Steele's mouthpiece—Harding—partly based the entire Spygate collusion hoax (and hung a fantastical book) on the fanciful speculations of a deeply out-of-touch relic from a bygone era. Supposedly, when Rezun heard of General Flynn's "Aquarium [GRU] drop-in," Rezun was "stunned" saying, "Oh my God, I had to eat my tie. . . . There's something fishy going on. Can you imagine a top Russian adviser being invited inside MI6 or to lecture at the CIA?" Rezun claimed, according to Harding's book, that the GRU was assessing Gen. Flynn for possible recruitment. And then we get the whole plot, handily attributed to a former GRU source: "Maybe the

[245] Harding, *Collusion*, 118.

Russians have some kind of material on [Gen. Flynn], or have him under control."[246]

Harding writes:

> Was this merely a friendly overture to a senior US general? Or—as Suvorov [Rezun] believes—was there something more calculating going on? The Steele dossier suggests that Kislyak's wooing of Flynn was deliberate, and part of a strategic US-facing operation. One of its aspects was to identify "sympathetic US actors." And, among other things, to bring them over to Moscow.[247]

This is how Steele wrote General Flynn into his dossier in August 2016, days after the "Lock Her Up" anti-Hillary Clinton chant at the Republican National Convention. Trips to Moscow by US spy chiefs are not such a rare event as the hysteria over Gen. Flynn made out. The ex-CIA director William Colby walked alone around Red Square in the 1990s.

After floating a grand conspiracy theory, Steele's mouthpiece Harding went immediately into the next stage of General Flynn's "treasonous path": "in February 2014 Flynn gave another lecture—this time in England. His host was the Cambridge intelligence seminar."[248]

Harding pivots awkwardly in his tale from Gen. Flynn in Moscow being targeted by the GRU in 2013 to 2014 and his chance encounter with me at Dearlove's dinner. So, what happened in Cambridge according to Harding? After going through a list of Russians who Harding says have been poisoned after visiting the Cambridge seminar, and a five-page buildup, Harding finally gets to the point:

---

[246] Ibid., 118–19.

[247] Ibid., 119–20.

[248] Ibid., 120.

General Flynn. The short passage featuring me in the book sits awkwardly because it is severely truncated by the legal action I served on Harding in 2017 following his *Guardian* article. After the lengthy buildup, the entire "excitement" is that Gen. Flynn sat with a female academic at a group dinner and "there is no suggestion she is linked to Russian intelligence."[249] Much more in the way of inventions and half-truths were originally intended by Harding and Steele, but I gelded that aspect of their tale with a threat of litigation.

The goal of Halper's investigation was to invent and then "find" the material the Russians were supposed to have on Gen. Flynn and then pin them down to known data points. I have to say there was a sad lack of imagination and originality in the geriatric Cambridge Club's Rumor Intelligence machine. Their story is that the sinister Russian intelligence organization has only one trick: to always compromise then blackmail the targets.

Donald Trump was smeared with a fake account of an encounter with prostitutes in Moscow and financial ties to the Kremlin. Gen. Flynn and I were smeared with a false allegation of an affair. Again, these "compromise stories" are loosely based on fables from the Mitrokhin Archive, supposed to be actual KGB operations, and the plots from cheap spy thrillers.

In one story from the Mitrokhin papers, President Nixon's personal physician was supposedly a planned target in a KGB "honeypot" sting at the ballet in Kiev whilst on an official visit to the Soviet Union. According to Mitrokhin, the Soviet security service planned to sit the doctor next to an attractive and willing lady.[250] The good doctor allegedly once mentioned in conversation that he found Russian girls

---

249 Ibid., 122.

250 The Mitrokhin Archive, The Churchill College Archive Centre

attractive. Sounds very reminiscent of Halper's fictional account of a dinner one night in February 2014 in Cambridge.

Central to Halper's apparently delusional conspiracy theory is the supposed role of Russian Ambassador to the United States, Kislyak, in the Gen. Flynn fable. In his diplomatic capacity, Ambassador Kislyak facilitated the 2013 Gen. Flynn official visit to Russia, while the Russian embassy coordinated the trip. That is international protocol for visiting dignitaries.

Conspiracy theorists transformed the career diplomat Kislyak into an international spymaster. Ambassador Kislyak was under surveillance as a result in 2015. As we have seen, the icing on the cake is the debunked Steele dossier suggests in 2016 that "Kislyak's wooing of Flynn was deliberate, and part of a strategic USfacing operation"[251]. Part of this supposedly sinister plot was to identify "sympathetic US actors"[252] "and, among other things, to bring them over to Moscow"[253]. In truth, Ambassador Kislyak simply extended diplomatic courtesies to General Flynn in the normal course of state business.

The next steps in the Russian crazy tale of wooing of Gen. Flynn was allegedly a series of paid speaking engagements. Two paid talks out of thirty Gen. Flynn gave to American companies assumed huge significance. They included a talk in the US on cyber security to Kaspersky Systems and another to Volga-Dnepr Airlines, a Russian cargo airline. The talks were organized by the prominent Washington-based speakers bureau Leading Authorities Inc, which Gen. Flynn

---

[251] Luke Harding, *Collusion*

[252] Steele dossier, August 10, 2016

[253] Luke Harding, *Collusion*

joined in January 2015. James Clapper and Andrew McCabe are clients of the bureau!

The speakers bureau arranged the Gen. Flynn trip to Moscow to attend a gala dinner for RT. He attended along with other foreign dignitaries such as Jill Stein, leader of the US Green Party. Interestingly and unreported is that the Russians were lukewarm to the idea initially and certainly did not throw money at the General. RT haggled the speaker's fee down with Leading Authorities before finally agreeing. Gen. Flynn would have missed out on the gig had his bureau not reduced the price.[254]

We know Gen. Flynn was briefed in advance and later debriefed by the Defense Intelligence Agency about his short Moscow trip.[255] Like many retired intelligence chiefs with security clearance, he was probably sent by the DIA, on a semi-official trip. The General returned from Russia with a thumb drive of documents which he gave to the Defense Intelligence Agency.[256] John Solomon reported:

> Before Gen. Flynn made his infamous December 2015 trip to Moscow—as a retired general and then-adviser to Donald Trump's presidential campaign—he alerted his former employer, the DIA. He then attended a "defensive" or "protective" briefing before he ever sat alongside Russian President Vladimir Putin at the Russia Today (RT) dinner, or before he talked with then-Russian Ambassador Sergey Kislyak. The briefing educated and sensitized Gen. Flynn to possible efforts by his Russian host to compromise the former high-ranking defense official and prepared him for conversations in which

---

[254] House Oversight Committee https://oversight.house.gov/news/press-releases/cummings-releases-new-documents-confirming-that-flynn-received-funds-from

[255] https://www.grassley.senate.gov/news/news-releases/grassley-calls-sunlight-flynn-case-justice-dept-shares-new-exculpatory-material

[256] Emily Shugman, The Independent April 27, 2017:*Donald Trump's former adviser Michael Flynn under investigation from Pentagon amid FBI probe*

he could potentially extract intelligence for US agencies such as the DIA.

When Gen. Flynn returned from Moscow, he spent time briefing intelligence officials on what he learned during the Moscow contacts. Between two and nine intelligence officials attended the various meetings with Gen. Flynn about the RT event, and the information was moderately useful, about what one would expect from a public event.[257]

Sydney Powell, Gen. Flynn's attorney, stated in court papers that the mysterious intelligence contractor Professor Mifsud was shadowing Gen. Flynn in Moscow.[258] An explanation for this operation could be that some in the intelligence community wanted to place Gen. Flynn under surveillance by having a trusted source report the American citizen had contact with a Russian intelligence target.

To avoid the complications of a FISA application, in which the target has to be validated as a foreign agent, always a non-starter with Gen. Flynn given that he was privy to every national security secret, a simpler route was followed to obtain intrusive "legal" surveillance. Professor Mifsud is a central character to Spygate who has disappeared since 2017. His testimony will demystify a great deal of the narrative.

The photo of Gen. Flynn sitting at a table with Russian President Putin was a gift to the Democrats and Christopher Steele. All the other characters around that table were assigned significance and a prominent and unlikely role in the conspiracy in the fake dossier. Putin speaks little English—Gen. Flynn, the same amount of Russian, so their conversation was extremely brief.[259] But the picture was probably

[257] https://thehill.com/opinion/white-house/423558-exculpatory-russia-evidence-about-mike-flynn-that-us-intel-kept-secret

[258] www.sidneypowell.com Legal filings

[259] https://www.reuters.com/article/us-russia-usa-putin/putins-dinner-with-michael-flynn-i-didnt-even-really-talk-to-him-idUSKBN18V0XZ

enough to activate spying on Gen. Flynn. Halper drew down his first expenses and began planning his mission to Cambridge in December 2016.[260] Was the original plan to put surveillance in place on Gen. Flynn if there was a contact with GRU leader Sergun? If that was the plan, it went off the rails. The GRU leader died in January. A new scheme was needed.[261]

Gen. Flynn would formally join the Trump campaign in February after he had been advising since the previous summer. The plotters and the media increased their shadow operation to undermine the General and potentially gain surveillance on the Trump campaign. This was a very serious matter as Gen. Flynn's deal with Donald Trump was to be his running mate. To the extent candidate Trump needed one, Gen. Flynn played the role of "attack dog" during the campaign. Gen. Flynn status as retired intelligence chief allowed him to attack Hillary Clinton over the use of a private server to conduct government business in 2015.

He doubled down on February, 16, 2016, by stating on CNN that Hillary Clinton should go to jail for the email affair. From his days at the DIA Gen. Flynn detailed inside knowledge of the workings of the Obama administration and Clinton's foreign policy bungles such as Benghazi. The billionaire Donald Trump was a dangerous political outsider whose wealth allowed him to be independent. The pair formed a lethal combination in the minds of the Deep State.

The Clinton response through the press was quick and defined the main attack themes on Gen. Flynn and Donald Trump way before any hacking. On March 9, 2016, Shane Harris penned an article in the *Daily Beast,* "Trump Embraces Ex-Top Obama Intel Official: Strange

---

[260] ONA Contracts, Sen. Grassley audit.

[261] Gregg Re, Catherine Herridge, "DOJ files detail Flynn-Russia contacts shortly before FBI informant sprang into action," Fox News (June 7, 2019).

Bedfellows." The quotes sourced from the now-familiar anonymous sources in the intelligence community seeded the fog of war. Harris links Gen. Flynn to the GRU from 2013, and then Trump/Flynn to President Putin.

Shane Harris, who is a very well-connected apologist for the intelligence community and a main collusion truther was briefed on the alleged consternation about Gen. Flynn's approved trip to the RT dinner. As I suspect, at the same time Halper was perhaps at work covertly fabricating intelligence, and no doubt, these placed media stories became an "independent" and confirming source part of a pattern of circular reporting. Harris was central to a number of attacks on Gen. Flynn and me in various publications sourced from Halper.

There is not the space in this book to explore the hacking controversy in detail. In May 2016, CrowdStrike, a private firm and not the FBI, was called in by the Democratic National Committee to investigate the "hacking attacks" on their server. Within days Fusion GPS appointed Christopher Steele, an "expert" on Russian intelligence, to help Hillary Clinton's campaign. By June 16, 2016, newspaper articles began stating Russia was behind the hack of the DNC.

On June 20, 2016, Christopher Steele produced his first memo: it was fake intelligence on Donald Trump later attributed to Vyacheslav Trubnikov.

Chapter Thirteen: "Nothing Is Coincidence When It Comes to Halper"

That which is crooked cannot be made straight: and that which is wanting cannot be numbered.

—Ecclesiastes: 1:15

"It seems a shame," the Walrus said,
"To play them such a trick,
After we've brought them out so far,
And made them trot so quick!"

—Lewis Carroll, "Through the Looking-Glass and What Alice Found There"

The trigger to unleash Halper appears to be a phone call Gen. Flynn made on January 5, 2016 to the Russian Ambassador Kislyak in Washington. Gen.Flynn was offering his condolences, a kind gesture to the Russians on the death of Igor Sergun, head of Russia's Military Intelligence (the GRU). Within four days Halper launched his espionage sting.[262]

Fox's Gregg Re and Catherine Herridge, reported that *"within days of a January 2016 Flynn phone call to Russian ambassador Sergey Kislyak...a Russian-born UK academic said FBI source Stefan Halper suddenly contacted her to gain information on Gen.Flynn. Asked about*

---

[262] "DOJ files detail Flynn-Russia contacts shortly before FBI informant sprang into action," Fox News (June 7, 2019).

the timing, a source familiar with the situation told Fox News, 'nothing is a coincidence' when it comes to Stefan Halper, and Kislyak was likely under US surveillance at the time of the contacts."[263] Just days after the call, Gen. Flynn's role informally advising the Trump campaign became widely known, Stefan Halper, the corpulent seventy-two-year-old, was going into the field to lure me into talking to him at a private dinner. Halper's first action was to send an agreed email to Professor Christopher Andrew in Cambridge on January 7, 2016 to set up the event. Halper was flying from his home in the United States for this curious dinner. Halper operates through cutouts, a third party his target trusts to arrange a contact. In my case Halper used my mentor and Ph.D. supervisor. Andrew forwarded the invitation to me on January 12. The plotter's goal was to have electronic surveillance in place on the then-Republican front-runner Donald Trump as soon as possible.

Under current law if an American has contact with a verified Russian intelligence target, it is perfectly legal to put them under surveillance. There is no need to involve the FISA court. The plotters needed a recently confirmed Russian intelligence contact with Gen. Flynn — and in a hurry. Gen. Flynn had no recent contacts with Russian intelligence targets so how did he become the unwitting "legal" route to monitor Trump's campaign communications? Halper was the man who set out to fix this tricky little problem. The cozy dinner was going to be the forum to establish that I was the Russian intelligence asset who maintained contact with Gen. Flynn.

Andrew proposed a dinner with Halper and his wife, Lezlee to discuss my research on either Saturday, February 13, or the following weekend February 20, 2016. Previously, Halper had shown no interest in my work pointedly sleeping through my presentations and I had never

---

[263] Ibid.

socialized with Halper. The proposed party was an incongruous gathering of mixed generations. As a further lure I was offered two nights of free accommodation in a Cambridge college room as an inducement. My initial response was to ignore the invitation hoping it would just go away. It didn't. I eventually had to formally decline after several tense and demanding phone calls with Andrew. His angry response struck me as extraordinary at the time, as I was not able to attend many more important engagements with no such comeback. Professor Andrew was never so angry with me. The reason I refused the invitation is because I did not like Halper. At the time I did not suspect this was part of the plot against Donald Trump or that Halper was an active spy. It was what happened afterwards that confirmed my suspicions about the invitation.

I had known of Halper since mid-2012 as we met at the Cambridge Intelligence Seminar. On each occasion we bumped into each other, he was rude to me to the point of being obnoxious. The seminar was held weekly in the oldest part of Corpus Christi College up a short, winding staircase. When he attended, Halper would arrive in the room sweaty and out of breath. He wheezes noisily; even when still. A dozen steps were too significant a physical challenge for him. Halper would mop his brow furiously with a pocket-handkerchief and survey the room before selecting the seat with the furthest distance from me and others he disliked. Everyone else joining the meetings were greeted by the group with a cheery, *"hello and, how are you?"* When Halper arrived, the response was a begrudging, *"Oh Hi, Stef."* He dragged a malign aura into the room.

The excellent academics at Cambridge easily smell out fraud so is that the reason Halper avoided contact with anyone except his minions? When I asked the senior members of the Seminar about him they either evaded or simply refused to answer any direct questions about Stefan

Halper's role or background. Everyone gave the impression they were scared of him. Halper was described as "very rich" and the "money" behind the Cambridge group. Today the response from the same people is along the line of *"Well, everyone knew Halper was CIA."*

Halper's "talk" to the Intelligence Seminar in 2015 was him reading from his book on China for an hour and a half in a painful monotone. The halting delivery suggested he was a stranger to the text. He sweated profusely throughout. Like many a pseudo-academic, he regurgitated a thesaurus to hide his pedestrian reasoning. After a lot of arm-twisting from Chris Andrew, I reluctantly accepted an invitation to attend a Formal Hall after Halper's talk.

Before the College dinner, the group met in an anteroom for drinks. Bad luck left the only empty chair next to my partner, so Halper was invited over by the host and he sat down. My partner tried to start a conversation, but rather than reply, Halper stared at us blankly, stood up, said, "Excuse me," and walked off. It was the only time in four years of being around Halper that he spoke to me. Despite the fact I had absolutely zero interactions with Halper, he later told the press and the FBI he knew me, and I was a Russian spy acting on the personal orders of Vladimir Putin to become the lover of Gen. Flynn.

Physically Halper could not resemble a corrupt station chief from a Tom Clancy novel more if he had "CIA" tattooed on his forehead. Following the unpleasant encounter, I researched his background on Google. Having read enough lurid stories about his past, I avoided any dealings with him. I am surprised others did not follow the same approach. When Halper whitewashed his own background, he emerged as a former Senior White House Official and distinguished academic with a wide array of connections. Yet when Halper was exposed in the press for entrapping campaign aides Carter Page and George

Papadopoulos, only the British citizen Dearlove, ex-head of MI6 put his hand up to defend him. Sir Richard is on the record claiming Halper is a "patriot and a good academic."[264] Richard Dearlove and Stefan Halper remain business partners.[265]

The Cambridge Intelligence Seminar is the retired Professor Christopher Andrew's longstanding hobby and his pet project. Since Andrew stepped back, no one has taught his famously popular Secret World Course on the history of espionage at the University. Intelligence history as an academic subject at Cambridge was dead, bar a few graduate students such as myself finishing up Doctoral dissertations.

The original purpose of the Seminar was a discussion group for students. As student numbers dropped, its original purpose evaporated. Attendance in comparison to the heydays a decade before was pitiful. The University of Cambridge fell way behind other centers in the academic study of espionage. An average turnout to the weekly event was a dozen academics to hear perhaps a friend of Andrew describe spying, for example, in the Napoleonic Wars. A pleasant dinner would follow the talk. The sad fact was the Seminar group was old. Funding its existence was an issue. A couple of thousand dollars was needed annually, and even that was proving increasingly tough to find.

The records show Halper was a co-convener of the Cambridge Intelligence Seminar from at least the fall of 2011. He may have given money to sponsor the Seminar to get this position. As the *Washington Post* reported in June 2018, he used his association with the elite University of Cambridge to provide cover for his espionage activities,

---

[264] Tom Hamburger, Robert Costa, and Ellen Nakashima, "Cambridge University Perch," *Washington Post* (June 5, 2018).

[265] Accounts of CSI filed at Companies House UK.

including his notorious Department of Defense (ONA) "studies," allowing him to claim he paid taxpayers' money to sources based abroad for information. The I.G. report revealed he became a paid FBI informer from 2008. Halper swanned around the world at the taxpayers' expense gathering "gossip" and manufacturing lies for the CIA and FBI.

Almost nothing happens in the quiet city of Cambridge, let alone anything that would alarm an intelligence service; yet Halper was on the books of the FBI as a paid informer for a decade. He was probably the best-paid informer in US history. In 2011 three distinguished visitors from FBI counterintelligence appeared at the Seminar. They came to talk about their roles in *Operation Ghost Stories.* The three were responsible for the capture of a large ring of Russian deep-cover spies in the United States. The arrests were seen at the time as a massive feather in the cap of the FBI. One of those visitors was Case Agent 1, now named by the reporter Adam Goldman of the *New York Times* as Stephen Somma, Stefan Halper's long-term handler during "Operation Crossfire Hurricane." Halper reported to Somma about his "acquaintance" with Gen. Flynn. Acquainted in this context implies he knows of, or is familiar with Gen.Flynn, which squares with the pair never having met but Halper knows something about him. Gen. Flynn has confirmed that he has never met Halper[266].

As we learned with the publication of the Inspector General's report, Halper told Carter Page he paid for Russian intelligence figures to speak at the Cambridge University seminar in 2012 and 2015. Indeed, the one who has received the most attention was the former Russian Foreign Intelligence Chief (SVR) General Vyacheslav I. Trubnikov.

---

[266] https://thefederalist.com/2020/05/07/fbis-memo-exonerating-flynn-proves-its-time-to-investigate-comeys-corrupt-confidential-human-sources/

Halper was the only member of the Cambridge seminar with connections to Russian intelligence.

The connections seem to date back to 2011. Halper was paid, no doubt very well, to produce a study by the Department of Defense on the "*Afghanistan End Game*," a key Obama election issue. According to a 2012 document, (in my possession) "*The DOD project on exit strategy, led by Dr. Stef Halper, included a series of productive round-tables in Moscow and demonstrated the opportunities for further dialogue as during V. I. Trubnikov's visit in May to the Cambridge Intelligence Seminar.*"

Halper appears to have co-operated with Trubnikov on this Department of Defense study, seeking Russian input on a drawdown strategy based on the Soviet experience. The long-retired Trubnikov is very well known to Western intelligence and diplomatic circles. He was appointed to the liaison committee to meet with CIA Deputy Director John McLaughlin after the collapse of the Soviet Union to co-operate on intelligence matters. The SVR met with the CIA and MI6. Trubnikov served under President Yeltsin and very briefly under his successor Vladimir Putin. He later became a deputy foreign minister and ambassador to India. In retirement, Trubnikov has been very active as a consultant, both in Russia and abroad.

The Cambridge Intelligence Seminar Program for May 2012 reads "*Ambassador Vyacheslav I. Trubnikov will comment on the challenges faced while directing the Foreign Intelligence Service, his tenure as Ambassador to India, President Putin and the likely course of Russia's relations with Britain and the US*"

Later in 2012 Sir Richard Dearlove and Halper authored a paid-for study titled "Dynamics of Russian and European engagement in the next 10 to 20 years." In the study the pair expressed some fascinating views. Dearlove and Halper, at least in 2012, saw the US and Russia as natural allies who had a *"joint interest in responding to the challenge posed by China's increasing economic, strategic and military power. This situation opens up new opportunities for strategic co-operation between the two countries."* The study states, *"closer relations with the United States"* is advocated by *"forces within the Russian elite, mainly from an intelligence background and including senior figures such as Evgeny Savostyanov [Russian Academician and former head of Moscow Region KGB-FSB], Vyacheslav Trubnikov [last (sic) head of SVR]."* The study goes on, *"These forces, separate from political power but nationalist and patriotic, think that it would be possible to convince Putin of such a course. Savostyanov and Trubnikov both engaged in frank and open discussions while visiting Cambridge in 2012."*

Could Halper have engaged in a spot of anti-Chinese freelance foreign policymaking in 2012 using a backchannel to Russia? Halper's FBI handler Stephen Somma, as well as his CIA controllers, surely would have been kept informed of these "frank and open discussions." Money made Halper advocate in 2012 closer ties to Putin and the Russians.

In May 2015 Trubnikov finally reappeared at the Seminar for a second visit. This trip was planned from late 2014. Trubnikov could not obtain a visa owing to sanctions imposed by the United Kingdom. In 2014 Halper implored Dearlove to intercede with the British government to ensure this visit took place.

According to Halper's emails, Trubnikov was refused entry to the United States and was hitting difficulties with the Brits. Christopher Andrew described Vyacheslav Trubnikov's visa ban as a bureaucratic oversight. The public program announced that *"With all issues relating to visas now sorted Vyacheslav Ivanovich Trubnikov, former Director of the Russian Intelligence Service (SVR), a former First Deputy Minister of Foreign Affairs and subsequently Russian Ambassador to India will speak on current relations between the Russian Federation and the West.*"

I was unable to attend. The talk Trubnikov gave in 2015 was reported to me as a massive disappointment to the Cambridge Club. They probably hoped for Russia-bashing. Instead, by all accounts, the ex-SVR head talked about the growth of Russian patriotism and his pride in the rebuilding of Russia.

The date of Trubnikov's visit may well prove another piece in the Spygate puzzle. From what we know of Halper's techniques and pattern, he looks at such innocent contacts as an opportunity. Halper has a record of embellishing his material, as I know to my cost. The visit occurred in late May 2015. I did not attend the talk and I have never met or had contact with Trubnikov.

As is standard practice for a paid intelligence source, Halper would have submitted a report. It is yet to be shown whether that was done via his "back channel"—an unscrutinized communication link to the US intelligence community —or officially. The conduit for the report either way might well have been Stephen Somma, Halper's FBI handler.

What Halper wrote in that report might be of extreme interest, not least because Christopher Steele later credits Trubnikov as being a source (in 2016) for several of the early fake stories in his dossier. Could Steele have been using fake material from his fellow FBI confidential human source Halper and claiming him as an "intelligence collector?" Steele openly told the State Department that General Vyacheslav

Trubnikov was one of the supposed sources of the now infamous dossier.

In her notes of a meeting with the chatty ex-British spy Christopher Steele, State Department official Kathleen Kavalec referred to the two Russian sources—former Russian foreign intelligence chief Vyacheslav Trubnikov and President Vladimir Putin aide Vladislav Surkov. Earlier the Department of Justice's and key Spygate figure Bruce and his wife Nellie Ohr learned from Steele that Trubnikov was a source but that Steele had never met him.

Whatever news Halper sent from Cambridge in the summer 2015, perhaps landed on fertile soil in Washington, for soon after, the now-retired Halper—recently liberated from his university responsibilities —submitted a proposal to the Department of Defense for a study costing just over $240,000. Not a bad earner for a man in his mid-seventies with plenty of time on his hands.

In contrast to the the narrative of being a top secret source, Trubnikov remained very communicative with the US and UK press. On June 28, 2016, NPR published an extract from an hour-long interview recorded earlier in the month with the ex-spymaster. This was held with reporter Mary Louise Kelly in Moscow. Apparently, the American journalist traveled all the way to Moscow on the off chance of a meeting with the ex-spy chief. The pair communicated the arrangements for the meeting by email. The conversation in the very public lobby of the Metropol Hotel was about espionage trade craft.

Mary Louise Kelly describes "The Metropol" as one of Moscow's grande dame hotels, just steps from Red Square, with polished dark wood, sparkling crystal decanters, and velvet armchairs. She asked the long-retired master spy to talk about his career and his thoughts on modern spy craft. "Today, to get any kind of secret paper, with the top-secret info—that's nothing," he said. "It is essential to penetrate into the brains of those who are leading the countries. And to penetrate the brains of foreign leaders—to predict your adversary's next move—Trubnikov says only human intelligence works."[267]

This oddly timed interview at the Metropol occurred just a few days before Vyacheslav Trubnikov's starring appearance in the Steele dossier in the first memo dated June 20, 2016. The memo allegedly describes information from Sources A and B, a senior Russian Foreign Ministry figure and a former top level Russian intelligence officer still active inside the Kremlin. "A" and "B" are "Trubnikov" just described differently. He is duplicated to bulk up the number of alleged sources.

The "explosive memo" goes on to say that the Russian authorities had been cultivating and supporting Donald Trump for at least 5 years and that the intelligence operation was both supported and directed by Russian President Vladimir Putin. Source A ("Trubnikov" described as a government official) says that the Kremlin had been feeding Trump and his team valuable intelligence on his opponents, including Hillary Clinton, for several years. According to Steele in June 2016, Source B ("Trubnikov" again now described as the former top level Russian intelligence officer) asserted that Trump's unorthodox behavior in Russia over the years had provided the authorities with enough embarrassing material to be able to blackmail him. Asked about rumors about a Russian dossier of 'kompromat' on Hillary Clinton being circulated, Source B confirmed the file's existence and that it had been collated by Department K of the FSB [268] for many years, dating back to her husband Bill's presidency.[269]

---

[267] Mary Louise Kelly interview with Trubnikov, https://www.npr.org/transcripts/483734866.

[268] Counter-intelligence and Financial Services.

[269] A story lifted from Boris Yeltsin's auto biography.

Steele lists his "sources" chronologically, so "Trubnikov" is both the first and second source, and used in his fake dossier to kick-start the Russia hoax. "Trubnikov" is not only included as two sources for the fake dossier but also described in the State Department notes in October 2016, as a participant in the operation to cultivate Donald Trump.[270] Given the efforts Steele later goes to in court to protect the identity of his "sources" why would he give away Trubnikov's name and why would an ex top Russian spy inform Steele about a live top secret operation he is participating in?

Then in March 2017, two months after the Steele dossier was first published by the US press, the BBC's Security correspondent Gordon Corera met up with Vyacheslav Trubnikov in Moscow. They discussed the century of suspicion in relations between Russia and the West for a radio program. They even discussed the allegations of Russian interference in the US presidential election. Steele and Halper's alleged secret source is not in hiding; in fact he is talking openly to the BBC. For the article and program aired on March 30, 2017, Gordon Corera records the Russian ex-spymaster saying, "It was the expansion of NATO to its borders. That was already the origin of real suspicions on our side."[271] The Russian view is that the West broke an agreement to expand NATO membership to countries on its border causing hostility.

The story then gets even more puzzling. NPR returns to Moscow in 2017 to re-interview the not-so-elusive and still-very-much-alive ex-spy Trubnikov. Once again, the pair meet up at the Metropol Hotel:

> KELLY: I met him last summer. I asked him to meet me again and tell me what he thinks about events unfolding in the US

---

[270] https://www.scribd.com/document/409364009/Kavalec-Less-Redacted-Memo

[271] https://www.bbc.com/news/world-europe-39339679

TRUBNIKOV: To be frank, I never expected that American society would be so deeply split. I never expected this. I considered this society more solid.

KELLY: You mentioned a split in American society and how surprising you find it. The fear in the United States is that Russia has also identified these divisions and is working to worsen them, to spread confusion, to make American democracy look bad. Is that true, do you think?

TRUBNIKOV: What for? In what sense Russia—what Russia gets from split American society?

KELLY: If you weaken your adversary, that can work to your advantage.

TRUBNIKOV: It is absolutely incorrect. It reminds me of very old anecdote about two neighbors. One neighbor has two cows and his neighbor has only one cow. So the neighbor who has one cow does not think in terms to have another one, but that one cow of neighbor would die. This is perverted logic which exists, unfortunately. But be absolutely sure today's Russia, at least the bulk of politicians here, do not think in such terms.

KELLY: You don't believe that a weakened America is to Russia's advantage?

TRUBNIKOV: To have a weak partner does not mean that you become stronger.

KELLY: Former Russian spymaster Vyacheslav Trubnikov. Although ask any CIA guy, they'll tell you there's no former KGB.[272]

There are multiple and clear contradictions between the various public statements of Trubnikov and the statements attributed to him in the fake Steele dossier possibly provided to him by Halper.

---

[272] https://www.npr.org/2017/06/09/532208376/russia-meddled-in-u-s-election-comey-says-during-senate-testimony

Of course, Spygate was a hoax from the beginning; there were no Russians involved. It began long before any "Russian investigation". Halper as a co-founding member of the "Cambridge Club" was out fabricating evidence. Absent any other suspect he may well have started the whole ball rolling with his invented "Rumor Intelligence" on Russian intentions in summer 2015 when he submitted his application to the Office of Net Assessments which allowed him to finance his activities. Could it be that Halper seeded the idea the Russians were up to something with a file of compromising material on Hillary Clinton which CIA Director John Brennan and the James Clapper Director of National Intelligence seized upon? My hypothesis is that Halper was being well paid from the US Treasury to "investigate" his own invented speculation. Halper would have been in his element. From 1980 onward, this was his forte. Halper might have gone out and planted clues to keep the taxpayer's money flowing into his bank account. Setting Gen. Flynn and me up with the help of his Cambridge buddies would be a vital part of the scheme.

Halper's fake investigation of Russian collusion seems near identical to the railroading of Carter Page to obtain the original FISA warrants and renewals. The Horowitz Inspector General report shows Halper and Steele supplied the probable cause. The FISAs were used to spy on the whole campaign, not just Carter Page, and they are illegal.

Halper's false allegations against me and Gen. Flynn fall into two parts. American citizens should enjoy constitutional protection from snooping by their government. Foreigners, even citizens of America's closest ally, do not enjoy any such protection from US surveillance.

An American who has contact with a foreign intelligence agent loses their constitutional protection if the agencies can satisfy themselves it represents a foreign intelligence threat. The then-director of National

Intelligence James Clapper outlined the criteria to obtain surveillance on an American citizen in a CNN interview:

> My concern in all this, as it was when I served as DNI, was the Russians and what the Russians were doing. And to the extent that there was surveillance of anyone . . . it was occasioned by contacts with Russians who were targets, validated foreign intelligence targets. And we sort of lost sight of that and the threat that the Russians pose because that's how this all started, is the Russian meddling.[273]

To find out what "the Russians were doing," the security services unleashed their one-man counterintelligence task force, Stefan Halper to the United Kingdom. The University of Cambridge became the unlikely frontline in the new Cold War. In this conflict, America was represented not by a crack investigative team but an untrained, chronically out of shape, wheezing storyteller with a history of failure and malfeasance. Halper had to establish the target Gen. Flynn, an American, had continuing contact with a Russian. Halper simply invented an account of what happened at dinner in 2014; a dinner he did not attend. He then perhaps used the very emails I was ordered to send to Gen. Flynn by Christopher Andrew as evidence of a continuing nefarious relationship, even hinting at blackmail.

The second step is Halper had to make me the validated "Russian" foreign intelligence target. Well, that was a really tough one and an impossible task. Halper attempted to stand up his ludicrous allegation that I was a Russian intelligence officer specifically from the GRU.

---

[273] James Clapper, CNN (April 12, 2019), transcript at https://www.realclearpolitics.com/video/2019/04/12/clapper_on_trump_spying_i_cant_speak_specifically_to_what_the_fbi_did.html.

In May 2020 the Department of Justice released an FBI document that shows to their credit that no one in Cambridge who was at the dinner in February 2014 would support Halper's fantastical account or had the slightest security concern about me. In fact, one of Halper's sub-sources he deployed against me, Dr. William Foster sat next to me at the Gen. Flynn dinner. Dr. William Foster has a clear recollection of the events of that evening.

In the summer of 2019, Dr. Foster told me his account of a stand-up row he had with Halper contradicting the published false accounts of the dinner. Halper was in Cambridge in February 2017 just as Andrew published an article for the *Sunday Times*. Foster brought the newspaper article to Halper's attention and disputed the account of the dinner. Foster told Halper that he was prepared to come out to correct all the many incorrect details in Andrew's account. Foster was left stunned by Halper's reaction. Halper exploded in anger and told him to keep his thoughts to himself.

Up to this point Foster considered Halper a trusted friend. Now he was alarmed. Foster realized his weekly "harmless" chats with Halper about me and others were far more serious than he ever imagined. Foster, like everyone at Cambridge, knew of Halper's CIA connections. But then the truth dawned on him. Foster realized he was an unwitting participant—a source in a black intelligence operation. Foster was browbeaten by Halper into staying silent until 2019.

The greater challenge for Halper was how to take me a British citizen their entire adult life, who was well known to the security services and Cambridge academics, and rebrand them as a Russian intelligence officer. I was very acquainted for years with every member of the "Cambridge Club" and closely associated with them.

Through my association with the Intelligence Seminar, I met a number of security chiefs and invited to visit secure buildings and handled materials in Western intelligence archives. The allegation that I was linked to Russian intelligence was not only a preposterous one but would be deeply embarrassing to the British authorities. Halper's lies made senior British intelligence figures (even some retired ones) look either complicit in a Russian intelligence operation or totally gullible imbeciles.

In particular, Dearlove was the ex-head of MI6 and an expert on Russian intelligence. Surely after all his years working behind the Iron Curtain, he would spot a spy straight away. No one other than the fraud Halper, not even Dearlove, reported any suspicious activity in the Cambridge seminar. Following the 2014 Gen. Flynn dinner, the Cambridge Club treated me as a person of trust, pulling me closer into their circle.

Halper began claiming my research into Soviet intelligence was too good to be the product of hard work. In his opinion my work was so ground-breaking it could only come directly from Putin. His claims were a joke. I published all my sources as any good historian is trained to do. My co-author Professor Christopher Andrew was the leading world authority on intelligence, and moreover, the historian the security services in the UK trust the most. He was the former official historian of MI5. Andrew worked with two Soviet-era defectors for MI6: the KGB archivist Vasili Mitrokhin and Oleg Gordievsky. It was not that Andrew felt any loyalty to me as he would later show, but he had his own reputation to protect. Andrew did not not go along with Halper's attack on my academic work as it would damage his own reputation.

What followed in the weeks after I rebuffed the opportunity to go to dinner with Halper was an Andrew-engineered termination of our extremely lucrative publishing contract with Basic Books and Penguin. He was in need of money for his retirement, and prior to February 2014, he worked very hard on our book calling me a superstar, praising my research. Now every word in our draft seemed to be a problem. He refused to sign the contract which would have triggered a large advance payment from the publisher we both needed. By April, he started to refuse to speak to me on the telephone and began negotiating through our exasperated literary agent. The agent and I initially put this behavior down to old age.Out of the blue Andrew suddenly asked me to send an email to the Seminar group to deny a rumor that I was somehow connected to Russian intelligence. To distract from Halper, Andrew blamed a colleague for being the source of this rumor, saying this fellow had early-stage dementia and was behaving oddly.

I learned later that bitter infighting broke out in the Cambridge Security Initiative (CSI). Disputes in this group of old men were common. Professor Neil Kent, another CSI fellow, had launched an academic journal and proposed a formal link with CSI. Christopher Andrew encouraged all his ex-students to participate.

I was not involved but was told that the issue was that the money for the journal came from a friend of Professor Kent a British citizen with Russian connections. The fighting got so bad Professor Kent resigned from CSI and led a rebellion. Christopher Andrew resigned from CSI, an organization he cofounded just two years previously and his legacy project. The dispute reached the ears of the Vice-Chancellor of the University and he instructed a ceasefire between the warring parties. By July 2016, there appeared to be an end to the dispute and a division of the spoils. CSI went one way with the "Cambridge Club" and the

Intelligence Seminar the other. In July 2016, Halper resigned amicably from the Seminar to retire and return to the US

In the meantime, as I discovered later, Halper intensified his spying on me. He began to interrogate anyone who knew me. One of his spies, my colleague Dr. Bill Foster told me in the summer of 2019 what happened. Halper is not a trained investigator; he is an agent provocateur. He arranged to meet Bill Foster weekly for a catch-up and gossip.

Foster was being paid by Halper to write a history of the CIA, which relied on access to the private papers and reminiscences of Halper about his father-in-law, Dr. Ray S. Cline, the retired deputy director. For an espionage historian, such access to a garrulous eye witness like Halper was fantastic. Foster found himself drawn into discussions that seemed innocuous at the time but later realized deeply compromised him.

Dr. Foster was sent out to solicit information about me. Inspector General Horowitz's report and declassified transcripts give a flavor of some of Halper's sledgehammer techniques. Halper asked Foster leading questions as statements, such as *How do you know that Svetlana is not a Russian spy?*" His approach is unsubtle in the extreme. He asked Papadopoulos *Trump and you are part of a conspiracy, right?*" Halper asserts an opinion but then reports others have the concerns. This can be gleaned from the later newspaper articles for which he was the only source.

Dr. Foster had to report weekly to Halper on what he discovered about my innocuous activities and views. Dr. Foster was shocked when he understood what he thought was just gossip was forming the basis of intelligence reports. Later he realized with horror that his gossipy chats might form a vital element of Spygate. Foster feared he was guilty of an unwitting monumental breach of trust by reporting private conversations of a student to a foreign intelligence asset, the CIA/FBI's Halper.

Moreover, Foster realized his comments had been given the Halper treatment of misreporting and false attribution. When at some point the University of Cambridge authorities became aware of Halper's activities, they were too frightened to do anything. They feared getting embroiled in expensive litigation with him. Dr. Bill Foster told me the University authorities believed Halper to be too rich to expose. They did what they do best: stuck their heads in the sand and hoped the scandal would go away.

In the meantime, I picked up the pieces of the book contract Andrew had torn up. I had to settle for much less than half the money, but at least now the book would be in my name only. My book was aimed at the US market, so I approached the only two people who saw my research in America. One was Gen. Flynn. I sent a forlorn hope email asking if he would agree to be mentioned in the proposal. Amazingly he agreed. I was anxious to finish the work as soon as possible as I was expecting my first child. I stopped going to Cambridge since, unexpectedly, all my teaching work dried up. Previously my feedback was excellent, so I was surprised.

The email I sent to Gen. Flynn on July 4, 2016, ended up somehow being referenced incorrectly in the Luke Harding's *Guardian* article. It is unclear to me who obtained a copy of the proposal that I sent to Gen. Flynn and provided the details to journalists. I am sure that Gen. Flynn didn't give the confidential book proposal to the *Guardian*. I suspect this is a concrete sign Gen. Flynn was under electronic surveillance before the opening of Operation Crossfire Hurricane. Harding is under investigation by Congress for possible CIA leaks for another article published in the same month.[274] Sara A. Carter later reported about the emails and the rest of his allegations:

> Numerous sources with knowledge of the allegations Halper made about Flynn, said that they were "absolutely" false and that Flynn and Lokhova only spoke for a short time at the dinner. Several email exchanges between Lokhova, Flynn and his assistant that took place after the dinner were generic in nature, as Flynn had asked her for a copy of a historical 1930s *(sic)* postcard she had brought to the seminar. "But it didn't matter that it wasn't the truth," said the former senior intelligence official. "It was already out there because of Halper's allegations and the constant leaking and lying of false stories of those to the media.[275]

In November of 2016, I was gripped like everyone by the cliffhanger US election. The coverage in the UK was universally pro-Hillary and anti-Trump. As the results started to come in, it became clear the coronation plan for President Clinton had gone off the rails.

---

[274] Sen. Chuck Grassley and Sen. Ron Johnson

[275] Sara Carter, "Whistleblower Exposes Key Player in FBI Russia Probe: 'It was all a Set-up'" (August 27, 2018).

Chapter Fourteen: Puzzles

And He said, That which cometh out of the man, that defileth the man.
For from within, out of the heart of men, proceed evil thoughts,
adulteries, fornications, murders,
Thefts, covetousness, wickedness, deceit, lasciviousness, an evil eye,
blasphemy, pride, foolishness:
All these evil things come from within, and defile the man.
—Mark: 7:20-23

"This is a war," Lemas replied. "It's graphic and unpleasant because
it's fought on a tiny scale, at close range; fought with a wastage of
innocent life"

—John Le Carré, *The Spy Who Came in from the Cold*

B efore their devastating betrayal of public trust by some in their former leadership, America's intelligence agencies derived their support broad support from conservatives. As students of intelligence studies at the University of Cambridge, we were taught that in a free Republic, unlike in authoritarian regimes, security services serve the people, not a ruling political party. We were told this distinction was the most significant difference between the intelligence agencies of the Soviet Union and those of the West.

During the Spygate scandal, America's intelligence agencies former leadership behaved more like the oppressive security services in totalitarian states, disgracing themselves in the process by acting politically, as agents of the Deep State. Without a reckoning, if after all the exposures of travesties and wrongdoing, the structures are left unreformed, this would represent a clear and present danger to the continuation of representative government. As it turned out in this affair, the former leadership demonstrated they cannot protect the Republic but instead attack its very foundations.

In 2016, some intelligence officials seemingly conspired and abused their positions of public trust to launch an operation with the sole purpose of discrediting the political opponents of the Democratic Party. Working hand-in-glove with a willing media, these corrupt bureaucrats leveraged the public's mistaken faith in their superior knowledge, competence, and patriotism to vilify their domestic enemies from behind a shield of secrecy.

The alliance with the media flowed both ways. Some in the FBI followed where the press took them in their investigation. In return and to this day, the liberal press apologists uncritically parroted what can only be described as propaganda. The effect on sections of the public is devastating. The spies, and journalists breathlessly poisoned the minds of millions of ordinary Americans to believe their own president and the Republican Party are traitors and work for a foreign power.

Some spies and journalists are professional betrayers. Russian collusion truthers filled the airwaves with a succession of frankly embarrassing allegations, as America tore itself apart. To a neutral eye, every step in the 2016 joint FBI and Department of Justice Russia collusion investigation looks misguided and puzzling. Why did the intelligence community reject every standard investigatory practice and instead embrace extraordinary methods? The only conclusion is Crossfire Hurricane was an intelligence operation, never a proper or genuine investigation following the evidence.

Contrary to the official narrative, counterintelligence investigations have "long runways,"[276] they do not "materialize out of thin air."[277] Allegedly it is the report from an outsider, the Australian diplomat Alexander Downer about his conversation with George Papadopoulos in July 2016, that was the catalyst for the investigation.[278] Downer made his report in an unusual manner to a friendly contact in the US State Department and not via official intelligence channels just a few days after the end of the "Spyfest" conference in Cambridge. There seem to be clear business and other links between Alexander Downer, Stefan Halper and Richard Dearlove.[279]

This chronology makes no sense in the light of my evidence. Devin Nunes and his investigator, Kash Patel, believe this FBI narrative on the origins of the investigation is purposefully misleading and a false chronology. They consider that this charade served two purposes: firstly, to conceal wrongdoing and secondly, to rationalize the withholding of documents from legitimate Congressional oversight. Nunes's team reached this conclusion because the FBI made such a big deal about the July 31 date. As part of their Congressional investigation, Nunes' team asked to be supplied with all pertinent documents dated before July 31, 2016, to which the FBI replied there

---

[276] Lee Smith interview with Kash Patel, *The Plot Against the President: The True Story of How Congressman Devin Nunes Uncovered the Biggest Political Scandal in US History.*

[277] Ibid.

[278] Report of Robert Mueller Special Counsel.

[279] Dearlove and Downer are both connected to the private security firm Hakluyt. Downer and Halper have shared a stage speaking about China.

are none. Nunes hit upon *The Curious Incident of the Dog in the Night-Time.* Sir Arthur Conan Doyle wrote a short story in 1892 called *The Silver Blaze,* explaining how Sherlock Holmes deduces the truth about "the dog that didn't bark":

> Gregory [Scotland Yard detective]: "Is there any other point to which you would wish to draw my attention?"
>
> Sherlock Holmes: "To the curious incident of the dog in the night-time."
>
> Gregory: "The dog did nothing in the night-time."
>
> Sherlock Holmes: "That was the curious incident."

In the Sherlock Holmes story, the detective solves the disappearance of a famous racehorse the night before a race and the murder of the horse's trainer. Holmes, like Nunes, solved the mystery by focusing on what was missing, rather than what was present. Holmes recognized that none of the people he interviewed mentioned the watchdog barked on the night of the incident. Holmes concluded if the dog did not bark, then the dog must have known the perpetrator and this led Holmes to track down the guilty party. Nunes realized he was finding mounting evidence of intelligence activity before the official start date of the investigation, but that did not fit the FBI narrative. Nunes refused to accept the Intelligence Community's denial and sought what they wanted to conceal.

The most significant evidence was about General Mike Flynn. Inadvertently, the press leaks about General Flynn and me during early 2107 helped confirm for Nunes what he suspected—there was something very wrong with the official narrative.[280] He was particularly struck by the contrast of alarming reports in the press that

---

[280] Nunes interview with Mike Huckabee (April 20, 2019), https://www.youtube.com/watch?v=hry1m62-9RI.

Flynn, a three-star general, was reportedly compromised by a Russian intelligence operative (myself), but at the same time Nunes was being told by the intelligence community that they had no pertinent intelligence. What could be more pertinent than a report that Donald Trump's key political ally, National Security Advisor with top-level security clearance was possibly a Russian asset? The unwillingness of some in the FBI to produce these (false) reports and later Special Counsel Mueller unwillingness to investigate them was a huge red flag:

> NUNES: The first Trump associate to be investigated was General Flynn. Many of the allegations against him stem from false media reports that he had an affair with the Cambridge academic, Svetlana Lokhova and Lokhova was a Russian spy.
>
> Some of these allegations were made public in a 2017 article written by British intelligence historian Christopher Andrew.
>
> Your report fails to reveal how or why Andrew and his collaborator, Richard Dearlove, former head of Britain's MI6, spread these allegations. And you failed to interview Svetlana Lokhova about these matters. Is that correct?
>
> MUELLER: I'm going to get—not going to get into those matters to which you refer.[281]

There should have been an enormous official reaction to the report that one of America's top spies was a traitor. Something is very wrong, and that is even before one realizes the source of the reports on General Flynn being compromised by Russian intelligence through an affair was Stefan Halper, the man who pops up everywhere in Spygate.

---

[281] Nunes questioning of Robert Mueller (July 24, 2019); see transcript at https://www.washingtonpost.com/politics/transcript-of-robert-s-mueller-iiis-testimony-before-the-house-intelligence-committee/2019/07/24/f424acf0-ad97-11e9-a0c9-6d2d7818f3da_story.html.

It is a standard procedure for the FBI to liaise with political campaigns immediately when security issues arise. Problems crop up all the time and might be as clear cut as warning a campaign about a suspicious donor.[282] Obviously, something as unusual and highly charged as Halper's fake report on General Flynn and his alleged contacts with Russian intelligence should have been resolved immediately.

The intelligence community could and should have talked to the Trump campaign about their concerns, about Russia and individuals on the campaign. They never did. Instead some in the FBI and DOJ aggressively and myopically pursued a strategy to obtain a FISA surveillance warrant to spy on the electronic records of the Trump campaign using a single confidential informer as the tool.[283]

Throughout the "Crossfire Hurricane" operation, some in the FBI and Department of Justice exhibited individually and collectively an alarming fanatical tendency to ignore evidence and presume guilt. At each point in the investigation where a sane person would say, "Let's just stop here," they just charged ahead. But when it came to "investigating" Donald Trump and his team, the FBI and DOJ investigators suppressed all common sense and the mountain of exculpatory evidence they gathered.

Seemingly, at no time in the investigation were there any adults in the room. The investigators acted like a cult. The investigation became a rush, cutting corners and riding roughshod over procedures to their holy grail of obtaining a Title 1 surveillance warrant by any means,

---

[282] Attorney General Barr interview with NBC's Pete Williams (December 10, 2019); see transcript at https://www.realclearpolitics.com/video/2019/12/11/ full_interview_ag_bill_barr_criticizes_inspector_general_report_on_the_russia_investigation. html.

[283] Ibid.

even illegally, to spy on the Trump campaign. A number of FISAs on the Trump team have now been declared invalid.[284]

The FBI launched their "official" investigation, Crossfire Hurricane, on July 31, 2016 and quickly deployed Halper as their chief investigator. His long-term FBI handler, Stephen Somma moved from the New York to the Washington field office to join the team.[285] In August, September, and October 2016, the FBI "miked" Halper, and sent him out to meet with various Trump campaign officials. Halper posed as an unlikely Donald Trump sympathizer desperate to help Donald Trump get elected. Halper circled around his chosen targets, weaving his web of deceit. He tricked his way into meetings, sometimes offering money, women or access to important people.

It was typical of this whole corrupt investigation that the simple, practical steps were ignored in favor of this charade. The goal was always to present "probable cause" to the FISA court that a Trump associate was an agent of a foreign intelligence agency. Eventually, of the five reasons offered to the court why intrusive surveillance was required,[286] the majority could be traced to Halper and the Cambridge Club. The search is still on for the exact predicate for unleashing Halper well before July 31, 2016.

The unseemly rush to access the campaign's electronic records was undoubtedly because the investigation was up against a ticking clock. By election day in November, it could all be too late. The FBI seemingly always ran with the idea that the GOP and Russia were planning a joint "October surprise." Their operation planted fake

---

[284] FISC January 23, 2020

[285] J. E. Dyer, "Spygate: Case Agent 1 and the essential 'operation' versus 'investigation' perspective" *Liberty Unyielding* (March 3, 2020).

[286] IG Report, Executive Summary

evidence of collusion to start an investigation hoping to find real evidence of collusion. There was never any evidence to support this supposition. The Crossfire team devoured the media stories placed by their own informers such as the one in *Politico* titled "Democrats fear 'October Surprise' as White House ponders hack response" dated August 5, 2016. In the article, Democratic Party strategists concocted an evil October surprise plan to release Hillary Clinton's emails that never was in Republican minds .

The release by Wikileaks of the DNC emails raised the fear that the next shoe to drop would be the leaking of Hillary's missing emails. Blaming Russia and the Trump campaign for this leak before it happened was an offensive and defensive strategy. Hillary's campaign was pushing Steele and Halper to lead the FBI investigation to focus on the October surprise and her emails. When October passed with no surprise, the FBI shelved their main theory but continued with the Collusion investigation.

The FBI seized upon the July 27, 2016 comments of candidate Donald Trump who triggered the liberal media at a press conference in Miami by saying "Russia, if you're listening, I hope you're able to find the 30,000 emails that are missing, I think you will probably be rewarded mightily by our press." Donald Trump was not giving orders to Moscow, he was masterfully trolling his opponent, Hillary. The FBI wanted to open an investigation on Donald Trump that day and duly did open one on his campaign (enterprise investigation) just a few days later.

For months in 2016, Halper assiduously cultivated the enigmatic Carter Page. During the long operation, lasting beyond the inauguration of Donald Trump, the two became friends. But all the time Halper feigned interest in the troubles of Carter Page, he was actually betraying him for money. Within days of joining the Trump campaign in March 2016, the then unknown financier Page became subject to a liberal press campaign targeting his Russian links. It all started with a critical profile piece in *Bloomberg News* published in March 2016. Page became Trump's "Mr. Russia" in the eyes of the media.

Carter Page espoused in a small number of public speeches a view that a reset in relations with President Vladimir Putin was needed. We now know Page was a CIA asset, gathering information on Russians which may explain his public views. A low-key FBI counterintelligence case was opened into Carter Page by the FBI within weeks of his joining the Trump campaign in March 2016, maybe as a result of his press attention. No one from the FBI informed the Trump campaign of their concerns.

Carter Page is a well-known figure to the US intelligence community. Somehow, the collusion obsessed fanatics concealed that he was a US intelligence asset, telling the court he was a Russian one. They suppressed and, in one case, altered evidence to support that false supposition.

The FBI twisted Carter Page's working with them against Russian intelligence assets into evidence against him. He was their best bet to get probable cause through a court to obtain a FISA. Page had visited Russia mid-campaign on a private visit. Once a first warrant was achieved, there was no turning back. The investigators just had to keep digging to find what they desperately needed to be there.

The start of Halper's operation against Carter Page predated "Crossfire Hurricane" by months. One event sticks out like a sore thumb and is unexplained. The first act against Page was to invite him to the University of Cambridge by an email sent in late May or early June, way before the start of the official investigation timeline of July 31, 2016. Page was lured into attending a mysterious conference held in early July 2016 by a cutout, a "student studying under Stefan Halper."[287]

The journalist John Solomon reported in *The Hill* on May 5, 2018, "Carter Page said conference organizers paid his airfare and provided him dorm lodging, and Halper spent time with him during the conference, then continued conversations with him for months."[288]

Page also told Congress in his testimony that "Cambridge University booked [him] a ticket."[289] In my experience of organizing University conferences, such events are financed by outside donors, not by ticket sales, and certainly not by the University.

According to Page's accounts, it is likely Halper paid, perhaps via a University account, for Carter Page's flights from Moscow to London and back to the US, plus accommodation, and expenses. Given the "intelligence" flow after the event, Halper and at least one colleague appear to have been working, perhaps for the CIA or some unknown others, laying out a bread crumb trail of "evidence." The Cambridge event was put together very quickly. Typically, these events are planned many months, or a year, in advance. Halper was the organizer of the event together with Steven Schrage who by all accounts pursued Page with emails and phone calls to ensure he would attend. Schrage was retired Professor Stefan Halper's last and most unusual Ph D. student.

---

[287] That doctoral student was Steven Schrage.

[288] https://thehill.com/opinion/white-house/390228-london-bridges-falling-down-curious-origins-of-fbis-trump-russia-probe

[289] Byron York, *Washington Examiner* (May 28, 2018).

Rep. Nunes talked about the clouds around Schrage to Maria Bartiromo on Sunday Morning Futures after the release of the Mueller Report on July 28, 2019 saying:

> You have an American citizen, somebody who's long been involved in politics, and the guy's name is Steven Schrage. Now, [he] knows that the House Intelligence Committee, the Senate Intelligence Committee, the FBI, we want to talk to anyone and everyone who was dealing with Carter Page and other Trump associates, especially in early 2016.
>
> Schrage is the one who invited Carter Page to this event. Schrage is the one who organized this event. So -- but instead of coming forward, a guy who's been involved in politics for this long doesn't come forward? I want to know, did he know about the Steele dossier at that time? When did he find out about the Steele dossier? Did he have control of the Steele dossier at any time? Did he give it to anyone?
>
> Those are the types of things that Steven Schrage needs to come clean on, because, you know, look, maybe he was just a guy working for minimum wage sweeping the floors around Cambridge. I highly doubt it.[290]

The dates of the conference were set for July 11–12, 2016. The event was held in two then-unused lecture rooms because the event was held outside the University's term time. It is very unusual timing for a prestigious event seeking to gather a large audience. The only people in Cambridge in July are the coach loads of day-trippers and swarms of tourists. These visitors flock in the thousands to choke the narrow streets around the landmarks such as King's College Chapel or take the chance to punt on the River Cam. Students are long gone. The University teaching staff is on their summer vacation. So, who was the expected audience for this unusual event?

---

[290] Fox News

The organizer Schrage is a fascinating character with his intelligence connections. Like so many in this tale, Schrage created a void, now filled with suspicion by failing to come forward to explain their actions. Schrage is a strong candidate for being perhaps the most overqualified PhD student ever. Before arriving at the University of Cambridge, his career found him working in the middle of many of the major US political and foreign policy events of the last two decades[291]. Schrage had direct experience with major presidential campaigns, even White House transitions and national security. He served on the 2008 Mitt Romney presidential campaign.

Schrage even taught National Security at the Georgetown School of Foreign Service in Washington, rated as the top global foreign policy master's program. He served as one of the Deputy Assistant Secretaries under Secretary Colin Powell at the State Department. In that role, he oversaw more than a thousand personnel across the globe and more than $2 billion in some of America's top priority global operations in the Middle East, Latin America, and Afghanistan. He has worked at the CIA's favorite think tank CSIS. Schrage is a friend of Cofer Black, ex-CIA top brass and board member of the Ukrainian energy company Burisma.

Schrage apparently collects degrees, having already conducted MBA and doctoral studies at Harvard Business School. He is a graduate of both Duke University and the University of Michigan Law School. As an expert, Halper's student appeared on major media outlets, including NBC's *Nightly News*, CNN, the *New York Times*, the *Wall Street Journal*, Fox News, the *Washington Post*, and *Bloomberg News*.

Since his bit part appearance in the 2016 scandal, he vanished. "Maybe [Schrage] was just a guy working for minimum wage sweeping the

291 https://www.milforddailynews.com/article/20100212/NEWS/302129875

floors around Cambridge. I highly doubt it," Rep. Devin Nunes has said. "And the fact that he hasn't come forward in two-and-a-half years is highly suspect."[292]

He apparently was holed up in the University of Cambridge completing another unnecessary degree. In February 2020, Schrage reappeared in the public eye at my talk at CPAC in Washington. He announced he was seeking to clear his name and felt used by his mentor, a familiar refrain from those who run into Halper's web.

Schrage has assiduously avoided contacting those looking for him despite an enormous hue and cry. He was not interviewed by the Mueller inquiry as one of their more than 500 witnesses.[293] The University of Cambridge is an obscure place to choose to research American politics, lacking any of the resources of say Georgetown, with its array of libraries and resource material. There are questions that need to be answered and another story that on its face does not seem to fit.

As Rep. Nunes explained why Schrage and the Cambridge Conference are a vital part of Spygate:

> BARTIROMO: Who is the mastermind of this story? Who is the mastermind of the plan to insert Donald Trump into Russia meddling, which we know Russia has been meddling for decades?
>
> NUNES: Well, I think we can say for -- let's talk about what we can -- what we know are facts, what we can say for certain. I think that's helpful.

---

[292] Fox News "Sunday Morning Futures" - Transcript: Interview with Rep. Devin Nunes July 28, 2019.

[293] Mueller testimony to Congress

We know the Clinton campaign, number one. So they're aware of a lot of this, right? They're involved in the creation of the dossier. They're hiring Fusion GPS. They hire Christopher Steele. That's a fact. So the Clinton campaign is involved.

We know the FBI is involved to some degree. We don't know exactly what they were doing before July 31, 2016. Why? Because they wouldn't answer the questions that we had over the last two years.

And, in fact, when we were getting close, we wanted transcripts, there were things that we wanted, those were not given to the United States House of Representatives under Republican control. Do you know why? Because the Mueller dossier team wouldn't let us have them.

So that's why I say, somebody needs to look at these characters that were on Mueller's team. I think they obstructed justice. They obstructed a congressional investigation. So that's number two.

We have -- we have the Clinton team. We have the FBI. There's also a third team that we know of. That is this Cambridge team, this group of British people that were there, these intelligence-related folks, including the American citizen, Steven Schrage, who organized this event.

They were involved in the character assassination of a three-star general, the former head of the director -- the director of intelligence, General Michael Flynn.

Was it to create a cover for the hit operation against Donald Trump's junior foreign policy advisor Carter Page that made Schrage seemingly send two invitations to attend the Cambridge conference to the small Trump campaign foreign policy team? Schrage first invited Stephen Miller, a senior Trump campaign advisor in May. The invitation to Page was sent on June 7, 2016.[294] Miller turned down the request. In the campaign calendar, July is the first, frantic month. There is a

---

[294] The Daily Caller News Foundation, https://www.dailysignal.com/2019/08/02/new-scrutiny-for-former-government-official-who-invited-trump-aide-to-cambridge/

mountain of work merely preparing for the convention scheduled for a week later.

On the other hand, unpaid advisor Carter Page had the time on his hands to swan off on a long international trip. Despite being told by his superior in the campaign, J. D. Gordon, not to go to Cambridge (and Moscow), there was no stopping Page. In advance of his fateful date with destiny in Cambridge, Carter Page set off on his extraordinarily poorly timed trip to Moscow. In the Russian capital, acting in his private capacity, he made at least two speeches at a Moscow Institute.

Page's ill-fated trip to Moscow was an absolute bonus to the plotters. The Cambridge leg of Carter Page's international trip has all the hallmarks of an elaborate intelligence sting operation. It is perhaps no coincidence that another of Halper's targets received a fully expenses paid trip to the United Kingdom as a setup. In the case of another campaign advisor George Papadopoulos, we now know it was the FBI who used taxpayers' money to trap him.[295] The question remains unanswered as to who planned and paid for Carter Page many weeks before the official start of counterintelligence investigations?

Carter Page's expenses, including flights and accommodation, were paid for him to sit in the audience at this "Spyfest" conference in Cambridge: this is an utterly unheard of practice. The University of Cambridge is a prestigious institution, so it does not pay its audiences to turn up to an event. A video available online shows the audience for the headline event of the conference was small. The event cost someone a great deal of money including the costs of flying dignitaries into the UK first class and five star hotel accommodation. Ticket sales for this event would come nowhere near covering the expenses.

---

[295] IG Report

The University lecture hall could hold a maximum of 110 attendees. A bigger venue that could hold 450 was hired for the headline event featuring a discussion between ex-Secretary of State Madeline Albright, lobbyist Vin Weber[296] and Steven Schrage. The video shows the lecture hall is practically empty. The obvious questions is: was Halper, the paymaster for this lavish and loss-making event using US taxpayer money and if so why?

The conference was entitled "2016's Race to Change the World: How the US Presidential Campaign Can Reshape Global Politics and Foreign Policy." The advertised speakers make a very impressive list, including Hillary Clinton's close friend Madeleine Albright, the former US Secretary of State; Tony Podesta's business partner and the "never Trump" Vin Weber, Republican Party strategist and former Congressman; Ambassador Peter Ammon, German ambassador to the UK; the "Cambridge Club's" Sir Richard Dearlove former head of MI6; Bridget Kendall, BBC diplomatic correspondent; Sir Malcolm Rifkind, former UK Defense and Foreign Secretary; and of course the FBI informer and CIA source, the "foreign policy expert" Stefan Halper.

What was the point of paying the CIA asset Carter Page to fly from Moscow to Cambridge to sit in the audience for an event? Halper disingenuously told his long-term FBI handler and the remarkably uninterested Stephen Somma that he 'just casually ran into' Carter Page at the Conference. Carter Page was already the subject of a counter-inteligence investigation opened in April 2016 but according to the IG report Somma had no interest in discussing the encounter with his source. According to Halper, it was the junior foreign policy

---

[296] Vin Weber is billed as a "Republican Strategist," although he would later profess he couldn't "imagine remaining a Republican if Trump becomes president," and promised, "if my vote decided the election, I would vote for Hillary Clinton over Donald Trump."

advisor who was so starstruck with the veteran electioneer that Page made all the effort to start a friendship. Halper said it was Page who invited him to join the Trump campaign, an invitation the veteran spy was considering. In a later interview with the *Federalist*, Page disputes this: "That is quite clearly not a correct characterization, I never asked him 'to be a foreign policy advisor for the Trump campaign... But, as written in the inaccuracy-laden IG report, that's an extraordinary mischaracterization."[297]

There is nothing in Halper's past or public pronouncements that would suggest the elitist Swamp dweller as a closet MAGA. The twin ideas of putting America first and draining the Swamp would be anathema to this globalist. The concept and implementation of "Draining the Swamp" is the end of fat paydays to Halper and his crew.

Carter Page was clearly upset by the revelation of Halper's account. He retaliated by giving an interview contradicting Halper's account to *The Federalist* where he revealed details of the VIP dinner at Magdalene College. According to what was told to Horowitz, it was Halper, not the FBI, who introduced Page as a potential person of interest in the Crossfire Hurricane team's first meeting with the confidential human source.[298] *The Federalist* pointed out a list of interesting follow-up questions:

> Did Halper hope to be tasked by the FBI with targeting Page? Was Halper tasked by another agency already? And did Halper exaggerate the content of his conversation with Page to make Page appear instrumental in the Trump campaign? If so, for what purpose?[299]

---

[297] Margot Cleveland, "Exclusive Carter Page Interview Raises Questions about 'Inaccuracy-Laden' IG Report," *The Federalist* (January 8, 2020).

[298] Ibid.

[299] Ibid.

In the Horowitz report, the FBI describes their encounter as follows: "Stefan Halper explained that, in mid-July 2016, Carter Page attended a three-day conference, during which Page had approached Stefan Halper and asked him to be a foreign policy advisor for the Trump campaign." According to the FBI records Halper said he was "non-committal" about joining the campaign.

Halper told the Crossfire Hurricane team, "he was expecting to be contacted in the near future by one of the senior leaders of the Trump campaign about joining the campaign." Of course, he was never approached by the campaign, and Carter Page denies asking him to be a foreign policy advisor. Page's July email to Sam Clovis supports this contention. In any event, the campaign by July was fully staffed.

Days before trapping Page at the elaborately staged conference, on Wednesday July 6, 2016, Halper made another speech in Cambridge to a small group. Halper outlined his predictions for the 2016 US presidential election. He had returned to Cambridge for the second time that year. The receipts he submitted to the Office of Net Assessments likely show the US taxpayer once again paid for Halper's "Spygate" travel expenses.

Based on the extract of Halper's talk, which is still online, the operative focused on the phenomenon which is "Trump's maverick candidacy" while also explaining the deficits in Clinton's campaign, which have caused the campaign to become almost too close to call. "Professor Stefan Halper concluded his talk by stating that if the media focuses on Clinton, she will lose, whereas if they continue to focus on Trump, he will lose. This will be true despite Trump's adept handling of the media resulting in him receiving two billion dollars' worth of free media coverage."[300]

---

[300] https://pembrokekings.wordpress.com/2016/07/09/the-p-stands-for-plenary/

Halper seemingly spotted early that without his help, Hillary Clinton's campaign was doomed because of the email scandal and the candidate herself was unlikeable. Clinton's personality would not carry her to the Oval Office. She could not win with a positive message. If Clinton was going to win, she would have to go negative and need the help of her legion of press allies.

Halper forecasted the eventual loser in the race would be the campaign the press focused on with the most negativity. He then set out to ensure as much negative press attention was shone on the Trump campaign as possible. The stick to beat Donald Trump with was Russia. It was, after all, the same dirty trick he apparently used years before on Bill Clinton with such devastating effect in the George Bush senior campaign.

At the Cambridge "Spyfest" event, Halper set out to make quite the impression on Carter Page. It was exactly the same strategy Sir Richard Dearlove unleashed on General Mike Flynn in February 2014. The unknown Page was incongruously a VIP guest at the conference. He was invited to a Sunday night prestigious, exclusive small elite candlelit dinner[301] at the medieval Magdalene College. He would have been Halper's guest as only members of College can issue invitations.

Halper is a life fellow and huge donor to the College[302]. At this cozy dinner, the little-known Trump campaign foreign policy associate was introduced to and sat amongst the "great and the good." The guests included Hillary Clinton's great friend US Secretary of State Madeline K. Albright. This flattering of a target's ego is an old espionage trick, a standard operating procedure.

---

[301] https://thefederalist.com/2020/01/08/exclusive-carter-page-interview-raises-new-questions-about-inaccuracy-laden-ig-report/

[302] https://thefederalist.com/2020/01/09/new-details-about-meeting-fbi-source-suggest-carter-page-was-set-up/

Spies believe their objects are all vulnerable to an approach. There are four methods characterized as MICE, Money, Ideology, Compromise, or Ego. Carter Page fell for the fourth. Halper trapped him by playing up to his vanity. Page wanted to be someone. So, the social misfit found himself catapulted into the company of a retired Archbishop, an ex-intelligence chief and political power brokers.

In Cambridge, Page was suddenly being listened to by people whose names he read in the newspaper. He was in a world way above his pay grade. No one so far has revealed what happened around the dinner table at Magdalene College on Sunday evening, July 10, 2016. Halper's standard technique would have been to encourage Page to speak. If Page played his role of being a pro-Russian advocate, the Russia hawks, of which there were plenty around the table, would have seethed. What Page said or did not say is irrelevant; what matters is he attended this event and "reports" could be made up.

Carter Page is aware that he was set up and an account of his words were passed on to a broad alliance of hostile forces. Halper seems to have distributed his version of Page's words far and wide. This is the key moment in the Halper operation when the intelligence and the Democrat political dirty tricks operation openly aligned. The informer may well have reported Page as an "agent of Russia" to his handlers at possibly the CIA, FBI, and likely Christopher Steele. Madeline Albright may have passed on Page's allegedly pro Russian views to the Clinton Campaign and the DNC to be used as attack lines.[303] Both "foreign policy experts" opinions got to the DNC dirty tricks outfit Fusion GPS.

A story was soon planted in the flagship fake news outlet, *The Washington Post*. On August 5, 2016 a Carter Page explosive,

[303] Page reported meeting Albright to the FBI. They took no interest, which is very surprising if they thought for a second that he was a Russian asset.

exclusive article authored by one of Fusion GPS's favorite journalists, Tom Hamburger, was published. The headline was "Trump adviser's public comments, ties to Moscow stir unease in both parties." The article stated, Trump's foreign policy advisor Page dumbfounded foreign policy experts by giving speeches harshly critical of current US policy toward Russia.

The *Washington Post* claimed implausibly that since being named to the Republican nominee's campaign team in March, the once virtually unknown Carter Page saw "his stature grow within the foreign policy world." Page's "position as a Trump adviser has catapulted him into the most prestigious policy events, such as a closed-door session co-chaired by former Secretary of State Madeleine K. Albright and Republican consultant Vin Weber at Cambridge University in July."

Wait a second, just how did an obscure conference in Cambridge become a "most prestigious policy event?" And who could have told the journalist Tom Hamburger the details of a close door session in this backwater of England?

The *Washington Post* article was published on the same day as left leaning *Politico* announced the Trump campaign was planning an "October surprise" plot to release Hillary Clinton's emails with the cooperation of a foreign hostile power, Russia.[304] Handily, there was the "facilitator" Carter Page, a Trump campaign official, with the dust of Moscow still on his shoes.

In the run up to publication and mirroring my experience with the press, Carter Page began receiving text messages, first from the *Wall Street Journal* and then from the *Washington Post* journalist Tom Hamburger on July 26, 2016. They were asking Page to confirm

---

[304] https://www.politico.com/story/2016/08/clinton-democrats-hacking-dnc-october-surprise-226743

details of the story. Pretending to confirm details with a target is a standard press tactic with a pre-packaged article. Page was later to complain at length to Halper in a conversation, secretly recorded by the FBI about the article, saying, "95 percent of it was complete garbage."[305]

Tom Hamburger was seemingly briefed directly by Halper or indirectly via Fusion GPS that Carter Page was "drawing alarm from more-established foreign policy experts who view him as having little real understanding about US-Russia relations." Those anonymous experts from "both parties" referred to in the article might well be Halper, Albright, and Weber. The voices from the shadows say they are "distressed" with Carter Page for his criticism of the US sanctions on Russia and praise for Russian President Vladimir Putin and his advisers.

By developing a fake narrative the *Washington Post* treated its readers to an elaborate and false conspiracy theory. This is how the fable goes: presidential candidate Donald Trump is depicted as an outspoken fan of the evil bogeyman Russian President Vladimir Putin. As Donald Trump was questioning longstanding US obligations to defend its NATO allies and Russia's goal was to disrupt or break up the Atlantic alliance they must be colluding. The readers were led to believe Donald Trump was asking for Russian help to find the deleted emails of his rival presidential candidate Hillary Clinton to help win the election. In return for Russia releasing Hillary's emails Donald Trump will weaken or break up NATO. Read in conjunction with the *Politico* article published on the same day, one could see Carter Page was being depicted as the conduit between the Trump campaign and Russian

---

[305] IG Report, 317; https://apps.npr.org/documents/document.html?id=6571534-OIG-Russia-Investigation-Report.

President Putin in their fiendish bargain. The fake collusion plot was being fleshed out in media stories.

The Trump campaign's National co-chair Sam Clovis was another early Halper target, well before the launch of the Department of Justice's "Crossfire Hurricane." Halper was giving every indication he was someone trying very hard to join the campaign. During the encounter between the aged academic and the Trump foreign policy advisor at the University of Cambridge, Carter Page says Halper asked to be introduced to the high-ranking Trump campaign official, Sam Clovis. On July 16, 2016, Page sent an email to Clovis:

> Professor Stef Halper spends part of the year in Virginia where he has a home in Falls Church; he's a big fan of yours having followed you [Clovis] on CNN and offered a range of possibilities regarding how he and the University might be able to help.

On the face of it, this email is utterly bizarre and raises many questions. Is Halper likely to be a big fan of Sam Clovis? How could a retired academic commit a British university to helping the Trump campaign? What exactly was the "help" that the Trump-hating Halper wanted to give a political campaign he deeply opposed?

It does not take more than a brief skim of his background as a globalist Swamp dweller to see that Trump's populism and Halper are irreconcilable. When Halper asked Page for the introduction to Clovis and the campaign bigwigs to offer assistance he was being disingenuous: on whose behalf was Halper acting in trying to join the campaign? Clovis didn't respond to the idea of Halper joining the campaign, so Halper later sent a second email.

Clovis made himself a bigger target for a wire-tapped visit by ace FBI informer Halper by being quoted in a *Washington Post* article: "I think what we are offering is a very clear, mature, adult, realistic view of the world."[306] Clovis was a Washington outsider, an Iowa talk-show host, and former Senate candidate unknown to Halper. It was Carter Page's name Halper dropped to gain access to Clovis. This is the email Halper sent to Clovis in August 2016 which contains some interesting claims:

> I am a professor at Cambridge University lecturing on US politics and foreign policy. I am what is called a "scholar practitioner," having served in the White House and four presidential campaigns—two as policy director. Over the past month I have been in conversation with Carter Page who attended our conference in Cambridge on US elections. Carter mentioned in Cambridge, that you and I should meet. I have enjoyed your comments and appearances in the media; you hit the sweet spot focusing Trump's appeal to working America. May I suggest that we set a time to meet when you are next in Washington. Meanwhile, all the best, Stefan Halper.

The email demonstrates Halper was happily pimping the University of Cambridge and faking political support to open the door to get inside the Donald Trump for President campaign. I am sure the University was "delighted" its name was misused in this way by the FBI's-paid deceiver.

Sam Clovis is convinced his meeting with Halper was part of the plot to ensnare campaign workers. "What they tried to do was nothing short of attempting to overturn the results of a duly conducted election and that is a despicable, shameful set of events."[307] It is striking that the day after his one meeting with Clovis in Virginia, Halper made contact with his next target, Papadopoulos as Clovis points out. "Asked if Prof. Halper was acting in the public interest by helping the FBI probe,

---

[306] https://www.washingtonpost.com/business/economy/trump-advisers-public-comments-ties-to-moscow-stir-unease-in-both-parties/
2016/08/05/2e8722fa-5815-11e6-9aee-8075993d73a2_story.html

[307] Ben Riley-Smith, "Spies, lies and secret recordings—how a Cambridge professor snooped on Trump campaign advisers," *Daily Telegraph* (March 5, 2020).

Mr. Clovis said: 'That's bull. There was nothing in the public good about trying to overturn an election. That's nonsense.'"[308]

Halper sent Sam Clovis various research papers about China which the campaign co-chair did not read after the meeting. Halper was up to something else. With an eye for an opportunity, whilst spying, Halper was simultaneously maneuvering for a diplomatic appointment if the unthinkable happened and Hillary lost. Halper attended one Trump campaign strategy meeting in August as part of a group of "experts" advising on China.

It was reported by Axios in May 2018 that after the election in November, Peter Navarro, the White House's top trade advisor submitted Stefan Halper's name for an appointment to an Asian ambassadorship (some say China) during the transition. It was Halper who pushed Peter Navarro to submit his name for consideration. This raises further questions: Was Halper the informer trying to get a position in the incoming administration on his own behalf or on behalf of the intelligence community? Would Halper have disclosed his multi-year relationship with the FBI and CIA and, specifically, his activities against the campaign, had he been appointed?

Back from her Cambridge adventure, on July 26, 2016, Madeline Albright gave a rousing speech at the DNC Conference in Philadelphia in support of her close friend of twenty years, Hillary Clinton. In a seven-and-a-half-minute talk, Albright praised Hillary to the skies. She then turned her fire on the rival candidate Donald Trump. Just as Halper had predicted the Democrats were going negative. Albright introduced the idea that a Trump victory would be a huge gift to the Russian President Vladimir Putin. Foreshadowing the Crossfire Hurricane investigation Albright claimed President Putin was eager to

---

[308] Ibid.

see candidate Trump win and mirrored the fake reporting of Steele and Halper. She even fanned the flames by saying that if Donald Trump were to be elected US president, Russia planned to occupy Eastern Europe! Just two weeks before Albright had sat round a table in Cambridge exchanging polite views on Russia with the "compromised" Carter Page and bit her tongue!

On the same day as Albright's speech Carter Page became alarmed by unexpected press attention culminating in the publication of hostile news stories about him. The allegations were preposterous as Page did not know the two senior Russian figures he was alleged to be in cahoots with. Halper and his prey were to bond over how unfair the press was being to Page. It is clear that at some point early on in their friendship Halper must have confided in Page about his intelligence links and relationship with the intelligence services.

The *Washington Post* reported Halper habitually name-dropped his intelligence connections. Everyone at the Cambridge Intelligence Seminar was tediously informed of his CIA connections via Ray S. Cline. To state the obvious, you don't become the co-convenor of the world's leading seminar on intelligence without strong intelligence connections. You were assumed to be an expert, either a retired practitioner or a historian. As part of his baited trap Halper even told Page he was connected to a bevy of ex Russian intelligence leaders and the Intelligence Seminar.[309]

The soon-to-be ex-Trump campaign advisor failed to realize it was, in fact, Stefan Halper who was the primary source of the press attacks led by Tom Hamburger. Hamburger is widely reported a long term close confidant and defender of Glenn Simpson of dirty-tricks-for-hire firm Fusion GPS and employer of Christopher Steele. The pair met at the

---

[309] IG Report

Philadelphia convention on July 26, 2016, and Simpson shared the content of the first Steele memos with him.[310] Hamburger left his meeting with Simpson fully briefed and started texting Carter Page. The journalist was even given Steele's name for future reference.

Hamburger and his colleague David Ignatius have worked with Halper for years, in Ignatius' case back as far as 1981. Coordinated and timely leaking to the press is one of the Halper's main tactics, which he returns to again and again. Fusion GPS was in Philadelphia meeting friendly journalists to urgently "change the message"on the embarrassing DNC leaks.[311] They succeeded. Hamburger broke the sensational story, briefed by the Clinton campaign's Rodney Mook on July 24, 2016 and just a week before the investigation started, that Russia hacked the DNC. Mook's message was "it's troubling that some experts are now telling us that this was done by the Russians for the purpose of helping Donald Trump."[312]

As part of the elaborate choreography Glenn Simpson of Fusion GPS later told Congress of the FBI's "independent corroboration" of the dossier. "We don't believe the Steele dossier was the trigger for the F.B.I.'s investigation into Russian meddling. As we told the Senate Judiciary Committee in August, our sources said the dossier was taken so seriously because it corroborated reports the bureau had received from other sources, including one inside the Trump camp."[313] Simpson

---

[310] Crime in Progress: Inside the Steele Dossier and the Fusion GPS Investigation of Donald Trump
Gregg Simpson Peter Fritsch

[311] ibid

[312] https://www.washingtonpost.com/politics/clinton-campaign--and-some-cyber-experts--say-russia-is-behind-email-release/2016/07/24/5b5428e6-51a8-11e6-bbf5-957ad17b4385_story.html

[313] https://thehill.com/policy/national-security/367166-fusion-gps-co-founders-say-they-were-shocked-by-contents-of-steele

said Steele was told by the FBI they had an informer, someone inside Trump's network, providing agents with information corroborating his own. Who other than Halper could it be?[314]

According to *The Atlantic* the dirty tricks outfit Fusion GPS is "embedded in Washington's professional class in a loose network of opposition researchers, journalists, ex-journalists, and past and present government officials. They've known one another for decades as sources and reporters, clients and contractors, friends and neighbors, colleagues and coworkers. They're part of an ecosystem in which tips and inside information flow back and forth. Participants have different motivations for taking part: ideological, financial, moral, or journalistic, to name a few."[315]

---

[314] Glenn Simpson before the Senate Judiciary Committee Meeting (August 22, 2017), https://assets.documentcloud.org/documents/4345522/Read-the-full-transcript-of-Glenn-Simpsons.pdf.

[315] https://www.theatlantic.com/politics/archive/2019/11/steele-dossier-fusion-gps/602341/

Chapter Fifteen: Three Sheets to the Wind

The time has come,'the Walrus said,

To talk of many things.

—Lewis Carroll, *Walrus and the Carpenter*

Yet have I ever heard it said that spies and tale-bearers have done more mischief in this world than poisoned bowl or the assassin's dagger.

—Friedrich Schiller

There are two key rules in intelligence: The first is that reputations of people are their most important secret. Rule two is that every agent is aware of rule one.

—*An Unknown CIA officer*[316]

Within seven days of the Cambridge Conference, an entirely false account of Carter Page's private trip to Moscow appeared in the infamous Steele dossier. The report is dated July 19, 2016. Both Steele and the journalists told the same lie. Page is depicted as the link-man between the Trump campaign and Russia.

---

[316] UPI *Russians knew about Lewinsky before public.* March 12, 2001.

According to the Steele memo, Carter Page had secret meetings with the giant Russian oil company Rosneft's CEO, Igor Sechin, and a second influential Kremlin political figure.

At these non-existent meetings, the Trump team's junior foreign policy advisor Carter Page is supposed to have been offered a file of *kompromat*, or compromising material on ex-Secretary of State Hillary Clinton. The genesis of the idea that such a file exists stems from an old Bill Clinton scandal. The fantastical quid pro quo the Russians wanted was relief from sanctions imposed by the United States. At this point the concocted story is about the threat of releasing a file of compromising material and there is no suggestion of releasing Hillary Clinton emails.

Spygate is peppered with spooky phrases and tradecraft such as "kompromat" to layer in some faux authenticity to otherwise wholly preposterous allegations. With all the "kompromat" and threats of blackmail contained in the ex-British spy Christopher Steele's report Stefan Halper's operation eclipses the dark operation in any spy tale. Among other bizarre and obscure language in the Steele memo of July 19, 2016, is the word *"demarche,"* which is an obscure diplomatic term of French origin meaning an initiative. The unknown author of that memo is clearly showing off a knowledge of State Department diplomatic language and terms Halper would know.

Russian oil executive Igor Sechin is falsely portrayed in the press as the "de facto deputy" of Russian President Vladimir Putin. Another lie is that Page met Sechin. No one just *meets* the CEO of a major oil company, let alone an unknown American like Carter Page on a private trip to Russia. Like chief executives all over the world, Sechin has an office of gatekeepers one has to navigate through before meeting the head. Anyone who knows anything about how business works would laugh at the claim that Page met Igor Sechin. There should never have been an investigation into Carter Page based on this claim.

Later, the FBI's own surveillance of Page proved the falseness of this ludicrous claim as they were unable to uncover a single email, text message, or communication of any kind between Page and Sechin.

Serendipity

For the FBI investigators, it was "serendipitous", just a happy chance, that Trump's junior foreign policy advisor Carter Page, a supposed Russian intelligence asset, struck up an unlikely and long-lasting friendship with the loathsome informant Halper. The two are polar opposites. Page also remained in contact with the mysterious 45-year-old PhD student Steven Schrage after the Cambridge event.[317] The clearly not impoverished student Schrage next popped up at the Cleveland Republican Convention to meet up with Page again. Is Schrage the eyes and ears of Halper's network?

Thanks to Inspector General Horowitz's report, we know a little more about Halper and his web. In the report, the FBI goes to enormous efforts, bordering on parody, to deny any political motive in anything they did. Horowitz has no power to probe. Implausibly, Halper stated to the FBI that the junior foreign policy advisor Page invited him to join Trump's campaign on the spot in Cambridge.

What is clear from the chronology is the meeting was crucial to the FBI investigation. The false allegations against Page was a critical step for importing the foreign-based operation back into the United States. Of course, it transpired later that all the "ties to Russian intelligence"

---

[317] Page told the Daily Caller that "he might have crossed paths with Schrage prior to the invitation, but he does not recall any specific encounters." https://dailycaller.com/2019/08/01/carter-page-cambridge-spy-halper-nunes/

turned out to be US intelligence efforts to entrap Trump campaign members, by which stage tens of millions of dollars had been wasted and lives ruined.

Some of Stefan Halper's activities which were covered by the Horowitz report were never probed with anything approaching rigor. One striking omission is any questions of the informer's fascinating network of alleged friends and associates. Is Halper a likely candidate as the source who fabricated the intelligence in the Steele dossier used to attack candidate Trump? If so, he requires investigating. It is my hypothesis Halper provided information now known to be false to Steele, claiming the source was a former head of Russian intelligence and such false information and reporting likely sent to the CIA/FBI to bolster their false narrative.

In a conversation over breakfast at the Mayflower Hotel in Washington, DC, July 30, 2016, one day before the opening of the official FBI investigation, Christopher Steele made an extra-ordinary claim in a conversation with Bruce Ohr of the Department of Justice and his wife, Nellie, of Fusion GPS.[318] He told them Putin had Donald Trump "over a barrel" and that an ex-head of Russian Foreign Intelligence was his source. Steele said he had never met the source himself. The suspicion about Steele's claim is confirmed when in October 2016 he told Kathleen Kavalec of the State Department that Vyacheslav Trubnikov was his source.[319]

The information given to Steele to put in his dossier was soon found by the FBI to be unverifiable, i.e. false. The most severe allegations about then-candidate Donald Trump being supported by Putin to win

---

[318] Bruce Ohr Congressional testimony (August 28, 2018); see transcript at https://dougcollins.house.gov/sites/dougcollins.house.gov/files/Ohr%20Interview%20Transcript%208.28.18.pdf

[319] FOIA reported by John Solomon The Hill.

the election are those credited to two separate "Source A and B" in the July 20, 2016 Steele dossier memo. Showing how unreliable these memos are is the descriptions of the alleged two separate sources but are actually that of one person. Trubnikov is described in two separate ways as a senior intelligence figure and a former diplomat. The memos attributed to the two personas of Trubnikov include claims the cultivation of Donald Trump began at least five years previously and even more serious allegations.

One claim attributed to "Trubnikov" (described in the FISA application as a sub-source) in the Steele dossier made it all the way to a Carter Page's FISA application. The FBI verified to the court that in 2016 a Steele sub-source said Russian intelligence had a file of compromising material, dirt on Hillary Clinton dating back to the 1990s. This is supposedly the file of compromising material that it is claimed falsely Igor Divyekin, a Kremlin official offered to Carter Page at a meeting that never happened. Interestingly, although there is no evidence that such a file exists, there is a very old story on the internet about compromising material used against Bill Clinton that is the basis of the later hoax. That story began in deceased Russian President Boris Yeltsin's memoirs published in the 1990s.

In his biography "Midnight Diaries" the former Russian President Yeltsin claimed that the Russians knew in 1996 of the Monica Lewinsky affair, two years before the scandal broke in the US Yeltsin said in November 1996 he had received an encrypted telegram from his intelligence service that reported Republican Party activists intended to plant an attractive young woman in the Clinton White House to entrap Bill. Yeltsin died in 2007 so he is probably not a Steele source.

On February 27, 1998 a Russian newspaper, Obshchaya Gazeta, (and later republished by the CIA's Foreign Broadcast Information Service) interviewed the former head of the Russian intelligence service, the SVR, Vyacheslav Trubnikov. Trubnikov confirmed that he knew of the Monica Lewinsky scandal before it broke in the US He is quoted by the CIA outlet saying

> You know, joking aside, our intelligence service some time ago anticipated that powerful pressure would be brought down to bear on the US president and that it would be exerted in various fields, including this one.[320]

The Russians were clear that they had heard about a Republican plot to embarrass the sitting US president. However, the CIA veteran analysts quoted in the article concluded that Russian intelligence was gathering compromising material on Bill Clinton. Could it be that Hillary was substituted for Bill in creating the idea of a file of compromising material dating back to the 1990s based on an internet search finding a decades old article?

Back in May 2015, one year before the Steele memo, Halper paid for Steele's alleged source Vyacheslav Trubnikov to appear in Cambridge at the Intelligence Seminar. It was a much delayed visit. The pair have previously collaborated on a research project in 2011 and met in Cambridge in 2012. Trubnikov is the alleged source of the allegation in the Steele Dossier that Putin had been cultivating Donald Trump since 2011. Did Halper and Steele use this meeting in 2012 as the basis for this false allegation? The new Fusion GPS book describes but does not name Steele's finest collector as "known to US intelligence and law enforcement."[321] The *New York Times* and *Washington Post*

---

[320] https://www.upi.com/Archives/2001/03/12/Russians-knew-about-Lewinsky-before-public/3173984373200/

[321] Glenn Simpson, *Crime in Progress: Inside the Steele Dossier and the Fusion GPS Investigation of Donald Trump* (New York: Random House, 2019), 82.

newspapers named Halper as both a long-term CIA and FBI source. In a meeting at the State Department in October 2016, Christopher Steele says the name he was given was Trubnikov as his main sub-source for his shattering and inaccurate July memos. It is impossible to imagine that the US intelligence community would not protect and reveal the name of such a crucial and vital source so openly in a FOIA.

Stefan Halper's Work with the FBI—Disciplinary Issues

The Russia collusion investigation was "a big hoax."[322] It was clear from the start and even more so after years of investigation there were no Russian intelligence agents meeting with the targeted Trump Campaign officials in 2016. The biggest single lie was that a Russian intelligence agent, might have recruited Gen. Flynn. Halper, a paid FBI informer was the inventor of those false reports. Halper's identity and what he did is still protected by the Deep State. Is the reason why Halper is protected because his fake intelligence is the foundation used to justify the ludicrous counter-intelligence investigation of Gen. Flynn?

By early January 2017 "the FBI said very clearly, there's not enough information here. Let's drop the case on Flynn and the very next day, there's an Oval Office meeting with Comey."[323] Instead of dropping the pointless case as there was no evidence, the investigation intensified and resulted in Gen. Flynn's persecution and ultimately prosecution. Worse was to follow; when the House Intelligence Committee requested information about Halper in 2017, the Mueller team responded by making the informer Halper a witness and refused to disclose any details to Congress. This obstruction of a

---

[322] Interview The Rubin Report June 9 2020

[323] ibid

Congressional investigation by the Mueller team is the subject of a criminal referral.[324]

The former acting Director of National Intelligence Richard Grennel, in his first interview since leaving office stated "the Obama Administration weaponized the intelligence agencies to go after their political enemies."[325] The foremost amongst the perceived enemies was Gen. Flynn.

Despite being central to the attack on Gen. Flynn and the whole FISA debacle, Halper still cannot be officially named. He is identified in a flurry of press reports but is referred to as "Source 2" throughout the Inspector General's report. It transpires unsurprisingly that his relationship with the FBI as with everyone was tempestuous.

Halper informed to the FBI for money on goodness knows who from 2008. Halper was fired for cause by the FBI in 2011 for "aggressiveness toward handling agents as a result of what Source 2 [Stefan Halper] perceived as not enough compensation."[326] Well, being greedy is par for the course for this informer.

More interestingly, he developed "questionable allegiance to the intelligence targets." These were relationships with the FBI targets he was being paid to inform on. However, Halper's exile from the flow of the FBI's money did not last long. He was re-opened as an informer just two months later by the crucial character in Spygate, FBI counterintelligence officer Stephen Somma.

---

[324] Interview with Fox News Rep Devin Nunes. July 28, 2019

[325] ibid

[326] IG Report, 313; https://apps.npr.org/documents/document.html?id=6571534-OIG-Russia-Investigation-Report.

Stefan Halper was handled by Stephen Somma from 2011 through 2016. The handler told the Inspector General that Halper, in one of the best understatements in history, can be "mercurial." As the dictionary says, this is a person subject to sudden or unpredictable changes of mood or mind, volatile, the list of unsavory adjectives goes on. Somma was strangely silent with the Inspector General about the details of Halper's long-standing relationship with ex-Russian intelligence figures.

Unsurprisingly given he laid for the trail of evidence of Russian collusion, Halper was willing to assist the FBI "without any hesitation." One assumes the money on offer from the FBI improved since 2008. The FBI's undisclosed stipend topped up the hundreds of thousands of dollars the Obama Administration paid Halper in 2015/16. Steven Somma told the Inspector General Halper has never given him any reason to doubt the veracity of his reporting! I fell off my chair when I read that gem. Steven Somma is according to all reports a real Spygate character responsible for a considerable amount of errors and omissions.[327]

Crossfire Hurricane Team's Initial Meeting with Stefan Halper on August 11, 2016

The official FBI version is that Halper's involvement in the Crossfire Hurricane investigation arose out of Somma's pre-existing relationship with the informer. The explanation is laughable. Despite having months to get their story straight, the information the Crossfire Hurricane team provided the Inspector General was still ridden with holes, evasions, and half-truths that make any sensible reader cringe, let alone a professional investigator.

---

[327] Case Agent 1 was primarily responsible for some of the most significant errors and omissions in the FISA applications," the IG report stated.

Somma only arrived in Washington, D.C., in early August to join the Crossfire Hurricane team.[328] He claims he had no experience in the "realm" of political campaigns. He said he lacked even a basic understanding of simple issues, for example, what the role of a "foreign policy advisor" entails. He seems an unlikely candidate to appoint to take the lead in a politically sensitive case. Seemingly there was no one even in the Washington FBI bureau qualified to help him get up to speed. Serendipitously, Somma had just the guy on his speed dial with a bit of time on his hands.

On August 10, the very day the team opened investigations into three campaign officials but significantly not Gen. Flynn, Somma proposed, a meeting with his source, the political operator Stefan Halper. Somma alleges he wanted to ask some basic questions because he knew Halper was affiliated with national political campaigns off and on since the early 1970s.

The FBI did not have the evidence to open a counter intelligence investigation into Gen. Flynn on August 10, 2016 Somma knew in advance of the meeting with Halper that his source had information about, and had met "one or more of the Crossfire Hurricane subjects". The "one or more" are Gen. Flynn and Paul Manafort. Halper claims (falsely) to have met Gen. Flynn in Cambridge in 2014[329] but certainly worked with Manafort on the 1980 Reagan campaign.

Seemingly and implausibly the FBI based in DC doesn't understand how political campaigns work, as on August 11, 2016, Somma and two other FBI officers met with Halper! Somma claimed to the Inspector General that the plan going into the meeting was to talk generally with

[328] IG Report; https://apps.npr.org/documents/document.html?id=6571534-OIG-Russia-Investigation-Report.

[329] In May 2020 Sydney Powell issued a statement that the General has never met Stefan Halper.

the informer about Russian "interference in the election, what he may know, and . . . to bring up Papadopoulos." Why does Somma claim that Halper knew anything useful about alleged Russian interference in the election unless they had discussed it before? On the face of it, the FBI expected Halper—a retired professor based at Cambridge, England for the last decade—might just happen to know about Russian interference in the US presidential election is a mystery we wish Horowitz probed. Horowitz is no Sherlock Holmes.

It was Halper who asked whether the FBI team had any interest in Carter Page. The investigative team claim they "didn't react because at that point, we didn't know where we were going to go with it."[330] The explanation is implausible as Somma suggested applying for a FISA on August 15, 2016 just a few days later claiming he had "a pretty solid basis" to do so. The team claim to have asked questions about how Halper knew Page. Sadly, we don't know the answers. The FBI showed no interest in the details of the whole conference in Cambridge when Carter Page had just returned from Moscow. The team asked Halper about George Papadopoulos. Halper said he had never heard of him but nonetheless was happy to set him up. There was little hurry to get that particular mission going.

Halper informed the Crossfire Hurricane team he knew Trump's then-campaign manager, Paul Manafort, for a number of years and he was "previously acquainted with Michael Flynn." In contrast to his earlier statement, Somma explained, "quite honestly . . . we kind of stumbled upon Stefan Halper knowing these folks." He said it was "serendipitous" and the Crossfire Hurricane team "couldn't believe [their] luck" that Halper "had contacts with three of their four subjects."

---

[330] IG Report, 315.

Follow-up Crossfire Hurricane Team Meeting with Stefan Halper on August 12, 2016

The next day, August 12, 2016, the same FBI team returned to meet with Halper. Somma now claims that based only on media reports, the FBI revealed their interest in Trump's foreign policy advisor Carter Page. They asked the ever-willing Halper to contact Page for a private meeting. The investigative team told the Inspector General they picked Halper as the informer, because of the unlikely and untrue story that the Trump campaign appeared interested in recruiting him. This was their cover story as to why Halper was in a perfect position to directly ask Page about media reports regarding links between the campaign and Russia. Somma was Halper's handling agent and must have asked what happened at the Conference in Cambridge especially as the media articles refer explicitly to that event.

The team also discussed with Halper his plans regarding trapping Papadopoulos. As we now know Halper ultimately clandestinely met with at least three members of the Trump campaign on behalf of the FBI Carter Page, George Papadopoulos, and Sam Clovis. The FBI secretly recorded Halper's conversations with each of these individuals. All the meetings were a disaster for the Crossfire Hurricane team in promoting the Russian hoax as the subjects deny any contacts with Russians. It is interesting that once the FBI start their secret recordings, Halper fails to generate any useful information in his interactions.

Opening on CROSSFIRE RAZOR

Between August 11 and 15, 2016 the Crossfire Hurricane team acquired new information that became the predicate to open the counter-intelligence investigation into Gen. Flynn. The investigation was unprecedented as Gen. Flynn had just retired from his position as Head of the Defense Intelligence Agency and held top security clearance. Gen. Flynn maintained his security clearance throughout the period he was under investigation which shows what a joke the whole exercise was. August 11 to 15 is the exact time period when the FBI met with Stefan Halper. On April 30, 2020 the Department of Justice disclosed a Closing Statement that revealed exactly what that new "evidence" they had gathered. The Confidential Source, Stefan Halper had made a false eyewitness statement to the FBI about events that he had not witnessed at the dinner in February 2014. Halper was not even at the dinner.

The heavily redacted statement contained preposterous details about events that not only did not occur but could not have occurred. The false statement falls into two parts. The first is a fake account of events after the Gen. Flynn dinner in Cambridge. The second part is Halper's alleged long held fantastical suspicions that this author is an agent of Russian intelligence.

In response the FBI seemingly checked me out through various intelligence databases both in the U.S and UK and drew a blank. They had previously checked Gen. Flynn. Illustrating how preposterous his report was, Halper could not even recall the year the event took place! An FBI agent performed a Google search to find the details. The report and its lies sat dormant from August 2016 until January 2017.

What is alarming is that the Crossfire Hurricane team had evidence that Halper was a liar in 2016 yet still attested in four FISA applications that he was a reliable source. Halper's handler even told the IG inspectors that Halper was reliable in their 2019 report! Halper was paid with taxpayers money throughout the Crossfire Hurricane investigation. Further the FBI Crossfire Hurricane team sat idly by when the very minutest details of his fake intelligence report were leaked to the newspapers in 2017 and 2018.

Stefan Halper's Meetings with Carter Page on August 20, 2016

The first secretly recorded meeting between Halper and Page took place on August 20, 2016. Eventually, the FBI used heavily edited highlights of some of the conversation for the Carter Page FISA Renewal Application No. 3, almost a year later in June 2017.

Somma instructed Halper to use the media articles to ask Page questions "regarding Russia and Hillary Clinton's emails." Halper was to find out if the campaign was planning an "October surprise," as was reported in the media. He was to ask Page if he maintained contacts with Russians (which Page did for his work for the intelligence community, which they knew) or knew whether the Russians were releasing emails to benefit the Trump campaign.

As happened with Papadopoulos later, Halper was trying to get Page to confirm on tape what he was falsely reported as saying at the Cambridge seminar in July in order to get a FISA. Most likely Halper had already reported Page as a Russian agent in the same way he reported me.

The August 20, 2016 meeting with Page was a bust in terms of proving the Russia hoax narrative. Halper learned where Page was staying while in Washington for campaign meetings. The information would be useful had the FBI acquired a FISA warrant in August as they planned to bug his room. Somma added, because "there were several emails sent back and forth thanking [Stefan Halper]," the FBI obtained

Carter Page's email address and telephone number, which could be used in the first FISA application.

Somma said, as a result of this operation, "we now had a successful contact between the established FBI source and one of our targets."[331] But they learned nothing as there was nothing to learn. Page had no ambition to seek a position in the administration if Donald Trump won the election. He had "literally never met" Manafort or said one word to him. Manafort did not respond to any of Carter Page's emails.

In fact, Page just complained about the negative, and highly personal, media attention he was receiving which ironically was probably organized by Halper. The victim was complaining to the perpetrator. Page described an article from the *Washington Post* (Tom Hamburger article published on August 5, 2016 [332] based on Halper's material described above) and how "95% of it was complete garbage."

Page also complained that next to Manafort who he called "public enemy number one," Page was being treated as "public enemy number two." Page said, as a result of a "hit job" in *Bloomberg News*, he was branded as "Trump's Russia Advisor" with "close ties with the Russian government," and that idea became "the consistent narrative ever since." None of this or other exculpatory evidence was presented to court in the FISA applications despite being a legal requirement. The FBI has now admitted the surveillance on Page was illegal.[333]

Inevitably Halper raised Hillary Clinton's favorite issue of the Trump campaign unleashing an "October surprise," placed by the Democrats

---

[331] IG Report, 319.

[332] https://www.washingtonpost.com/business/economy/trump-advisers-public-comments-ties-to-moscow-stir-unease-in-both-parties/
2016/08/05/2e8722fa-5815-11e6-9aee-8075993d73a2_story.html

[333] From page 317 of IG Report; https://apps.npr.org/documents/document.html?id=6571534-OIG-Russia-Investigation-Report

in the media. Page responded to Halper about the October surprise in the 1980 presidential campaign showing he knew all about Halper's past. Masquerading as a veteran Republican strategist trying to help the campaign, Halper asked if the Trump campaign could access information that might have been obtained by the Russians from the DNC files, adding that in past campaigns, "we would have used it in a heartbeat."

Halper was planting collusion on the Trump campaign. But Carter Page called it "the conspiracy theory about . . . the next email dump with . . . '33 thousand' additional emails." Halper even went as far as to ask, "well the Russians have all that, don't they?" to which Page responded, "I don't, I-I don't know."

The exchange shows an attempt to entrap Carter Page and to hurt the Trump Campaign by getting Page to admit that he had Russian intelligence contacts and was a Russian asset himself. Halper then steered the conversation toward how he paid for the ex-head of the SVR Vyacheslav Trubnikov to speak at the Cambridge Intelligence Seminar and asked if Page knew anyone of that type who might be interested in coming to Cambridge. Unsurprisingly, Page didn't.

Page is a CIA asset who espouses pro-Russian views to gain confidences. Given that Page was supposedly under suspicion as a Russian intelligence asset and the FBI later verified him as such, it seems very strange Halper would bring up his connection with Vyacheslav Trubnikov (the alleged Sources A and B in the Steele dossier) so casually. If Trubnikov was a source and if Page was a Russian asset, Halper put his connection in severe danger. Of course, none of this was true; it was Halper's fables. The whole discussion is a deceit.

Rejecting the FISA Request

It was always Somma's goal to obtain a FISA warrant on someone in the Trump campaign as soon as he joined the operation. He obsessively spearheaded an effort to obtain the warrant on Carter Page as soon as early August. On August 15, 2016, the agent raised the idea with others at the FBI of applying for a FISA order on the Trump campaign's junior foreign policy advisor. Somma wrote in an email cited in the Inspector General's report that there was a "pretty solid basis" to believe Page, who was a CIA asset, was working as an agent of Russia.

It was allegedly based on Page's past business dealings in Russia for the CIA and the trip he made to Moscow in early July 2016 plus his known interactions years earlier with a Russian intelligence officer which was an operation on behalf of the FBI. The FBI knowingly bundled one of their own and sent him down the river.

This gives an idea of how little actual evidence is needed to unleash the most invasive powers of the state against an individual. The secret recording of the August 20 meeting between Halper and Page was to provide the clinching key evidence. The attempt never got off the ground.

Halper "couldn't get Carter Page to say anything about the Russians" commented FBI Chief Counsel Jim Baker on reading the transcript. Halper succeeded in obtaining far worse material as far as the FBI were concerned "extra crap we didn't really want political stuff that needed to be minimized."[334] In every response to the Inspector General, the FBI are obsessively covering up just how much illegal snooping was conducted on the political campaign.

---

[334] IG Report, 320.

Second Time Around with Carter Page on October 17, 2016

The second secret recorded meeting between Halper and Page took place in a rush on October 17, 2016, just four days before the FBI obtained their first FISA warrant. Polling day was less than a month away. Halper's sting on another Trump campaign advisor George Papadopoulos had misfired spectacularly. By now, Page was long gone from the Trump campaign after all the negative publicity Halper had a hand in placing in the press.

The Crossfire Hurricane team claim they learned Page was planning a foreign trip. At this point the investigative team, despite all the evidence, were still pushing the story that Page is a Russian asset while knowing he works for the CIA and now suspected he may be going abroad to meet an individual with ties to Russian intelligence.

The FBI's Crossfire Hurricane team did not even bother to get a complete transcript of the meeting but instead "wrote up only the pertinent parts of whatever meetings occurred just because . . . doing a full transcript would have taken too long." Given the importance of this matter, this is surprising. During the meeting, Page who was no longer working for the Trump Campaign under questioning from Halper mentioned he would like to develop a research institute to be "a rare voice that talks against this consensus of Russian containment."

In talking about how he might fund this institute, Page told Halper, "I don't want to say there'd be an open checkbook, but the Russians would definitely . . ." then, according to the partial transcript, the sentence trailed off as Page laughed. Halper stated, "they would fund it

—yeah you could do alright there," and Page responded, "Yeah, but that has its pros and cons, right?"[335]

The members of the Crossfire Hurricane team seized upon Page's vague comment of having a potentially "open checkbook." This information from the October 17, 2016 meeting between Halper and Page was firmed up to become a definite idea. The "open checkbook" became the centerpiece of the successful FISA application.

Beating the Dead Horse: December 15, 2016

The third secretly recorded meeting between Halper and Page took place on December 15, 2016. This was several days after Page returned from giving another lecture at the New Economic School in Moscow, the same venue at which Page spoke July 2016.

During their lunch meeting, Halper asked Page again about the "think tank" they discussed in their October 17, 2016 meeting. Page replied to Halper that the Moscow-based New Economic School was "possibly" going to help with the financing. When Halper referred back to Page's comment made during their October 17, 2016 meeting —about Russians giving Page a "blank check" for the think tank— Page stated he "didn't know that he went that far." By denying the comment, Page was actually contradicting the key "evidence" in the FISA application.

The Final Meeting with Carter Page on January 25, 2017

The final taped meeting between Halper and Carter Page took place on January 25, 2017. None of the information from this meeting was

---

[335] Ibid., 360.

included in any of the FISA applications. Page even asked whether Halper had ever "come across that [Steele] guy." Halper told Page he did not know Christopher Steele.

Halper focused again on whether Page made any progress on the think tank. Halper tempted Page that if he "could bring some Russian money to the table . . . [Halper] might be able to help ... get some US money."

The only subject of the Crossfire Hurricane investigation mentioned during the January 25, 2017 conversation was Gen. Michael Flynn. Halper asked Page if he knew Gen. Flynn "pretty well," and Page responded "no." This exchange was just two days after the infamous FBI interview of Gen. Flynn at the White House.[336]

Stefan Halper's Meeting with Sam Clovis on September 1, 2016

Halper reached out to Sam Clovis, a high-level official on the Trump campaign, the national co-chair in a last attempt to join the Trump campaign. It is a particularly egregious approach by a wired-up FBI informer, as Sam Clovis was not even a subject of the investigation. Halper succeeded in arranging a meeting with Sam Clovis using his University of Cambridge cover on September 1, 2016, and their meeting was secretly recorded by the Crossfire Hurricane team.

It is not clear why or how Sam Clovis would divulge any information to Halper that could have been of use to a real investigation. Halper was most likely trying to join the campaign. Back to his favorite theme, Halper asked Clovis whether the Trump campaign was planning an "October surprise." It is not clear why the FBI thought a senior Trump advisor would give away campaign strategy to a complete stranger. The high-level Trump campaign official Clovis

---

[336] Ibid., 364–65.

responded that the real issue was the Trump campaign needed to "give people a reason to vote for him, not just vote against Hillary."[337] Luckily for Donald Trump, Clovis had no interest in hiring Halper and his bag of tricks.

Stefan Halper's Meetings with George Papadopoulos

Getting desperate but still in no hurry, the FBI launched the entrapment scheme they had been discussing since August the day after the Clovis meeting. Near the end of the campaign, Halper invited George Papadopoulos to meet with him in mid-September 2016 in London to discuss a fabricated project. The FBI paid for this elaborate jaunt. According to the distinguished attorney Jonathan Turley, this is problematic. Steven Somma said the Crossfire Hurricane team thought it would play to "Papadopoulos's ego to help take part in a project." The fake project was based on Papadopoulos's past writings about the Leviathan oil fields located off the coast of Israel and Turkey. The FBI, through Halper, covered the undisclosed costs of Papadopoulos's travel, including flights and accommodation and paid him $3,000 of FBI money for an "academic" project.

Halper and the Crossfire Hurricane team were trying to re-create the conditions that resulted in George Papadopoulos's alleged comments to Alexander Downer, the Australian diplomat. Halper and the Crossfire team tried to get their target drunk whilst providing a woman to flirt with him. Somma said that by rendering Papadopoulos to another country, he might "feel a little freer to talk outside the confines of the United States and . . . repeat that conversation" he had with Alexander Downer apparently in the restroom. However, rather than get their target inebriated the short evening drinking session with

_____

[337] Ibid., 367.

Papadopoulos left the informer worse for wear. Halper commented to the tape "I'm three sheets to the wind," as he headed out into the night.

An American citizen working on a major political campaign was lured to a foreign country to be secretly recorded. In the meeting Papadopoulos reported to a newspaper that Halper blurted out "Trump and you are involved in a conspiracy, right? You are helping Trump in a conspiracy, right?"[338] In the event Papadopoulos rebutted all of Halper's accusations. Halper's clumsy entrapment led Papadopoulos to conclude Halper "was going to go and tell the CIA or something if I'd have told him something else. I assume that's why he was asking. And I told him, absolutely not....it's illegal."[339]

In one of his schemes Halper recycled old intelligence to entrap Carter Page and George Papadopoulos by recalling his 2012 conversations with retired senior Russian intelligence figures. Was one of Halper's ruses whilst posing as a Trump supporter to suggest to junior campaign associates that he, Halper had contacts with Russian intelligence that could be used as a conduit? It is difficult to understand why Halper repeatedly brings up these Russian intelligence contacts with Page and Papadopoulos.

With the Crossfire Hurricane team listening Halper attempts to insert collusion into the taped conversations but only succeeded in exposing himself as a US intelligence asset. Halper asked Page, the first target of his operations in August if he knew any Russian intelligence figures that Halper could invite to the University of Cambridge to give a talk. The approach to Papadopoulos in September 2016 was even more bizarre. Utterly, incongruously Halper suddenly starts boasting to the

---

[338] https://www.telegraph.co.uk/news/2020/03/05/spies-lies-secret-recordings-cambridge-professor-snooped-trump/

[339] ibid.

young campaign advisor in the midst of a taped conversation about his connections to retired senior Russian intelligence officers, as if Papadopoulos should know these characters from the Cold War.

HALPER: Slava Truvnikoff [Trubnikov] Do-do you, do you know Truvnikoff? Truvnikoff was the director of KGB...

PAPADOPOULOS: Mm-hmm.

HALPER: and the FSB. He was, ah, deputy foreign minister at another point and he was a Russian ambassador to India. So I brought him to Cambridge to talk to us about how-how their intelligence service works. He was very forthcoming. I mean he's retired now and he's, ah, ah very much a, um, sort of an international participant in nuclear disarmament.

PAPADOPOULOS: But, he's a private citizen?

HALPER: He's a private citizen but he's, ah, really plugged in. Knows a lot. And, ah, is very helpful, ah, in all kinds of ways. So, he's a friend of ours at mm and I have to say that I've enjoyed his friendship all over the world. I've met him everywhere and we've talked from time-to-time. And another one that I've, I've come to know pretty well is, um, a guy named, ah, ah Evgeny Savostyanov was the head of the Moscow KGB and now he's in [Laughs] He's a real, a real swordsman, you know, [laughing] And, ah...

PAPADOPOULOS: How did he make that transition?

HALPER: Well, you know, he finished up in his organization and he went out to and entered some um he's a bright guy. Um I guess just the exotic nature of who he was helped him along. [laughs] Then I've developed a friendship with a really senior KGB general, a four-star general named Leonid Sherbarshin.[340] Did you know him?

---

[340] Leonid Sherbarshin died in 2012 so the chances of Papadopoulos aged 24 at the time of the Russian's death knowing him are zero.

PAPADOPOULOS: No.

HALPER: Interesting man. A very, very bright guy who was the architect of the Russian effort in Afghanistan. So, um, and then. I knew another one named Yuri Totrov[341] who was a, ah, KGB, ah, officer who actually figured out a system to track American CIA agents around the world.

Did Halper cross the line from being an informer and acting as an agent provocateur fermenting a conspiracy that did not exist?

The members of the Crossfire Hurricane team who traveled for the operation included Steven Somma, Case Agent 2, and the attractive "honeypot" Azra Turk. The written plan for the operation stated that Papadopoulos would meet with Halper to discuss the project and "there will be ample opportunity and various angles to have Papadopoulos expound on the initial comments made in May 2016 to the FFG regarding the anonymous release of emails by the Russians that would damage the Clinton presidential campaign."[342] When Downer reported to his contact at the US State Department in July 2016, about a meeting in May with Papadopoulos he was acting "rogue"[343] and independent of the Australian government. It is wrong as the FBI and Mueller did, to characterize Downer's information as coming from an official friendly foreign government source. Malcolm Turnball, the Australian Prime minister at the time revealed in April 2020 that Downer raised his concerns at the US embassy in London without government approval. Turnball, added that "Trump was

---

[341] Totrov was a "discovery" in the CIA vault of Jonathan Haslam and features in his article "How to explain the KGB's amazing success identifying CIA agents in the field? Paranoid CIA heads blamed Soviet moles, but the real reason for the repeated disasters was much simpler." Salon Magazine September 26, 2015.

[342] Quotes from Halper's Meeting with Papadopoulos are from IG Report, 329.

[343] https://www.smh.com.au/politics/federal/downer-raised-russia-concerns-at-us-embassy-without-government-approval-20200416-p54kho.html

endorsed as the Republican candidate on 19 July, and that prompted Alexander [Downer] to call on the US charge d'affaires (standing in for their ambassador) and tell him about the Papadopoulos discussion. He had no authority from Canberra to do this, and the first we heard of it in Australia was when the FBI turned up in London and wanted to interview Downer." There is an established channel for such tip offs which Downer knows but avoided using. It is hugely ironic that it was Halper who deployed a "honeypot" against a US citizen when he falsely claimed Russian intelligence did so against General Flynn in Cambridge in 2014.

Brunch Meeting with Stefan Halper and Papadopoulos, September 15, 2016

On September 15, 2016, Halper arranged a brunch in London as part of the scheme to lure Trump campaign official Papadopoulos the Trump campaign official abroad and entrap him. Halper had suggested Papadopoulos produce an academic paper focused on the geopolitical dimensions in the eastern Mediterranean, including the energy sector and Russia's engagement with the Israelis. Halper offered him $3,000 to write a paper and asked for Papadopoulos to complete it within three weeks. The money for this ruse was paid by the US taxpayer via the FBI.

Starting the meeting, Halper tried a bit of charm, telling Papadopoulos that Carter Page "always says nice things about you." Papadopoulos replied to Halper that although Page was one of the campaign's "Russian people," Page "has never actually met Trump . . . [and] hasn't actually advised him on Russia."

When Halper raised the subject of the key target Gen. Flynn, Papadopoulos said innocuously that as part of his role the General "does want to cooperate with the Russians and the Russians are willing to…embrace adult issues." As for his own non-existent connections with Russia, Papadopoulos told Halper he thought "we have to be wary of the Russians." Halper started asking Papadopoulos about the possibility of the public release of additional information that would be harmful to Hillary Clinton's campaign.[344] Throughout their discussions Papadopoulos denied any suggestion of collusion between the Campaign and the Russians. The trap was a bust from the start.

A Delightful Evening with Stefan Halper, a "Honeypot" and Papadopoulos: September 15, 2016

On the evening of September 15, 2016 Halper, the FBI "honeypot," and Papadopoulos met for pre-dinner drinks. When Halper asked about Wikileaks, Papadopoulos commented that with respect to Assange "no one knows what he's going to release." Papadopoulos stated, "no one has proven that the Russians actually did the hacking," Later in the conversation, Halper asked Papadopoulos directly whether assistance "from a third party like Wikileaks, for example, or some other third party like the Russians, could be incredibly helpful" in securing a campaign victory. Papadopoulos responded:

> Well, as a campaign, of course, we don't advocate for this type of activity because, at the end of the day, it's, ah, illegal. First and foremost, it compromises the US national security, and third, it sets a very bad precedence [sic]. . . . Espionage is, ah, treason. This is a form of treason. . . .

---

[344] Quotes from Brunch Meeting are from IG Report, 330.

The FBI suppressed the comment and withheld it from the FISA court.

When Halper raised the issue again, Papadopoulos added this exculpatory evidence —also concealed from the court: "no one's collaborating, there's been no collusion and it's going to remain that way."

The meeting with Papadopoulos ended with a fresh effort by Halper to push himself forward for a position in the Campaign and a future administration. Halper elicited another offer to introduce the retired professor to more members of the Trump campaign team, and to set up a follow-up meeting the next time Halper was in Washington, D.C. Despite, saying to Papadopoulos that he did not "really want to be in government again" Halper pushed hard because he was "wanting to help on China"[345] and willing to provide Papadopoulos with written materials, such as speeches and pre-position papers, which might be helpful on foreign policy issues. This pitch to a campaign official was the FBI's informer Halper's fourth attempt to get a position in a future administration.

The *New York Times* reported through the Crossfire Hurricane apologist Adam Goldman that "British intelligence officials were also notified about the operation . . . but it was unclear whether they provided assistance."[346] The FBI probably planned to arrest Papadopoulos, if he repeated what he was supposed to have said to Halper's acquaintance Downer. Goldman reveals the flirtatious Ms. Turk, a "sexy bottle blonde in her thirties who wasn't shy about showing her curves,"[347] was sent to take part in the operation to pose

---

[345] Quotes are from IG Report 331–32.

[346] https://www.nytimes.com/2019/05/02/us/politics/fbi-government-investigator-trump.html

[347] Geoff Earle, "Trump 'spy' scandal deepens: 'Curvy blonde' undercover FBI investigator targeted aide George Papadopoulus at London bar and asked 'Is the campaign working with Russia?'" *Daily Mail* (May 2, 2019).

as Mr. Halper's assistant "because placing such a sensitive undertaking in the hands of a trusted government investigator was essential." The botched operation in London made the FBI Counter Intelligence team the laughing stock of the world, showcasing the depths they were prepared to sink to get at candidate Trump. The FBI's Turk later emailed Papadopoulos, calling their meeting the "highlight of my trip" and said "I am excited about what the future holds for us :)."[348]

In his recorded discussions, Halper acted as a provocateur and not an investigator. Was the goal of these recorded meetings to provoke a drunken response to use as "evidence" perhaps as part of an October surprise? Halper failed in his mission and when he did, according to Papadopoulos he started getting angry and aggressive.

His clumsy and sinister meetings with Campaign Foreign Policy Advisor Carter Page, National Co-Chair of Donald Trump's campaign in the 2016 presidential election Sam Clovis, and the most junior team member George Papadopoulos should have destroyed any theory of collusion. But as Attorney General Barr pointed out in an important interview with the *Wall Street Journal* in December 2019, the plotting continued:

> This is the meat of the issue. If you actually spent time to look into what happened I think you would be appalled. Remember they say "Okay, we are not going to talk to the campaign. We are going to send people in wire them up and have them talk to the individuals." That happened. That happened in August, September, and October, and it all came back exculpatory. People said, "I don't know what you are talking about." It is exculpatory not only as to the relationship with the Russians but as to the specific facts. And that A) they never did anything about that, they just pressed ahead, but B) they never informed the court. They

---

[348] https://www.nytimes.com/2019/05/02/us/politics/fbi-government-investigator-trump.html

were told they didn't have probable cause to get a warrant, so they took the Steele dossier, which they had done nothing to verify, and they used that to get the warrant. It just collapsed everything. They withheld from the court all the exculpatory information, and they withheld from the court information about the lack of reliability of Steele. The real interesting thing here, and to me the major takeaway, actually is after the election. Because in January Steele was dealing with one person. He only talked to one person and that is what we call the primary sub-source. And it was that person who had the so-called network of sub-sources. When they finally got around to talking to him, he said, "I don't know what Steele is talking about. I didn't tell him this stuff," or "It was mostly barroom talk and rumor. I made it clear to him that this was my own suppositions or theories." And at that point, it was clear that the dossier was a sham. So what happens? What happens at that point? They don't tell the court. They continue to get FISA warrants based on that dossier. And more damning is they actually filed a statement with the court saying, "We talked to the sub-source and found him credible and cooperative." And that they put it into bolster. . . . When actually what he was being truthful about was that the dossier was garbage.[349]

The FBI turned full circle in their efforts back to using Steele's dodgy dossier as prima facia evidence that Carter Page was the agent of a foreign power. Even at this late stage in October the plotters still could not bring themselves to believe candidate Trump could win, but the private polls were too close to call. Even Donald Trump's supporters only realized they were in the lead with one week to go to the election.[350]

_____

[349] Attorney General William Barr interview with *Wall Street Journal*'s Gerard Baker (December 10, 2019).

[350] Interview with Devin Nunes.

In the Washington bubble in which elitists such as Halper and the Crossfire Hurricane team lived and worked, they rarely came across Trump supporters or understood how Hillary was unappealing to swathes of Americans. Was the plan, an "October surprise" to help Hillary get across the line by leaking the investigation with evidence from the Halper tapes? "Just went to a Southern Virginia Walmart. I could SMELL the Trump support" is one of FBI's Peter Strzok's most infamous texts.

The Crossfire Hurricane team relied on three sources to gain a FISA warrant which were   reporting the same information, their Holy Grail since August 2016 on Carter Page and the Trump campaign: Steele's dossier of unverified and untrue accusations including leaks placed in the press by Steele and Halper with the help of Fusion GPS, and lastly highly selective parts of Halper's secretly taped interviews. From this point the Crossfire Hurricane team's actions such as using unverified, concocted intelligence illustrate the desperation bordering on insanity to ensure Hillary's victory.

Chapter Sixteen: Director Brennan

Let them alone: they be blind leaders of the blind. And if the blind lead the blind, both shall fall into the ditch.

Matthew 15:14

A desk is a dangerous place from which to view the world.

—John le Carré

O n June 23, 2017, the *Washington Post* published an important "resistance" propaganda article titled "Obama's secret struggle to punish Russia for Putin's election assault."[351] This article provides a tremendous insight into the telling lack of activity in the Obama White House in the period from August 2016.

After the debacle at the Democrat Convention, Hillary Clinton's campaign was putting intense pressure on President Obama's White House to back their account of Trump campaign collusion with the Russians. But President Obama was in no mood to get involved or at least not publicly. He viewed Donald Trump as a joke candidate and a no-hoper in the election. Obama must have felt he could just sit back and do nothing publicly; privately he was well aware of the FBI investigation launched on July 31, 2016 into his political opponents. The then President was briefed by Director Comey in early September,

---

[351] Gregg Miller, et al., "Obama's secret struggle to punish Russia for Putin's election assault," *Washington Post* (July 23, 2017).

perhaps even with the specific fake intelligence provided by Halper on the Trump campaign officials. Peter Strzok texted Lisa Page to say that he was preparing a briefing for the FBI Director to which she replies that the President wanted to know everything about their investigation.

The *Washington Post* article, perhaps sourced from the ex Director himself, describes how it was CIA intelligence generally and John Brennan in particular who were pivotal in events. Although the FBI launched the Trump-Russia conspiracy probe, it was John Brennan who aggressively pushed it to the Bureau, breaking with the CIA charter by interfering in domestic politics. Brennan is responsible for supplying information to the FBI counterintelligence investigators in early 2016 that was false. Brennan sounded the "alarm" about alleged Russian collusion to the White House in early August, and managed the US intelligence community's response. To bolster his claims, Brennan is reported saying he had:

> sourcing deep inside the Russian government that detailed Russian President Vladimir Putin's direct involvement in a cyber campaign to disrupt and discredit the US presidential race. But it went further. The intelligence captured Putin's specific instructions on the operation's audacious objectives — defeat or at least damage the Democratic nominee, Hillary Clinton, and help elect her opponent, Donald Trump[352]

"The CIA breakthrough came at a stage of the presidential campaign when Trump had secured the GOP nomination"[353] at exactly the same time and using the same trigger as Downer reported his conversations with Papadopoulos!

---

[352] https://www.theguardian.com/world/2019/sep/14/oleg-smolenkov-alleged-us-spy-gave-russia-the-slip

[353] ibid

Another damning piece of evidence against Brennan is that he supplied then-Senate Minority Leader Harry Reid with the incendiary information Reid released in letters late in the election campaign.[354] After President-elect Trump's unexpected victory, Brennan oversaw the hasty production of the ridiculous Intelligence Community Assessment. Then after leaving office, Brennan sought work as a prominent analyst for MSNBC, where he launched waves of attacks on the sitting president, even going so far as to accuse Donald Trump of "treasonous" conduct. Despite his public utterances under oath Brennan has so far produced no evidence of collusion.

In the first days of August 2016, CIA Director Brennan sent a white envelope with "extraordinary handling restrictions"[355] to the White House. For dramatic effect, the envelope carried "eyes only" instructions that its contents be shown to just four people: President Barack Obama and three senior aides. Inside it was what the *Post* describes with huge exaggeration "an intelligence bombshell"[356]

It was likely nothing of the sort. Just days after the opening of the Crossfire Hurricane investigation Brennan produced his timely intelligence bombshell. As le Carré says "Topicality is always suspect." The bombshell was likely Halper's fake "intelligence," ascribed to the ex-head of the SVR Trubnikov, the most well-known ex-Russian intelligence officer on the Washington foreign policy circuit. It was almost certainly the same intelligence that forms the June 20, Steele memo attributed to Trubnikov. Was Halper the original source for both? Later in September 2019 the CIA's secret alleged

---

[354]https://www.realclearinvestigations.com/articles/2019/11/15/the_brennan_dossier_all_about_a_prime_mover_of_russiagate_121098.html

[355] Greg Miller, et al., *"Obama's secret struggle to punish Russia for Putin's election assault,"* *Washington Post* (June 23, 2017).

[356] Ibid., https://www.washingtonpost.com/graphics/2017/world/national-security/obama-putin-election-hacking/?utm_term=.ab1819a0fdf6

Kremlin super spy, one Oleg Smolenkov was exposed by Agency friendly US press outlets. But Smolenkov has to be ruled out as the super spy. Oleg Smolenkov was far too junior in the Kremlin hierarchy to be privy to Putin's inner thoughts. A more troubling question is how can Smolenkov be the CIA's top intelligence asset in the Kremlin and also working for the Steele network providing the same information?

"Mission Impossible" style, the *Post* breathlessly reports, "the material was so sensitive that CIA Director John Brennan kept it out of the president's daily brief, concerned that even the restricted report's distribution was too broad. The CIA package came with instructions that it be returned immediately after it was read. To guard against leaks, subsequent meetings in the Situation Room followed the same protocols as planning sessions for the Osama bin Laden raid."[357] The *Washington Post* is trying to persuade us Brennan produced some top-notch intelligence. But did he?

Well, not judging by the reaction. No serious players in the White House or the intelligence community believed Brennan. His pseudo–Tom Clancy drama fell flat on its face right at the outset. Damningly, the *Post* confirms, "it took many months for other parts of the intelligence community to endorse the CIA's view." Even then, the support was minimal from only three out of seventeen agencies. The NSA only supported some of the conclusions.

Clearly, few believed the alleged Kremlin source could have access to the information Brennan was reporting. Even worse for Brennan the White House administration did not believe him either. It was only *after* the election, facing the nightmare scenario of losing his legacy, did President Obama tell the public, in a declassified report, what

---

[357] Ibid.

officials learned from Brennan in August. So much for the intelligence bombshell—it was a total dud.

The *Post* article describes Brennan's intelligence on Putin (that Halper perhaps fabricated) as extraordinary on multiple levels, including as a feat of espionage. "For spy agencies, gaining insights into the intentions of foreign leaders is among the highest priorities. But Putin is a remarkably elusive target. A former KGB officer, he takes extreme precautions to guard against surveillance, rarely communicating by phone or computer, always running sensitive state business from deep within the confines of the Kremlin."[358]

In the 2017 Washington Post article, officials described the President's reaction to John Brennan news as "grave" but did nothing. Obama "was deeply concerned and wanted as much information as fast as possible," a former official said. "He wanted the entire intelligence community all over this." But in 2016, all President Obama did at the time was suggest that John Brennan the then CIA Director should mention his concerns on an already-scheduled phone call on August 4 to Alexander Bortnikov, Director of the FSB, the post-Soviet successor to the KGB.

Brennan's phone call with Bortnikov was mostly about Syria. Brennan claims he used the final part of the conversation to raise the issue of Russian interference. Brennan allegedly told his FSB counterpart that Americans would be outraged to discover Moscow was trying to meddle in their democracy and said the effort would backfire. Bortnikov denied the Russians were up to anything but told him he would pass on his message to Russian President Vladimir Putin. Brennan told Congress:

---

[358] Ibid.

I next raised the published media reports of Russian attempts to interfere in our upcoming presidential election. I told Mr. Bortnikov that if Russia had such campaign underway, it would be certain to backfire. I said that all Americans regardless of political affiliation or whom they might support in the election cherish their ability to elect their own leaders without outside interference or disruption. I said American voters would be outraged by any Russian attempt to interfere in [the] election.

Finally, I warned Mr. Bortnikov that if Russia pursued this course, it would destroy any near-term prospect for improvement in relations between Washington and Moscow and would undermine constructive engagement even on matters of mutual interest.

As I expected, Mr. Bortnikov denied that Russia was doing anything to influence our presidential election, claiming that Moscow is a traditional target of blame by Washington for such activities. He said that Russia was prepared to work with whichever candidate wins the election. When I repeated my warning, he again denied the charge, but said that he would inform President Putin of my comments. I believe I was the first US official to brace the Russians on this matter. [359]

That's it, folks—the entire reaction to the huge intelligence bombshell. If you believe the Brennan myth, the chances of the source spying for the CIA in the center of the Kremlin surviving undiscovered following a tip-off to the Russians from the head of the Agency would be nil.

Then, in the face of this "grave" political crisis, President Obama departed for an August vacation to Martha's Vineyard. Obama eventually instructed aides to get a high-confidence assessment from US intelligence agencies on Russia's role and intent and seek bipartisan support from congressional leaders for a statement condemning Moscow.

---

[359] Brennan testifying before Congress (May 23, 2017) at http://transcripts.cnn.com/TRANSCRIPTS/1705/23/cnr.03.html.

Even the *Washington Post* admits, "Despite the intelligence the CIA had produced, other agencies were unwilling to endorse a conclusion that President Vladimir Putin was personally directing the operation and wanted to help Trump." Because of the source of the material, the NSA was reluctant to view it with high confidence."[360]

With President Obama gone on vacation, John Brennan moved swiftly to schedule private briefings with congressional leaders. Brennan gave personal briefings to the "Gang of Eight", high-ranking US senators and members of Congress regularly apprised of state secrets. Breaking with tradition, he contacted them individually, rather than as a group.

His briefing with Harry Reid was extraordinary. The Democrat Minority Leader was used as a conduit to the press. As the journalist Kimberley Strassel says in the *Wall Street Journal* "the CIA director couldn't of course himself go public with his Clinton spin—he lacked the support of the intelligence community and had to be careful not to be seen interfering in US politics."[361] In his late August briefing, John Brennan told the Senate Minority Leader Russia was trying to help Mr. Trump win the election, and Trump advisers might be colluding with Russia.

Within a few days of the briefing, Harry Reid wrote a letter to James Comey of the FBI, which immediately became public. "The evidence of a direct connection between the Russian government and Donald Trump's presidential campaign continues to mount,"[362] wrote Sen. Harry Reid, insisting the FBI use "every resource available to investigate this matter."[363] Sen. Harry Reid divulged the first

---

[360] "Obama's secret struggle," *Washington Post* (June 23, 2017).

[361] Kimberly A. Strassel, "Brennan and the 2016 Spy Scandal," *WSJ* (July 19, 2018).

[362] Ibid.

[363] Ibid.

allegations contained in the infamous Steele dossier. Sen. Reid warned on August 27, 2016 that Russia may be trying to "influence the Trump campaign and manipulate it as a vehicle for advancing the interests of Russian President Vladimir Putin."[364]

Significantly, Sen. Reid's August 27, 2016 letter contained references to an unnamed Trump campaign aide traveling to Moscow and allegedly meeting with two sanctioned Kremlin figures. The unnamed aide is of course Carter Page. John Brennan denies any allegation suggesting that he saw the information in the Steele dossier before December 2016. So how did Brennan know about the Carter Page allegation that he passed on to Harry Reid if not from the Steele dossier? Who could be another source connected to the CIA with the identical information? Who could possibly have the fake Page intelligence and report both to Christopher Steele and John Brennan?

Although Brennan has claimed publicly, he "provided the same briefing to each of the Gang of Eight members,"[365] Rep. Devin Nunes (R-Calif.) says that is not true. Nunes, who was then the chairman of the House Intelligence Committee, is quoted in journalist Lee Smith's excellent book, *"The Plot Against the President"*, saying, "Whatever Brennan told Reid, he didn't tell me."[366]

Sen. Harry Reid's two leaked letters show the extent to which John Brennan maneuvered behind the scenes on behalf of Hillary Clinton to push the idea of the collusion conspiracy theory to a public audience. Brennan must have wanted this information to go public or so Sen Harry Reid believed. Michael Isikoff and David Corn, the collusion hoaxers write in their book *Russian Roulette* that Reid "concluded the

---

[364] https://fas.org/irp/congress/2016_cr/reid-comey.pdf

[365] Lee Smith, *The Plot Against the President* (New York: Hachette, 2019), 91.

[366] Ibid., 92.

CIA chief believed the public needed to know about the Russia operation, including the information about the possible links to the Trump campaign."[367] Brennan seemingly helped to generate the collusion investigation and then inserted it into American politics right at the pivotal point of a presidential campaign in August through October.

Hillary Clinton campaign's opposition-research firm Fusion GPS followed up the Brennan leak by briefing its media allies about the very dossier that they had dropped off at the FBI. As an election ploy on September 23, Yahoo News's Michael Isikoff ran the headline: "US intel officials probe ties between Trump adviser and Kremlin." Not only was the collusion narrative out there in the press, but so was evidence the FBI was investigating.

In late September 2016, the White House decided to step into the election fray by announcing the intelligence community had reached "unanimous" agreement that election interference was a Russian operation directed by President Vladimir Putin. Obama had directed his spy chiefs to prepare a public statement that was issued in October. A three-paragraph statement was issued by Jeh Johnson, Secretary of Homeland Security and James Clapper. It read "The US intelligence community is confident that the Russian government directed the recent compromises of e-mails from US persons and institutions, including from US political organizations," the statement said. "We believe, based on the scope and sensitivity of these efforts, that only Russia's senior-most officials could have authorized these activities."[368] The American public ignored it.

---

[367] Kimberly A. Strassel, "Brennan and the 2016 Spy Scandal," *WSJ* (July 19, 2018).

[368] Greg Miller, et al.,"Obama's secret struggle to punish Russia for Putin's election assault," *Washington Post* (June 23, 2017).

The post-election atmosphere at the Obama White House was grim, according to the *Washington Post* "it was like a funeral parlor"369 according to one official as the team began to anticipate the damage Donald Trump might inflict on President Obama's policies and legacy. On December 6, the lame duck President Obama ordered a "review" by US intelligence agencies of Russian interference in US elections, with a plan to make some of the findings public.

As described by Lee Smith in his book "The Plot against the President," the whole exercise in December was a stitch up and marked the start of the coup. The plan was to delegitimize the incoming President and present his administration with a foreign policy crisis. The tools were the intelligence services and press leaks.

Just three days after its official start, the *Washington Post* on December 9 was the first newspaper to be able to report the conclusion of the Intelligence Community Assessment. The story was headlined "Secret CIA assessment says Russia was trying to help Trump win White House." The writers included the journalist with the most stunning and accurate insights into the workings of John Brennan's mind, Gregg Miller.

The door was ajar for every fake news outlet to add spice to the tale. All the stories dutifully followed the defeated candidate's Hillary's narrative blaming her failure on Russia citing intelligence officials as sources. At the start of the new President's term, the non-existent "Russia's collusion in the election" was portrayed as the crime of the century and used as a lever to attempt to topple the new President.

But this extreme reaction was not the one the Intelligence Community reached straight after the election in November as Rep. Nunes explains:

369 Ibid.

After the election we were briefed on the election interference, which by the way is quite common.The DNC got hacked and the Podesta's emails got hacked, it's totally normal it happens every single day to all politicians, all political parties, all government agencies. We've been warning for years about the Russians, the Chinese, the Iranians, the North Koreans, other non state bad actors they are constantly going to be looking to hack anything relating to US government just to gather intel and steal secrets, not to mention a lot of the corporations and technology companies in this country. With all that said, we all got briefed —it's right after the election, all the Agencies are in there, it's all normal, nothing new that has happened nothing unusual everything that we know, it was all predictable, what we know about the Russians what they always do. Maybe people have not talked about it all these years but none of it was unusual.[370]

Out of the blue in late December 2016, just before the inauguration of Donald Trump, lame-duck President Obama approved a draconian sanctions package against Russia, including the expulsion of diplomats and the closure of two diplomatic compounds. President Obama decided on the expulsion of thirty-five diplomats claimed to be suspected spies. Obama announced the punitive measures on December 29, 2016, while on vacation in Hawaii. It was an act of such magnitude it was tantamount to declaring a new Cold War. As Lee Smith points out:

> the administration wasn't retaliating against Russia for interfering in a US election; the action was directed at Trump. Obama was leaving the president elect with a minor foreign policy crisis in order to box him in. Any criticism of Obama's response, never mind an attempt to reverse it, would only further fuel press reports that Trump was collaborating with the Russians.[371]

---

[370] Interview with Rep Devin Nunes DC leaks

[371] Lee Smith "The Plot Against the President."

By the end of December, President-elect Trump's incoming administration faced a full blown crisis and numerous accusations in the press sourced from anonymous intelligence officials about its alleged contacts with Moscow. Around the time Obama imposed sanctions, Donald Trump's designated national security adviser, Gen. Michael Flynn, spoke to the Russian ambassador Kislyak by phone as was his job. Gen. Flynn's statements about that conversation later cost him his job in the White House.

The Intelligence Community Assessment report Obama commissioned was released a week later, on January 6, 2017. It was based largely on the work done and previously leaked to the press by the task force organized by CIA Director John Brennan. The ICA established and made public what the Agency already concluded in August:

> Putin and the Russian government aspired to help President-elect Trump's election chances when possible by discrediting Secretary Clinton." [It also carried a note of warning:] "We assess Moscow will apply lessons learned from its Putin-ordered campaign aimed at the US election to future influence efforts worldwide.[372]

At the center of this now-controversial document was a statement, the United States' "seventeen intelligence agencies" all agreed Russian President Vladimir Putin ordered intervention to prevent Hillary Clinton's election and to install Donald Trump. The statement was a lie.

Only handpicked members of three agencies were involved in the assessment. Brennan's CIA, Comey's FBI had high confidence in the politically charged finding. Admiral Roger's NSA would only agree to moderate confidence in the assessment. Moderate means hardly any confidence at all. It transpired that the whole assessment hung on the information supplied by one unverified human intelligence source,

---

[372] Intelligence Community Assessment

allegedly from the Kremlin. The NSA had no information themselves from intercepts (SIGINT) to support this key contention. The NSA gave only moderate confidence to the finding because they doubted the alleged source could know what was in President Vladimir Putin's head. The NSA's chief, Admiral Rogers experienced extreme difficulty obtaining any information from the CIA about their secret source.[373]

Who was this ultra-secret source? Most likely it was Stefan Halper posing as Trubnikov. As previously described, there is evidence that the name in the August 2016 Brennan envelope might well be former head of SVR Trubnikov, which would have been based on the word of Halper.

In September 2019, a story was leaked to the "collusion truthers" in the media and then quickly shelved. Out of thin air, articles appeared saying Brennan's super spy was living openly in Virginia just outside D.C. A line of journalists descended on this Russian and his family. The story is utterly bizarre. "Oleg Smolenkov, 50, is said to have had access to papers on the Russian president's desk and to have been instrumental in confirming to American intelligence that Mr. Putin personally ordered interference in the 2016 US presidential election."

This is of course the same Russian president who we have been told by the Washington Post with equal confidence never commits anything to paper. Smolenkov was a junior Kremlin official in charge of travel arrangements who the CIA exfiltrated. According to media reports the Russians were a bit worried when he disappeared whilst on vacation in Montenegro and alerted Interpol. Apparently they dropped the inquiry when they found on the internet Smolenkov alive and well. It was reported in the Washington Post that Smolenkov had just bought a

---

[373] https://www.nytimes.com/2019/12/19/us/politics/durham-john-brennan-cia.html

house in his own name in the United States. So, this super spy was not hiding and not the source close to Putin.

The sources of the main conclusions of the ICA were the liars and leakers Steele and Halper. In the recently declassified Appendix A to the ICA the analysts reveal how much the report relied on this pair and their concoctions. "The most politically sensitive claims by the FBI source [Steele] alleged a close relationship between the President-elect and the Kremlin. The source claimed that the President-elect and his top campaign advisers [Flynn] knowingly worked with Russian officials to bolster his chances of beating Secretary Clinton; were fully knowledgeable of Russia…and were offered financial compensation." Three other unverified and unverifiable allegations whose origin is probably Halper were included that:

> The FBI source claimed that the Kremlin had cultivated the President-elect for at least five years; had fed him and his team intelligence about Secretary Clinton and other opponents for years.

> The FBI source also claimed Russian authorities possessed … a compromising dossier on Secretary Clintons.

> The FBI source claimed that secret meetings between the Kremlin and the President-elect team were handled by some of the President-elect advisors.[374]

On May 23, 2017, Brennan revealed details about his pivotal role in the origins of Spygate to Congress. For the whole of 2016 he claimed the CIA was receiving intelligence independent of Steele about possible Russian collusion with the Trump campaign. The former CIA Director Brennan's message in his testimony was he was the one who had the intelligence causing the early concerns that Russian "officials" may have successfully recruited an aide from Donald Trump's campaign to help in the Kremlin's efforts to influence the 2016

---

[374] Appendix A ICA Declassified June 2020.

presidential election. By applying a simple process of elimination, there is only one aide who fits the bill, General Mike Flynn. *The Washington Post*, a media ally of the CIA, through Gregg Miller confirmed Brennan was referring to Gen. Flynn.[375]

Brennan is adamant that he received his intelligence *before* the summer of 2016 (the official start of the FBI investigation) and passed it on to the FBI. Brennan said based on his intelligence, he saw a conspiracy involving the Trump campaign—and as a result, he believed "there was a sufficient basis of information and intelligence that required further investigation" of the campaign by the FBI.[376]

What intelligence did Brennan pass on before July 2016 about Russian collusion with the Trump campaign to the FBI? The now ex-director stated authoritatively to Congress, "there was intelligence that the Russian intelligence services were actively involved in this effort" to "try to suborn individuals, and they try to get individuals, including US persons, to act on their behalf, either wittingly or unwittingly . . . and I was worried by a number of the contacts that the Russians had with US persons." [377]

Perhaps the "contacts" the cryptic Brennan is referring to in Congress include the small number of work emails I exchanged with General Flynn at the request of Christopher Andrew. The CIA must have been over-excited at the invitation to speak again in Cambridge I sent to

[375] https://www.washingtonpost.com/world/national-security/cia-director-warned-russian-security-service-chief-about-interference-in-election/2017/05/23/ebff2a7e-3fbb-11e7-adba-394ee67a7582_story.html

[376] https://www.realclearpolitics.com/video/2017/05/23/gowdy_grills_john_brennan_do_you_have_evidence_of_trump-russia_collusion_or_not_brennan_i_dont_do_evidence.html

[377] Brennan Testimony to Congress (May 23, 2017); excerpts at https://www.washingtonpost.com/world/national-security/cia-director-warned-russian-security-service-chief-about-interference-in-election/2017/05/23/ebff2a7e-3fbb-11e7-adba-394ee67a7582_story.html.

Gen. Flynn on behalf of the Cambridge Intelligence Seminar—
especially when Halper falsely reported the entire Seminar was
penetrated by a Kremlin front company.

Brennan outlined to Congress "the Russian plan," Gen. Flynn's
"treasonous path" was based on the "intelligence" he claims he saw:

> It is traditional intelligence collection tradecraft in terms of
> HUMINT, which is to identify individuals that you think are either
> very influential or rising stars, and you will try to develop
> relationship with them. And the Russians frequently will do that
> through cutouts or through false flag operations. They won't identify
> themselves as Russians or as members of the Russian Government.
> They will try to develop that personal relationship. And then over
> time, they will try to get individuals to do things on their behalf.[378]

The Republican congressman Rep. Trey Gowdy, an ex-prosecutor,
spoiled the party by demanding to know whether Brennan's evidence
of collusion was "circumstantial or direct." "Brennan ducked the
question by lecturing the lawmakers that the CIA engages in
intelligence gathering and assessments, not criminal investigations and
prosecutions. His motif was "I don't do evidence." Brennan hedged
that he knew only of "contacts and interactions." The ex-director
added there are "contacts that may have been totally, totally innocent
and benign as well as those that may have succumbed somehow to
those Russian efforts." "Often," he added in an ominous moment
pregnant with innuendo, "individuals who go along a treasonous path
do not even realize they're along that path until it gets to be a bit too
late."[379] He was of course referring to Gen. Flynn and myself.

---

[378] Ibid.

[379] Brennan Congressional Testimony May 23, 2017

Chapter Seventeen: Poisonous Pens

Ye are of your father the devil, and the lusts of your father ye will do. He was a murderer from the beginning, and abode not in the truth, because there is no truth in him. When he speaketh a lie, he speaketh of his own: for he is a liar, and the father of it.

—John 8:44

He that filches from me my good name robs me of that which not enriches

him, And makes me poor indeed.

—William Shakespeare, Othello Act 3 Scene 3

Towards the end of July 2016, Halper resigned from his role in the Intelligence Seminar. He was clearing the decks ahead of starting his work on Operation Crossfire Hurricane. Halper wrote this entirely innocuous memo to Professor Christopher Andrew:

> I wanted to write to say that I can no longer be a "Co-Convener" of the Intelligence Seminar. It has been most enjoyable these past several years, and I wish you continued success. I look forward to seeing you next time I am in Cambridge.

There was no mention or even hint in his July 2016 resignation email of devilish Russian plots, Kremlin front companies, Mata Hari–like spies seducing the speakers or ensnaring the good people of the University of Cambridge. Halper held an honorary position as a co-

convenor of the prestigious group but the role was undemanding. To my knowledge he gave one very boring talk which was poorly attended about China and brought in one speaker in four years. Halper still has the unique distinction of being the only person to arrange for a former Russian intelligence officer to speak at the Seminar, not just once but twice. Halper, after all is the only foreign spy to penetrate the seminar.

Halper's role was otherwise so minor in the Seminar organization that his departure was not even formally announced to the members. The history faculty no longer taught intelligence, so all the graduate students were associated with the Department of Politics and International Studies. No one missed his lurking presence.

It was agreed with Chris Andrew many months before that another convener, Peter Martland, would also step down at the end of the academic year in July 2016 due to his financial difficulties and ill health. Peter Martland was Christopher Andrew's unofficial assistant and administrator of the Seminar. Seemingly all the old men associated with the Seminar were retiring and cutting back on their commitments in a planned way. Halper and Martland no longer appeared as conveners in the program distributed in September 2016.

In the previous months they had all been falling out with each other. There were continued petty disputes over what seemed like nothing that blew up into storms to vanish just as quickly. It was impossible to keep track of who fell out with who, let alone the reason. My last speaking appearance at the Seminar before the operation was in late 2015 and my attendances in 2016 tailed off.

Halper might have presented himself as an eminent academic to his prey in 2016, but the year before he wound down the last of his official Cambridge activities and retired. He was finished at the University of

Cambridge. He now lives full-time in Great Falls, Virginia, just minutes down the road from the CIA headquarters in Langley. Since his exposure as a key long-term FBI informer in May 2018, the University of Cambridge hides from any association with the foreign spy once buried in their midst. When pressed, the authorities who once employed him duck the issue, saying the connection with Stefan Halper was severed at the end of the 2015 academic year.

Cambridge has given Halper the unique distinction of expunging any reference to him from their official websites. He has also been erased from his other academic role in the US If you ask questions about Halper of the University authorities, they push off your inquiry to Magdalene College with a polite but firm "no comment." Magdalene College is in full hand-wringing mode. I contacted the Master of the College, its honorary head, the retired head of the Church of England Lord Rowan Williams, former Archbishop of Canterbury about Halper. His response was shock.

Although Halper remained associated with the seminar, in mid-2015 he retired back to his home in the United States. He was the sleepy Cambridge Security Initiative's representative in the United States. The Cambridge Security Initiative was a washout, a failure. Despite all the early hopes for the project at launch, its achievements were a conference with the US Department of Defense and the publication of an article on the role of cash in the economy.

The bright young academics who signed up on the promise of a steady stream of paid work were deeply disillusioned. No work, let alone money came their way. No one even commissioned a study on Russia despite the new Cold War. It mattered not a jot to the directors who suddenly one day in 2016 abolished our roles and fired us all without saying a word. Chris Andrew resigned from CSI in the summer of 2016.

That was far from the end of the Stefan Halper resignation story. He left the University of Cambridge with a bang, not a whimper. After the presidential election on November 8, 2016, Halper took dramatic action to further the Russian hoax conspiracy by defaming me and General Mike Flynn and to advance his wholly fabricated story across multiple platforms. Halper used his experience and skill as an intelligence asset to undertake his defamation campaign in the press. Halper seeded the media, who already harbored an extreme bias against and ill-will toward President Trump with extraordinary stories and disinformation. Journalists told me and others that Halper was their source.

Halper's tales were false and defamatory statements about me and General Flynn—statements eagerly republished with no evidentiary support and for the sole purpose of advancing the sensational and false narrative of Spygate. Halper was identified by the journalists as their source.

Halper identified himself directly in a *Financial Times* article in December 2015. In other articles he would be described, for instance, as "a former senior US official with knowledge of the matter"[380] or "a person associated with the event"[381] claiming detailed personal knowledge of the matters. Halper fits the bill, as not only was he the only ex-American government official with connections to the Seminar, but also someone who knows everything about the FBI investigation.

---

[380] Carol E. Lee, et al., "Mike Flynn Didn't Report 2014 Interaction with Russian-British National," *Wall Street Journal* (March 18, 2017).

[381] The curious wording of the WSJ points to a seminar organizer being the source.

On December 16, 2016 (around the time Dearlove was meeting with Christopher Steele at the Garrick Club in London)[382] the confidential secret FBI source, Halper managed to score himself a front-page story in the habitually unread weekend edition of the *Financial Times*. As it is known in the UK, the *Financial Times'* circulation at the weekends, is approximately zero. The story was released at an absolute low point in the journalist cycle, published in the no-news part of the year. The article was a placeholder, not breaking news. Despite their splash headlines on the front page of the newspaper, the editors knew the story whiffed.

The publishers' in-house legal team added noisy disclaimers openly admitting they were unable to verify Halper's tale. The legal department and editor added cast-iron legal protection to their article. They added the line "The Financial Times has been unable to independently substantiate their claims, and no concrete evidence has been provided to back them."[383] This is legal speak for "we in absolutely no way at all stand by this story." The editors caveated the dud spy scandal and quickly recast the story as an academic rivalry to protect themselves.

The supposedly "super secret" FBI source kick-started an international media scandal with his fable including his delightful picture in the *Financial Times;* no one and certainly not Halper resigned from the Cambridge Intelligence Seminar because of a "spy scare." There were no spies penetrating the Seminar, other than Halper. Anyone, let alone an experienced intelligence asset such as Halper knows you call the authorities with these suspicions, not the newspapers. Certainly, the ex-head of MI6 knows the correct procedure. Even the newspaper

---

[382] Simpson and Fritsch's *Crime in Progress* and multiple press reports.

[383] Sam Jones, "Intelligence experts accuse Cambridge forum of Kremlin links," *Financial Times* (December 6, 2016).

knew it. Halper tried his hardest to invent and promote a vintage spy scare storm at the University of Cambridge invoking powerful images of Kim Philby the infamous Soviet spy.[384]

The resignation of the ex-head of MI6 Sir Richard Dearlove from the Cambridge Intelligence Seminar was placed as the headline to lure the readers in. It is hard to follow the logic of the nonsense story until the reader understands it is part of a sophisticated operation. Every artifice was deployed, including pictures of the 1930s Cambridge traitors to adorn the newspaper story to bulk it out. Halper claimed ridiculously, that the core of the British way of life was under attack by Russian intelligence seeking to spread their malevolent influence. Members of the British Parliament were reported duly alarmed and began demanding public inquiries.

Halper was the only person quoted on the record in the article to endorse the absurd allegations. At the time of the press article, he was still employed as a confidential source to the highly secret and sensitive FBI investigation. Instead of being "confidential," Halper the informant was putting himself together with his photograph on the front pages. The article started with a provocative introduction: "A group of intelligence experts, including a former head of MI6, has cut ties with fellow academics at Cambridge University, in a varsity spy scare harking back to the heyday of Soviet espionage at the heart of the British establishment."[385] Wow, that's a must-read—Britain's finest institution undermined by the Russians. Who exactly is the spy causing the scare? The *Financial Times* had its tiny weekend readership choking on their breakfast cereal. Seemingly the story was designed only to be read by other journalists as a placeholder.

---

[384] Kim Philby: British Intelligence Officer and Soviet Spy, https://www.britannica.com/biography/Kim-Philby

[385] Ibid.

Crucially, you wonder about the credibility and possible sanity of the key FBI source Halper simultaneously promoting twin Russian conspiracies aimed at both the heart of the British and American establishments. There was no conspiracy in the UK; there was not even an investigation, but in the US the myth lived on for another two years. If you take a close look at this fictional *Financial Times* story, it is easy to understand Spygate and Halper's pattern of behavior.

In his typical style, Halper boosted his own importance by claiming in the article that he was both an intelligence expert and "a senior foreign policy adviser at the White House to presidents Nixon, Ford and Reagan."[386] Even when selling disinformation, Halper had to tell the world he was once important. If there is going to be media attention, he wanted it all to himself. Stefan Halper cannot ever be upstaged. At that stage was an active undercover confidential paid human source to the FBI. In December, 2016 he put himself on the front pages six months into their most important and sensitive investigation in its history.

Halper reveals himself to the world as a delusional man or a liar, asserting on the front page of a British national newspaper, the "Russians" are running a fantastical intelligence operation in Cambridge. Halper expected that the story would be picked up in the United States. The FBI had just sacked their other confidential source, Christopher Steele in October for getting his name in the press as an FBI asset, and now the other one, Halper was out of control. This was getting embarrassing for the FBI. Halper is quoted directly in the article saying he stepped down from the Seminar due to "unacceptable Russian influence on the group." The chronology of events undermines his claims. What was the "Russian influence" that caused Halper to resign? Even stranger is the timing of this article. What is the

---

[386] Ibid.

connection between Halper's false FT story and Christopher Steele's efforts around the same time to promote a false story of an affair to Senator John McCain? Was Halper, like Steele seemingly ordered by forces in the FBI to leak stories to the press?

With this newspaper splash, Halper identified himself as the one person in the world who uncovers every fiendish Putin plot. In comparison to uncovering Russian collusion in the US election, this is probably one of his minor discoveries. Of course, Halper does not alert the authorities in the UK. MI5 which is British counterintelligence do not descend on the University in a fleet of unmarked cars. Using one of his old journalistic tricks, of which he is a master, he provided both on and off-the-record quotes. He often masquerades as "people familiar with" in articles. In his unmistakably pompous prose style, Halper anonymously contributed this passage on the critical importance of our insignificant group to UK national security. "They [Halper and his Cambridge Club friends] fear that Russia may be seeking to use the seminar as an impeccably-credentialed platform to covertly steer debate and opinion on high-level sensitive defense and security topics." [387]

The few attendees of the Seminar woke from their slumbers and laughed uproariously at this nonsense, such as the description of the Cambridge Intelligence group as "an academic forum for former practitioners and current researchers of western spy craft" and there "could be a Kremlin-backed operation to compromise the group." Halper's favorite spy word is "compromise," and his other hallmark is the use of the conditional tense.

---

[387] Ibid.

Here are the titles of the talks that in Halper's view President Putin was seeking to influence in the fall of 2016: "Confusion and Opportunism? British Intelligence and the Battle of the Somme"; "Intelligence, policy and the move towards attritional counter-insurgency against the IRA in 1971"; and "Espionage in World War I: spy fact and spy fiction."[388] None of these events look likely to attract much of an audience, let alone the attention of the Russian or any other security service.

The only conclusion is the chief investigator for Spygate, Halper deployed his feverish paranoid imagination to come up with this doozy of a conspiracy theory. He is responsible for this gem, "a newly established publishing venture may be acting as a front for the Russian intelligence services." It is possible to see how the outlandish suggestions of the Steele dossier were put together when this man turned his mind to the task.

Buried deep down in the article to receive little prominence is a quote from Christopher Andrew, who ran the Seminar, destroying at a stroke Halper's allegation of a Russian covert operation to compromise the Seminar. He described the accusations as "absurd."

At this point, if you were FBI agent Steven Somma, Halper's handler, or CIA Director Brennan, and you were conducting a real investigation —you panic. Halper is your main Confidential Human Source. What is his face doing in the press, associated with such a scandal? Christopher Steele has been fired for leaking to the newspapers in October and now your second key source is involved in a publicity storm. The FBI takes no action against Halper; instead they continue to use him and promote Halper as a credible witness for the Mueller inquiry.

---

[388] Cambridge University History Faculty website, https://www.hist.cam.ac.uk/seminars/seminar-pdfs/2016-2017/intelligence-mt-2016.

The *Financial Times* article revealed Halper to the world as a pusher of absurd conspiracy theories. Halper's credibility is publicly in shreds. He has just accused the official historian of British counterintelligence, MI5, without any evidence of being a Russian agent or a Kremlin stooge. Andrew is one of MI5's most trusted confidants. A measure of the regard was the first talk Sir Jonathon Evans gave when he retired as the Director of MI5 in 2014 was to this group.

This is, of course, nothing new to the man who made the same type of allegations about president-elect Trump, National Security Advisor Gen. Flynn, and a host of others. Halper has just promoted and stood up a flimsy and easily disprovable fantasy in the press in his own name. Halper showcased to the world, by pushing crazy stories that when it suited he saw Putin's handiwork everywhere.

If this were normal times Halper should have been treated for paranoia or delusion. But the FBI did not get concerned. Despite Halper's public lies in the press, the Crossfire team carried on using him. His FBI handler Steven Somma repeatedly verified Halper to the FISA court as reliable and presented him to Mueller inquiry as a witness.

The truth is the Cambridge seminar by 2016 was an irrelevancy, surviving way past its sell-by date. The discussions were entirely unclassified, open to the public and the few attendees were charming but mostly vintage academics. The entire annual budget was a couple of thousand dollars for drinks and room hire. There were never any sensitive defense or security topics on the agenda. Most of the dozen attendees were already in their seventies. Speakers appeared to plug books or because they were friends.

What was Halper up to by going to the press in December 2016 about events allegedly occurring months before in July? The answer lies in the article: "Spurred by the mounting concern over Russian meddling in the US presidential election, western spooks are rushing to try and get a fuller picture of the Kremlin's strategy for manipulating information to influence opinion.[389] In the article, Stefan Halper falsely links his earlier resignation from the Cambridge Intelligence Seminar to the Russia Collusion hoax he had helped start. Did he name himself as one of the Western spooks rushing to get a fuller picture?

There is a long tradition of CIA operatives placing fake stories in foreign newspapers to get them picked up and reported in the United States. The originator of this stratagem was Halper's father-in-law, the CIA's Ray Cline. Tellingly, Senator Chuck Grassley is investigating if *The Guardian,* a UK newspaper was used in this way by the CIA during Spygate. Halper planted a big lure in the story for the US media to feast on in follow-up articles.

Halper mentioned his then-favorite bogeyman General Mike Flynn the President-elect Trump's selection for National Security Advisor as a "recent attendee of the intelligence seminar." That's despite the fact General Flynn attended the Seminar nearly three years before the article, when he was the head of Obama's DIA. General Flynn was being set up as the target to delegitimize the electoral result. Halper planned for his friends in the US to jump at the chance to embroil General Flynn in a new Russian spy scandal. The story had a sting in its tail. Halper planned and placed a second follow-up story.

In releasing this piece, Halper burnt the reputations of his friends and ex-colleagues in a monumental act of betrayal on a very public bonfire. His resignation email sent in July 2016 made no mention of any concerns about Russian interference. There was none. No one resigned from the Seminar for a sinister reason. Russian intelligence must have bigger fish to fry than subsidizing seventy-year-olds' Friday

---

[389] The *Financial Times* (December 16, 2016).

drinking sessions. Subverting Professor Andrew's supper club was not going to rank among the greatest operations of Russian intelligence.

On the day the *Financial Times* article published in December 2016, Andrew emailed Halper to find out if the newspaper had misquoted him:

Dear Stef,

I am somewhat shocked by the comments attributed to you in today's FT. I can well imagine that you've been misquoted but do need to know as a matter of urgency what you actually told the FT. The Seminar remains grateful to you for taking the initiative in arranging the visits and talks to the Seminar by the former head of the SVR, Vyacheslav Trubnikov. I'm sure we both continue to believe that his visits in no way compromised the integrity of the Seminar.

Andrew's email pointedly reminded Halper that in 2015 it was only he who invited and paid for the former Russian intelligence officer to attend the seminar—Vyacheslav Trubnikov, the ex-Head of the SVR. The email was an indication Andrew was not going down without a fight. The organizers knew, Halper, not a Russians was the only active foreign spy to penetrate the Seminar and mount an operation in Cambridge. According to Andrew, Halper never replied to the email.

Behind the scenes in the UK, press reports suggested there was some consternation in security circles following Donald Trump's unexpected electoral triumph. Several Spygate roads lead to the UK. A week after President Trump's election win in November 2016, according to the conservative British daily *The Daily Telegraph,* Christopher Steele briefed Sir Charles Farr, who then chaired Britain's Joint Intelligence Committee, about his investigation of the Trump campaign. Given that Steele told David Kramer around the same time about Halper's lies, did this briefing included the "intelligence" about the 2014 dinner and the allegation I was a Russian spy in contact with the senior Trump campaign advisor General Flynn? It is reported by the Telegraph that Farr passed Steele information to other high-level British intelligence officials, including MI5 Director Andrew Parker and MI6 Director Alex Younger. The British security services confirmed to the FBI that they have no derogatory information on either myself or Gen. Flynn.

Nine months pregnant, I was dragged into the row by Christopher Andrew caused by Halper's *Financial Times* story to help defend his reputation. A group of friends tried to offer him informal advice on how to navigate the crisis. Christopher Andrew was outraged and insulted that anyone would believe such ludicrous accusations. At stake were his reputation and legacy. In 2016 I had no idea the *Financial Times* article was part of a co-ordinated media operation to attack Gen. Flynn and undermine the President elect. I was told the article was the result of a dispute between academics over money.

We advised the panicking Andrew to contact lawyers, his intelligence contacts and friendly journalists for help. But no one would come forward and speak up publicly to support Andrew because Dearlove, a dominant figure, was named in the press as one of those who resigned. I was later told everyone in the Cambridge intelligence group was simply too scared to speak out. Fresh scandalous news stories kept on appearing in the press day after day. Andrew had another plan. He went to see Dearlove and, I was told, made an arrangement to end the press attacks on him. Just as quickly as the stories appeared, they just stopped. Dearlove apparently spoke to the newspaper editors.

The *Financial Times* story embarrassed the University and its chief administrator, the Vice-Chancellor. The Vice-Chancellor was furious and in full panic mode. The University of Cambridge was dragged into a major spy scandal by a small bunch of warring old retired men. The

Vice-Chancellor ordered the matter quashed. He sent an emissary, Dr. Bill Foster, to knock heads together. A face-saving solution was brokered but rejected. CSI and the Seminar went their separate ways. As abruptly as the ludicrous situation arose, it stopped. Halper was privately identified as the source of the articles and a cover story was placed about Cambridge community describing everything as a petty academic dispute over money.

The sting in this story was that a second, more damaging follow-up news article was planned by the informer. In his hits, such as on Carter Page, Halper always places a story and a follow-up. Having stirred up a major spy scandal at Cambridge, Halper identified me as a real Russian spy embedded in the University to the UK press.

Halper told Sean O'Neill, a chief reporter with *The Times* of London, Britain's oldest national daily newspaper, that I was a Russian spy. On December 19, 2016, O'Neill called me and repeated the false accusation. Nine months pregnant I was shocked to receive a call from a top journalist threatening to print a false story that would destroy my life. In horror, I got a leading UK libel lawyer to say I would sue his newspaper for defamation if they printed anything. The story was never printed.

The *Financial Times* article with all its absurd allegations was planted by Halper to create a false narrative about a Russia sleeper agent at the University of Cambridge and link this all to Gen. Flynn. The Seminar had to be painted as a juicy target for a Russian intelligence operation. Clearly it was all utter nonsense. It all goes to show how far Halper was prepared to go to dirty up Gen. Flynn and the absurd weakness and baseless foundations of the Crossfire Hurricane operation.

I did not appreciate at the time that the Flynn angle placed in Halper's *Financial Times* story was part of a wider operation. I asked

Christopher Andrew what Halper was up to many times afterwards, but he closed down the conversation. Andrew desperately wanted the matter closed. I was told the dispute was a local university infighting that got out of hand.

On Friday, January 20, 2017 at Corpus Christi College Dearlove and Andrew gave a joint talk at the first Intelligence Seminar as if nothing previously happened. It was "to mark the Inauguration in Washington of President Donald J. Trump."[390] It was billed as taking place less than half an hour before the control of the nuclear codes will pass to President Trump. Andrew spoke on "The Transfer of the Nuclear Codes" while Dearlove gave "Reflections on the Intelligence Transition." The program reminded everyone that three years ago General Michael Flynn, the new president's National Security Adviser, gave a presentation to the Seminar. Dearlove was back as a co-convenor.

At the talk, Dearlove raised no concerns about Donald Trump and Gen. Flynn. The pair claimed credit for spotting Gen. Flynn, the soon-to-be appointed National Security Advisor, as a rising star and inviting him to the Seminar.

 Donald Trump's stunning election victory in November 2016 took the partisan plotters by surprise and to another, higher level of activity. There was only a short hiatus to regroup and come up with a new plan based on their informants' "intelligence." The infamous "insurance policy" was cashed in and found to be woefully inadequate. "Operation Crossfire Hurricane" was a dismal failure. Halper's false reports about General Flynn being compromised by me on the orders

---

[390] Cambridge University History Faculty website

of Russian intelligence were so ridiculous they were not even investigated.

Unleashing Halper to entrap innocents had found nothing but inconvenient exculpatory evidence, which would, in upright investigations have stopped the operation in its tracks. Halper created a fresh problem for the FBI. Most of his reports had to be deliberately suppressed from the FISA court as it was essentially exculpatory for Gen. Flynn, Carter Page, Papadopoulos and any other targets of Crossfire Hurricane. Electronic searches conducted under FISA warrants proved no collusion between the Campaign and Russia. The Trump campaign had not produced an "October surprise." Rather than reach a sane conclusion that there was no Russia collusion with the Trump campaign, the coup plotters doubled down. They needed to keep their investigation going at all costs in the hope of actually finding a crime. The Crossfire Hurricane team continued the fruitless investigation for years as part of Special Counsel Robert Mueller's team who knew from day one there was nothing to find. The final act of this expensive farce of the Russia fixing narrative was that the legal case brought by Special Counsel Mueller against alleged Russian government controlled troll farms (claimed responsible for the social media campaign that supposedly swung the 2016 election) collapsed in March 2020.

Acting DNI Richard Grenell recently declassified transcripts showing that under oath to the House Intelligence Committee no-one in the Obama administration had seen any evidence of Russia collusion.[391] But publicly many like the former Director of National Intelligence James Clapper, they kept the myth alive. Clapper said to *Vox* reporter Sean Illing on May 31, 2017: "I'm not saying collusion didn't happen.

---

[391] https://nypost.com/2020/05/07/transcripts-reaffirm-no-collusion-between-trump-and-russia/

I'm simply saying we don't have definitive evidence yet."[392] After a year of investigation, all Clapper had was "suspicion": "I saw the frequency of meetings between people in the Trump campaign and people with ties to the Russian government. . . . But I saw no smoking-gun evidence of collusion before I left the government, and I still haven't. There is a lot of circumstantial evidence and reasons to be suspicious, but no smoking gun as of yet."[393] Under oath Clapper said "I never saw any direct empirical evidence that the Trump campaign or someone in it was plotting/conspiring with the Russians to meddle with the election." In June 2020, after declassifying the transcripts Richard Grenell called out lead hoaxer Rep Eric Swallwell and Democratic member of the House Intelligence Committee:

> I'm talking about how you lied to the American people over and over again. You said publicly you saw lots of Russian collusion. But the many Republicans and Democrats you questioned under oath all said they saw NO COLLUSION. You knew what they said in private. You lied.

Despite lacking the evidence to support their Trump-Russia collusion narrative, a chorus led by Hillary Clinton decided on a new strategy to publicly delegitimize the election result. Clapper articulated the Swamp's absurd thought process whilst promoting his book:

> speaking as a private citizen, having left government service and knowing what I know about what the Russians did, how massive the operation was, how diverse it was, and how many millions of American voters it touched. When you consider that the election turned on 80,000 votes or less in three key states, it stretches

[392] https://www.vox.com/2018/5/31/17384444/james-clapper-trump-russia-mueller-2016-election

[393] Sean Illing, "Former top spy James Clapper explains how Russia swung the election to Trump," *Vox* (May 18, 2017).

credulity to conclude that Russian activity didn't swing voter decisions, and therefore swing the election.[394]

A colluder was defined as anyone who said anything negative about the defeated candidate Hillary Clinton during the election. Clapper was grasping at straws in January 2017: "There were striking parallels between what the Trump campaign was saying and doing and what the Russians were saying and doing in the run up to the election. It's almost as though there was an echo chamber, particularly with respect to anything about Hillary Clinton."[395] The plotters had re-characterized the natural rough-and-tumble rhetoric of electoral politics as evidence of sinister traitorous crimes by the Trump campaign. Anyone who challenged this partisan conclusion was called out as being complicit in the conspiracy. It was the stuff of hysterical medieval witch trials, where the accused had to die to prove their innocence.

President Trump's opponents employed projection: "Don't look at me, look at him." After the election real moves were underway to remove an elected US president and the plotters pointed to their fake conspiracy to hide a coup underway in plain sight. The media were fed a feast of stories by the leaders of the intelligence community based on the fake "intelligence" of Steele and Halper.

At stake over many months were the votes of sixty-three million voters who exercised freedom of choice, legitimately electing a president. The survival of the whole system of democracy hung in the balance. If there is no acceptance of an election result and peaceful transfer of power, it is the end of the democratic process—a soft coup.

---

[394] Ibid.

[395] Ibid.

The "obstruction of justice" coup plot was born just after the election. First up, departing President Obama tried to persuade incoming President Trump not to appoint General Flynn as his National Security Advisor. It was, on the face of it, a dumb strategy Donald Trump was hardly going to take hiring decisions from a fierce political opponent.

According to reports leaked in 2017, Obama did not say a word to his successor about the FBI investigation into his campaign. Instead President Obama used his meeting in November 2016 at the White House to warn Donald Trump about Gen. Flynn's contacts with Russians. Those "contacts" were an oblique reference to the FBI counter-intelligence investigation underway against the General. The predicate for opening the investigation as Rep. Nunes stated was Halper's false report that Gen. Flynn had a Russian girlfriend. It is still hard to imagine how my innocuous email invitation for General Flynn to speak in Cambridge in 2015 or the proposal for my history book *The Spy Who Changed History* might have ended up being part of a warning passed between the two most powerful men in the world. Incoming President Trump was not buying what his predecessor Obama was selling. The campaign received no official warnings from the FBI about Russian intelligence contacting his campaign team. The gambit was of course that Donald Trump would not take the hiring advice; but if he ignored the warning, he could be smeared later as incompetent or complicit.

The next stage in the plot, as described in the previous chapter was to focus as much public and press attention as possible on Russia and on General Flynn. The lame duck administration became a hive of activity to make "Russia collusion" incoming President Trump's Achilles' heel. President Obama had weaponized the intelligence agencies against the President elect and Gen. Flynn with the Intelligence Community

Assessment and its damming conclusions based on dodgy "intelligence" from unverified sources.

Following a meeting on January 6, 2017 Gen. Flynn became Donald Trump's lead investigator into the Russia hoax. FBI Director Jim Comey, CIA Director John Brennan, DNI James Clapper, and head of the NSA Admiral Rogers presented the conclusions of the Intelligence Community Assessment to the incoming administration. The meeting turned inevitably to what was the evidence of "Russian collusion?"

Then FBI Director Jim Comey explained that based on their sources, Russian intelligence had twin files of compromising material on the presidential candidates. In an FBI memo on January 7, 2017, Jim Comey recorded that a "member of Trump's national security team" (Gen. Flynn) asked whether the FBI was "trying to dig into the sub sources" to get a better understanding of the situation. Comey replied "yes". [396] But in fact, the FBI hadn't verified the primary sub-source. It became clear to the plotters that the incoming President Trump's team would begin to push to find out all about the dodgy Steele dossier and the non existent sub-sources. As he would lead the charge, the plotters needed to remove Gen. Flynn from his position as National Security Advisor and in a hurry.

At the end of the meeting, Jim Comey took the President-elect to one side and "warned him" the press was likely to publish certain salacious allegation about him. In his warning Comey was prescient. On January 10, 2017, "Buzzfeed" published not just the scandalous parts but the whole Steele dossier.

"Passing the baton" to Gen. Flynn as the incoming National Security Advisor from Susan Rice was on January 10, 2017. According to Sydney Powell this was the day that Clapper ordered Ignatius of the

---

[396] IG Report page 180.

Washington Post using words "to the effect of" take the kill shot on Gen. Flynn.[397] To help Ignatius, Jim Baker who Powell describes as "Stefan Halper's handler" at the Office of Net Assessment might have leaked the details of the conversation with Kislyak to the *Washington Post* according to Powell.[398] Clapper had requested "unmasking" of Gen. Flynn on the day of the calls with Kislyak on December 28 and again on January 7, 2017. The FBI and Department of Justice tried desperately to characterize the conversation between Gen. Flynn and the Russian Ambassador as possibly illegal; maybe a violation of the ancient and unused Logan Act. It was not, as the Department of Justice always knew the Logan Act was a non-starter. No one has ever been prosecuted for an offense under the old Act.

David Ignatius of the *Washington Post* took "the kill shot" on Gen. Flynn on January 12, 2017. Ignatius revealed a massive classified security breach in his innocuous titled "Opinion" piece "Why did Obama dawdle on Russia's hacking?" Ignatius was briefed on the obscure Logan Act. Ignatius, the alleged CIA mouthpiece wrote:

> According to a senior US government official, Flynn phoned Russian Ambassador Sergey Kislyak several times on Dec. 29, the day the Obama administration announced the expulsion of 35 Russian officials as well as other measures in retaliation for the hacking. What did Flynn say, and did it undercut the US sanctions? The Logan Act (though never enforced) bars US citizens from correspondence intending to influence a foreign government about "disputes" with the United States. Was its spirit violated?

As a preamble, Ignatius had trotted out the usual Russia collusion conspiracy theories somehow pretending that a full investigation was

---

[397] Fox News https://www.youtube.com/watch?v=q1fAAsUDaBg

[398] ibid

required to find the truth. It was almost as if the Crossfire Hurricane investigation, which had found nothing after six months had never happened. No-one has yet been held to account for this outrageous and flagrant leak of classified information.

On January 13, 2017, three days after publication of the dodgy dossier, the FBI finally got around to interviewing Steele's primary sub-source. What the FBI learned at the meeting, and immediately suppressed confirmed what they already knew: the whole dossier was one big sham. The FBI worked hard to keep the fiction going that the dossier was real and the investigation must continue. It was now more urgent that ever that Gen. Flynn be removed.

Two days before the inauguration of Donald Trump as the forty-fifth President of the United States, Gen. Michael Flynn sat down in a Washington restaurant with a very hostile reporter from *The New Yorker*. Gen. Flynn began the meeting with: "What's the purpose of this thing?"[399]

Of course Russia was the subject. Gen. Flynn told the reporter, "We have to figure out how to work with Russia instead of making it an enemy. We have so many problems that we were handed on a plate from President Obama." He identified the negative attention on him as part of a larger plot against Donald Trump. "I'm a target to get at Trump to delegitimize the election," he said. The press had him "damn near all wrong." Reporters were just chasing after wild theories, while neglecting to consider his career as a decorated Army officer. "You don't just sprinkle magic dust on someone, and, *poof*, they become a three-star general," he said.[400]

---

[399] Nicholas Schmidle, *"Michael Flynn: General Chaos,"* New Yorker (February 18, 2017).

[400] https://www.newyorker.com/magazine/2017/02/27/michael-flynn-general-chaos

Just two days into his job as National Security Advisor Gen. Flynn was the victim of an ambush interview with the Crossfire Hurricane team from the FBI. The former FBI top brass Jim Comey and Andy McCabe organized the hit. Gen. Flynn believed he was helping his colleagues in the FBI to find the leakers of his highly classified and appropriate conversations with Russian Ambassador Kislyak. Instead the FBI and Mueller used the interview later as a pretext to bring criminal charges against the General. The Department of Justice has now reviewed the matter and withdrawn the prosecution. As we shall see later the former leadership of the FBI and the press were unrelenting in their efforts to have Gen. Flynn removed.

The "edited 302", the FBI record of the meeting is a frustrating document, one of the worst interrogation records I have seen. Although testimonial, it stands in court as a true account of the interrogation neither of the two FBI agents, Strzok and Pientka noted down the specific questions they asked. It would seem Gen. Flynn was quizzed about his relations with Russia following the familiar thread of the "Treasonous Path." Quite what an official meeting in Moscow in 2013 has to do with tracking down a leaker of a 2016 phone call cannot be explained. Gen. Flynn was seemingly asked did you have "contact with other Russians?" Given that the Crossfire team planned weeks earlier to end their ridiculous investigation into the man who was a guardian of the nation's top security secrets because they had found nothing derogatory what was the point of the interview? Of course, it was a planned trap to force his resignation and end the risk to the bigger plot to force out President Trump.

Gen. Flynn's eventual resignation only opened the door for further media attacks on the President. Senator John McCain, an anti-Trump Republican and the chairman of the Senate Armed Services Committee, said the Gen. Flynn fiasco was a "troubling indication of the dysfunction of the current national-security apparatus"[401] and raised further questions about President Trump's administration's intentions toward Russian President Vladimir Putin. Sen McCain had a central role in the laundering the Steele's dossier. Recently released Congressional testimony revealed that Senator John McCain's emissary David Kramer travelled to meet Christopher Steele in the United Kingdom at the end of November 2016. In addition, Steele passed on a malicious lie that General Flynn was having an extra marital affair with a Russia woman living in the United Kingdom. Just where could Steele acquire that nugget? You need look no further that Stefan Halper, its fabricator. Senator McCain passed the dossier and no doubt the lie to the Director of the FBI James Comey.

The press attacks on Gen. Flynn came thick and fast sourced from some ex-colleagues. The vitriol stemmed from one election campaign event when, twenty minutes into the speech, Gen. Flynn mentioned Hillary Clinton, the convention audience responded with chants of "Lock her up!" Gen. Flynn nodded, and said: "That's right—lock her up." He went on, "Damn right. . . . And you know why we're saying that? We're saying that because, if I, a guy who knows this business, if I did a tenth—a tenth—of what she did, I would be in jail today."[402] The convention speech was the reason Gen. Flynn was inserted into the dodgy dossier as Steele told Luke Harding:

> His speech was a piece of hubris that would haunt Flynn in the months to come—an invitation, practically, to the gods to strike him down for his folly, self-ignorance, and foolish pride. The mood inside the hall was frenzied. "We do not need a reckless president who believes she is above the law," Flynn told delegates. They broke

---

[401] KCUR of NPR (February 14, 2017), https://www.kcur.org/2017-02-14/flynn-may-be-called-to-testify-before-senate-intelligence-committee

[402] https://www.realclearpolitics.com/video/2017/12/01/flashback_aug_2016__flynn_if_i_did_a_tenth_of_what_clinton_did_i_would_be_in_jail.html

into chants of: "Lock … her … up!" Flynn looked stern, nodded, and said: "Lock her up, that's right!" Clinton's use of a private email server meant she was a threat to the "nation's security," Flynn told the crowd, to further cries of "Lock her up!" He went on: "Damn right, exactly right, there's nothing wrong with that…. And you know why we're saying that? We're saying that because if I, a guy who knows this business, if I did a tenth, a tenth, of what she did, I would be in jail today. "So, crooked Hillary Clinton, leave this race now!" Even by the standards of the 2016 contest, this was a defining low—an inglorious and squalid attack from a man who, unbeknown to Republican supporters and the American voters, was actually on Moscow's payroll.[403]

One of the great lies in the post election *New Yorker* hit piece is this:

> Several months after General Flynn returned from his Moscow trip, he hoped to reciprocate by inviting several senior G.R.U. officers to the United States. Clapper, the director of national intelligence, cautioned him against it. Russia had recently annexed Crimea, and Russian special-forces operatives were fomenting a violent clash between rebels and Ukrainian troops in eastern Ukraine.[404]

His ex-boss and sworn enemy James Clapper, in briefings, was pressing hard against Gen. Flynn to suggest he was a Russian puppet. The invitation to the GRU leadership was issued months before the trouble in Ukraine. Clapper was implying Gen. Flynn was in the pocket of Russia to add fuel to the fire of negative press attention.

If General Flynn had remained the National Security Advisor, the Russia hoax would have been exposed in early 2017. Multiple witnesses have told Congress that a week before Donald Trump's inauguration in January 2017, Britain's top national security official sent a private communique to Gen. Flynn, addressing his country's

---

[403] Luke Harding Collusion

[404] "General Chaos," *New Yorker* (February 18, 2017).

participation in the counterintelligence probe into the now-debunked Trump-Russia election collusion and the new National Security Advisor. The then British National Security Adviser Sir Mark Lyall Grant stated in the memo, hand-delivered to incoming US National Security Adviser Gen. Flynn's team, that the British government lacked confidence in the credibility of former MI6 spy Christopher Steele's Russia collusion intelligence. The Steele dossier and his information about the affair depended on the credibility of its alleged author and his former employer was scathing. The British authorities dammed the FBI's informers and undercut all the poisonous media stories written by compliant journalists briefed on Steele and Halper's lies.

Chapter Eighteen: Media Storm

For there is nothing hid, which

shall not be manifested; neither was anything kept secret, but that it should come abroad.

—Mark 4:22

A nation of sheep will beget a government of wolves.

— Edward R. Murrow

I was recovering slowly from childbirth when the fierce media storm broke over me in February 2017. I start my Spygate suffering clock on February 28, 2017. It was three years exactly from the event where I met General Flynn for the only time. It is over three years and counting since the misery began. There is seemingly no end in sight.

In September 2016, I was thrilled to win publishing contracts with the large US publisher Norton and Harper Collins in the UK for my history book, *The Spy Who Changed History.* I was juggling to deal with a newborn and writing in brief spurts to a fast-approaching deadline for my first ever book. Nothing in my life before prepared me for the terrible events that were about to happen. I was not following the news as I was living life in an exhausted blur.

Looking back on the events in 2016, I was told Halper formed a clique in Cambridge who was talking hurtful trash about me and others around the university. I thought little of it at the time and was told to ignore the old men who were just fighting amongst themselves. I did not know, nor could have known these evil old men were part of an intelligence operation ordered from on high targeting the US election.

The outsiders who entered the rough and tumble of American politics in 2016 underestimated how vicious it was going to be. Making the centerpiece of a political campaign attacking the Washington swamp was always taking the fight to the enemy on their own ground. Donald Trump and Gen. Flynn entered the battle to roll back a system seen as corrupt in the very belly of the beast. Even President Trump expresses surprise at how evil his opponent is. The Swamp made the rules of the Washington political game and has the tools spread across the branches of government fights tenaciously. The Swamp sees Donald Trump as a difficult phase, and his time will pass. Whilst he is in the Oval Office, the Deep State will resist.

I had no choice, nor did my family to be involved in Spygate. I was left with no other option but to fight once my identity was stolen by Stefan Halper and his masters for their perfidious purposes. I was the first to know Spygate was a hoax. When the accusations began, I knew I was not a Russian spy or Gen. Flynn's lover. I never worked for Russian intelligence. I thought if someone is using the ravings of a loopy old man to go after Gen. Flynn, then there was something terrible going on. My struggle was to get my message out and to clear my name. I want a normal life for my family.

I went into hiding when my picture was plastered all over the front pages attached to the most scandalous stories. I was forced from my home by the overzealous attention of reporters banging unceasingly on my door. I was forced into hiding with my baby. For months I hid in England until she was big enough to flee abroad. For three years, she has known no peace, no permanent home. We have traveled the globe hoping one day the nightmare will end. I pray one day everyone will wake up and see the truth. We crave a normal life.

Why did Halper pick on me? Halper was inventing "Russia Collusion" to attack Donald Trump. I was the only woman at the dinner when Gen. Flynn visited Cambridge and I had been born in Moscow.

Between February 28 and March 4, 2017, as part of what was a coordinated operation, I was approached by three major "liberal" US media outlets. The team from the *Wall Street Journal* was led by Carol Lee, Chief White House Correspondent, and Russia collusion truth master Shane Harris. The *New York Times* rolled out Security Correspondents Matthew Rosenberg, and chief among Gen. Flynn haters, Adam Goldman. The *Washington Post* deployed the CIA's very own "kill shot" through character assassination David Ignatius. In the UK, Christopher Steele's ally, the *Guardian*'s Luke Harding, was given the story.

Wall Street Journal

The attack on Gen. Flynn was so important that the extremely connected White House Correspondent for the *Wall Street Journal*, Carol Lee, lead the charge on an untrue article in March 2017. The article was a vital component of the ongoing coup attempts. The storm the *Wall Street Journal* unleashed on me was deliberate and a small part of a much bigger plan.

Working alongside Lee was Shane Harris, a propaganda mouthpiece for the agencies, the pair came to be in touch with Stefan Halper. The introduction was either direct or via Fusion GPS who has close connections to the *WSJ*.

Matt Rosenberg of the *New York Times* confirmed to me Stefan Halper approached US media outlets with various stories about me in December 2015. In Halper's evil tales, Gen. Flynn may have been compromised by Russian intelligence whilst visiting Cambridge in 2014. Halper falsely stated that he witnessed this author, a supposed Russian spy approach Gen. Flynn at a conference, sit next to him at a dinner, and that the two embarked on an affair. Halper said the approach might have been successful, falsely claiming that Gen. Flynn failed to report the contact with me

Halper was not a witness, as he was not even at the event, yet reported he was to the FBI. Halper added that I organized Gen. Flynn's trip to Moscow for the Russia Today gala. As a final twist he said that I was connected to an alleged hacker, Guccifer 2. The tales were all lies. Halper was able to provide my name and my email address to the journalists. Stefan Halper wanted to remain hidden as an anonymous source for these stories.

This was a planned hit on Gen. Flynn. The alleged events were supposed to have occurred in 2014. The so-called investigative journalists were not the slightest bit concerned about the gaping holes in their source's mendacious story. The fact that no security agency had taken any action against General Flynn for being supposedly compromised by Russian intelligence caused them no issues. This is surprising for the crack national security team at the *WSJ* knew Gen. Flynn was privy to all America's top secrets. Further, the newspaper was unable to find a second source to back up even the simplest of Halper's false assertions. The *Wall Street Journal* article even makes it clear the Defense Intelligence Agency officer present at the dinner dismissed the whole story. It is a deeply damaging story that is unsupported by any evidence, so why did the Wall Street Journal publish it?

The chronology leading to publication is that on February 28, 2017, and again on March 1, 2017, reporters from the *Wall Street Journal* contacted me by email desperate to discuss "my relationship" with General Flynn. At the time, I was in bed looking after my four-week-old newborn while very ill. I have not had a "relationship" with General Flynn. I met the General once at a pre-approved event three years before.

The *Wall Street Journal* "journalists" put the damaging allegation to senior academics at Cambridge that your author and General Flynn had an affair. The *Wall Street Journal* was informed all the accusations were untrue and they knew it. With every reason to doubt Halper's veracity, the *Journal* still published Halper's false story.

Early on the morning of March 1, 2017, I got a strange email from Professor Andrew telling me the *Wall Street Journal* was contacting members of the University of Cambridge regarding "outrageous" allegations about me and others. Andrew emailed me as follows:

> Dear Svetlana, Neil [Kent] rang me this morning and has probably briefed you by now about WSJ. Because I refused to speak to them when they rang, I had no idea they were following such an outrageous story. Understandable, perhaps if Neil is right about the source, but nonetheless appalling best wishes Chris.

I called Andrew at his home in Cambridge, but he claimed to be so distressed he refused to speak to me. Andrew was not upset for me but for himself. Andrew was not silent for too long. His spirits rallied and he recovered quickly and sent me another bizarre email later that day. It stated:

Dear Svetlana, I've been contacted by WSJ and refused all comment. David Ignatius of Washington Post is in the UK at moment. I've known him for years and trust him. I've given him your email, and he accepts that if you don't wish to respond, that's an end to it. I've told him you've signed a US contract for a blockbuster and that this will later be a big story for him. He trusts my judgment on that! Flynn's career for years past is obviously going to continue to be investigated. David has an inside track on that which I think he'd share with you if you're interested.

I called Professor Kent later that morning and what he told me about his conversation with the *Wall Street Journal* was so shocking I had to get him to repeat it twice. Before speaking to me, the *WSJ* called Kent on his mobile phone. He told me he was at a noisy dinner and could not really hear the questions being put to him.

The journalists were looking for someone to put a name to the story. It is an old trick. The journalists put a number of Halper's statements to him as part of a pre-packaged article and asked him to stand them up. They started off innocuously with "Were you at the dinner with General Flynn in 2014?" "Was Svetlana Lokhova there?" "Is she Russian?"

Professor Kent was next told a series of lies Halper had concocted. Could Kent confirm what the *Wall Street Journal* had been told that I approached Gen. Flynn at the start of the dinner; that I sat next to Gen. Flynn; that I left with Gen. Flynn and finally that I had an "inappropriate relationship with Gen. Flynn. Professor Kent exploded at them and said the whole story was nonsense. He told me the *Wall Street Journal* were accusing me of being a modern-day Mata Hari, the legendary seductress executed as a German spy by the French during the First World War. I immediately contacted a lawyer, and we prepared a statement to issue to the *Wall Street Journal*.

On March 1, 2017, I received an email from the *WSJ*, which stated "I'm a reporter at the Wall Street Journal and am researching a story that will likely mention your relationship with . . . Gen. Michael Flynn."

I had no relationship with Gen. Flynn so, my partner issued a flat denial to the *Wall Street Journal* inquiry as follows:

> I am writing on behalf of my long-term partner Svetlana Lokhova. Ms. Lokhova is currently unwell, and your inquiries have made that condition worse. She is recovering from the recent birth of our daughter. Your baseless allegations have been relaid [sic] to me by two third parties whom you have seen fit to contact. The allegations are deeply upsetting and hurtful to Ms. Lokhova and our family. The underlying assumptions behind the allegations are preposterous. Having discussed this matter with Ms. Lokhova, I can assure you that they are without any foundation. Further, it is likely that your source is acting maliciously in inventing these falsehoods.
>
> Re. General Flynn
>
> Ms. Lokhova has met General Flynn on only one occasion at a dinner in Cambridge in February 2014. The dinner was attended by upwards of a dozen people, and she had a twenty-minute public conversation with General Flynn and others. They have not met or spoke since then...
>
> The *WSJ* butchered my total denial of their false Halper based allegations printing only the parts that suited them in the article. The level of detail I provided in my statement did not fit their prepackaged story. I forwarded the identical statement to David Ignatius at the *Washington Post*. Ignatius thanked me and later represented that he had no interest in publishing anything, as there was nothing to publish.

Despite my hopes to the contrary on March 17, 2017, the *WSJ* published an article written by Carol E. Lee, Rob Barry, Shane Harris, and Christopher S. Stewart, titled *"Mike Flynn Didn't Report 2014 Interaction with Russian-British National."* The sources of the *WSJ* article were, of course, Stefan Halper, shrouded in various anonymous guises and Christopher Andrew.

The gist of the *Wall Street Journal* article was I engaged in unlawful or suspicious interactions with General Flynn on behalf of the Russian government that should have been reported to the Defense Intelligence Agency. The article implied I had attempted to recruit Gen. Flynn on behalf of Russian intelligence. The *WSJ* article is intentionally laden with falsehoods in order to support Stefan Halper's preconceived fake narrative. The article referred to the February 2014 dinner as a "UK security conference."[405] It was not; it was a work dinner. The article stated that General Flynn's contact with me at the Cambridge dinner "came to the notice of US intelligence" showing it was a leak of highly classified information from a live Criminal investigation.[406] This has not been investigated. Halper fabricated his allegations in August 2016 years after the dinner he did not attend. The article falsely stated I was a "foreign stranger," when in fact I am a citizen of the United Kingdom.

Moreover, my name, the fact I was invited to the dinner by the spymaster Dearlove, and I would show my research were all pre-reported to the Defense Intelligence Agency. The article falsely insinuated and implied General Flynn and I engaged in "anomalous behavior" and there were inappropriate interactions between us.

The *WSJ* article also falsely stated I had worked for "Russia's state-controlled Sberbank" and had been leaked that the "contact" between General Flynn and me at the February 2014 dinner might be the subject of the FBI's "wide-ranging counterintelligence probe into any

---

[405] "Mike Flynn Didn't Report 2014 Interaction With Russian-British National," *WSJ* (March 18. 2017), https://www.wsj.com/articles/mike-flynn-didnt-report-2014-interaction-with-russian-british-national-1489809842

[406] Ibid.

contacts Trump campaign personnel may have had with Russian officials."

The *Wall Street Journal* article further falsely implies I had an ulterior motive in attending the dinner and I "approached Mr. Flynn at the start" (untrue) and "sat next" to him (false) with a view to gathering information from him on behalf of the Russian government. The article portrays me and my behavior as so suspicious it leaves the reader with no doubt I was an agent of an "adversarial power": Russia. The *WSJ* article was republished thousands of times on Twitter. It was instantly and universally understood to imply that General Flynn and I had engaged in wrongdoing.

On March 17, 2017, Bill Palmer, author of the *Palmer Report*, republished the *Journal*'s false statements in an online article titled "Exposed: Michael Flynn has been secretly meeting with Russians since his time at the DIA." Palmer stated "the Wall Street Journal is now reporting that Flynn's pattern of covertly meeting with Russians dates back to his final days at the Defense Intelligence Agency before he was fired." Palmer captured the defamatory implication—the gist— of the *WSJ* article:

> Flynn met with a young Russian woman named Svetlana Lokhova while at a conference in the United Kingdom in 2014. If this Russian woman came out of nowhere and approached Flynn, then he would have been expected and required to report the encounter when he got home. These are the kinds of tactics often used by foreign spies and are therefore reported and tracked—particularly when it involves the head of the DIA. But instead, there is no record that Flynn reported the meeting, thus suggesting that the meeting involved something on Flynn's part that he didn't want the US government knowing about.
>
> This raises several questions. Was this Russian woman (source: Wall Street Journal) sent to this UK conference to recruit Michael Flynn for the Kremlin?

On March 19, 2017 Professor Kent emailed the *WSJ* to correct the grave errors of their article falsely attributed to him. Kent stated as follows:

> Rob, hi! I have just had an opportunity to look at a photo which was taken by someone at the dinner with Mike, but which is under Chatham House rules and therefore I cannot forward it. It clearly shows that Peter Martland sat on Mike's right hand and that Christopher Andrew sat on his left. I was on the far-left corner, so didn't really take this on board. However, one would have expected that the two principal conveners of the seminars would have sat on either side. The dinner was a formal dinner with assigned seating, so it would have been impossible for Ms. Lokhova to have approached him. Moreover, I should add that to the best of my knowledge, she is a British national of Russian origin. I would assume that *everyone who attended that dinner was clearly acceptable to Sir Richard Dearlove and posed no security risk; otherwise, they would not have been allowed to attend.* Finally, to repeat what I said in our telephone call, the innuendo that you suggested that Ms. Lokhova might have had some "inappropriate" contact with Chris, Mike, or Sir Richard is not only shocking to me but preposterous! But why you came to me as a third party on the end of the table, who cannot even remember where Ms. Lokhova sat, I still can't quite understand. Anyway, I hope this clears up any loose ends. It would be great if you could amend your article to reflect this.[407]

In spite of repeated requests to retract or correct the *WSJ* article, they refused (and still refuse) to take any action to mitigate the damage caused to me. In various, and sometimes animated conversations, the *WSJ* claimed they were only out to get Gen. Flynn and claimed not to understand why I was upset for being libeled and defamed as collateral

---

[407] Email from Neil Kent to Wall Street Journal.

damage. When it was pointed out that their readers in the comment section were naming me as a spy, the reply was their readers were "idiots;" especially those who post comments on their articles.

Christopher Andrew's Article in the *Sunday Times*

When reading the *Wall Street Journal* I discovered Christopher Andrew had authored a false article about Gen. Flynn featuring me for the *Sunday Times*. It was a huge unforgivable act of betrayal on his part. "It is easier to forgive an enemy than to forgive a friend" said William Blake.

I had known Professor Andrew since I was eighteen and first arrived in the United Kingdom. I started a new life in a new country escaping from the collapsing Russian economy and the ensuing chaos. Chris was more than a mentor for my academic career. He was a man I greatly admired both intellectually and because he was a Christian. I knew not only him but his large extended family. As he grew older and his health declined, I used to watch out for him. His betrayal of me was absolute.

On February 13, 2017, General Flynn resigned as National Security Advisor. Stefan Halper and the FBI saw General Flynn's resignation as the catalyst and opportunity to accelerate their defamatory campaign and solidify the belief that "Russian collusion" was real to get at President Trump. Halper had seemingly enlisted Christopher Andrew and Richard Dearlove in his scheme to defame General Flynn and me. On February 19, 2017, Andrew published his article in *The Sunday Times* of London, titled *"Impulsive General Misha shoots himself in the Foot."* The article did not mention me by name but ensured enough details were included to ensure I was easily identifiable. I later discovered Andrew claimed that he had even provided my name and email address to the *Sunday Times* in case they wanted to contact me for "comment". I never heard from *the Sunday Times*.

Christopher Andrew included many lies about me and General Flynn and the article was deliberately laden with sexual innuendo including that I showed Gen. Flynn an "erotic postcard" and that the General was "especially struck" by me. Utterly untrue. Andrew falsely stated General Flynn asked me to travel with him as a translator to Moscow on his next official visit and General Flynn signed an email to me as "General Misha." It was a placeholder for future articles and a false "witness" account.

Halper and Andrew knew the statements in the article were false. Neither of these men ever heard General Flynn ask me to travel with him to Moscow as a translator or otherwise. General Flynn never invited me, nor am I a translator, and I am sure the DIA have their own translators. Moreover, Andrew was copied on my email communications with Gen. Flynn. Gen. Flynn never signed a single email, "General Misha."

Halper and Andrew emphasized the phraseology "General Misha" (the diminutive of Mikail the equivalent of Mike) because they knew these words would receive international attention from the media and users of social media. The words were sexy and unforgettable. The co-conspirators knew the words implied and would be immediately understood to mean there was an intimate relationship between Gen. Flynn and myself. Indeed, the defamatory phrase "General Misha" Andrew invented has been repeated millions of times and lives in infamy on the internet.

Andrew refused, and still refuses, to correct his article. I have approached him directly and via mutual friends many times. His friends say his refusal to withdraw the article is the vanity of an old man who will not admit to any error. He later falsely claimed the article was written to head off "fake news" stories. I assume what he is referring to is that he was blackmailed or compromised into writing the article. In truth, Andrew wrote the article and published in concert with Halper as part of the conspiracy to defame and smear me and promote, underpin, and support those stories that would advance the coup in progress.

The *Washington Post*

Here is how the fake news masters *Washington Post* came into my life. On March 1, 2017, the same day the *Wall Street Journal* was accusing me behind my back to my University colleagues of having an affair with Flynn, the legendary *Washington Post* columnist David Ignatius emailed me out of the blue. At that point, I had never heard of David Ignatius. But for some reason Andrew, who I now understand is a friend of David Ignatius, gave him my personal email address and pushed hard that I speak to the journalist. The pair had discussed Gen. Flynn and me as Andrew's email reproduced above shows. Andrew knew all about Ignatius' role in bringing down Gen. Flynn, the "inside track." This was the same professor who was so ill earlier that morning and distressed he could not come to the phone to speak to me. The carrot for me to dish dirt on Gen. Flynn to the *Washington Post* was the idea that Ignatius would promote my book! It transpired that Ignatius flew to England in early March 2017 to "investigate" the fake story about Gen. Flynn with Andrew. Here is the email setup:

> At the suggestion of my friend Christopher Andrew, I am writing to ask if you would be willing to talk with me about Mike Flynn. A bit of background about me: I am a foreign affairs columnist for The

Washington Post. I also have a longstanding interest in intelligence issues, have written ten spy novels, and in this role was invited by Christopher to speak to his seminar a dozen years ago, where I met a lot of smart graduate students, a group in which Christopher says you're one of his best students ever. I promised Christopher that I would tell you that if you decide you don't want to comment, that's fine, and I will so note. But if you'd be willing to chat, I will be careful and accurate. I'm in London Wednesday but fly back to D.C. Weds afternoon at 4.20 from LHR. I could come to Cambridge Weds am, or talk on the phone if you're somewhere else.

David Ignatius. The Washington Post

I had no idea about David Ignatius's pivotal role in bringing down General Flynn. I was surprised by the approach, as Andrew knew, given I was nursing a newborn, was not sleeping and had no interest in events outside my own small world. But given it was a second approach from a US newspaper on the same day, I was now highly suspicious. My partner had issued a statement on my behalf, which is a flat denial of any inappropriate relationship with General Mike Flynn. I sent that to Ignatius. He responded, saying he understood.

I suspect he was disappointed because I think he was angling for a "no comment" response. But he published nothing as he told me later, he interviewed other "witnesses" who were at the Gen. Flynn dinner and found the story to be a dud. More likely, as we shall see later, he was called off as Brennan's testimony to Congress was postponed. David Ignatius is not just a friend of Christopher Andrew, he has known Halper for forty years and clearly knows Dearlove. In later articles he quotes Dearlove. Readers will recall Dearlove famously claims he does not talk to the press.

After the *Wall Street Journal* published their story, it was followed with an article by "collusion hoaxer" Luke Harding from the

Guardian. I got back in contact with David Ignatius to ask if he was planning to publish anything. He said no as there is nothing to the story and if anyone else from the press contacted me, I was to say he, David Ignatius, investigated the claims and found them false.

Roll forward to May 22, 2018, when Halper was exposed as the key FBI operative by the press. Ignatius of the *Washington Post* suddenly wrote me an email, "I'd like very much to ask you about Stefan Halper." Ignatius's sudden interest in discussing Halper with me is very interesting. Ignatius is closely aligned with the CIA and some like to joke he has his own parking spot at their HQ. I suspect the Ignatius's interest was self-preservation. He had already traveled once to England in March 2017 to follow up on the fake story from Christopher Andrew. I imagine he wanted to find out in advance what I might say as he knew I was an eyewitness to Halper's activities.

We spoke briefly on the phone while he was at an airport. I caught him off-guard with a direct question: "So how did he know Stefan Halper was a spy?" To which he said, "I always found him very reliable." Then he abruptly hung up and we have not spoken since.

Ignatius was part of an exhaustive full cover press operation to protect Halper and diminish his role. Ignatius and others from the *Washington Post* wrote a series of defensive articles and made television appearances on the likes of NBC before and after Halper was exposed. Ignatius described Halper correctly as a "middleman" in the spy game; but also said he was not James Bond and falsely described Halper as "a gossipy Professor".[408]

---

[408] David Ignatius, *"How the Trump echo chamber pushes bit players like Stefan Halper to center stage,"* Washington Post (May 22, 2018).

Ignatius confirmed in his article that Halper is the source of what Rep. Devin Nunes describes as RUMINT (rumor intelligence). Ignatius desperately tried to downplay Halper's product to the level of idle tittle-tattle, neglecting to say the Pentagon paid him almost a million dollars for what Ignatius would have you believe is inconsequential. This was in fact the "intelligence" Halper was paid to provide the FBI to open a counterintelligence investigation into Gen. Flynn.

Through Ignatius the CIA-approved mouthpiece Halper was not a super spy. Halper has the "role of would-be influencers,"[409] which of course is exactly what Ignatius is. Through Ignatius the CIA would have you believe there is nothing to see here as Halper is unimportant. These influencers "start off as connectors and facilitators, but gradually (and implausibly) they move to the center of the story." This is Ignatius's finest work: Halper is "the mouse that roared"![410]

David Ignatius conceals from his readers that he has been connected to Halper for four decades and uses him as a source—a relationship that maybe started when he received a cash prize from Halper in 1981.[411] There is no mention in his article of him flying to Cambridge on a fool's errand in 2017 to publicize Halper's "gossip." Ignatius wrote:

> Those who know Halper describe someone closer to a gregarious busybody and academic eccentric—an intellectual who jostles for first billing on a book cover—than a mole burrowing toward Trump's inner circle. Like many underemployed ex-professors, he likes to gossip and perhaps that made him a good intelligence source.[412]

David Ignatius pivots and projects the blame onto the president:

---

[409] Ibid.

[410] Ibid.

[411] CIA.com

[412] Ignatius, *Washington Post* (May 22, 2018).

It's outrageous that Trump has encouraged "outing" this putative intelligence source [Halper]. And this latest attempt to deflect special counsel Robert S. Mueller III's investigation only adds to suspicion that Trump has something very big to hide.[413]

And could it be Dearlove in feint disguise using his favorite words *disconcerting contacts* or is it perhaps Halper's fellow informer Christopher Steele quoted by Ignatius here? "A former British intelligence officer who knows Halper well describes him as "an intensely loyal and trusted US citizen [who was] asked by the Bureau to look into some 'disconcerting contacts' between Russians and Americans."[414]

The *Guardian* Article

I learned from a mutual friend that Luke Harding, *Guardian* journalist began stalking Christopher Andrew at the start of March because my friend saw the unlikely pair huddled together in deep conversation. Chris kept from me any mention of this approach from the notorious conspiracy theorist Luke Harding and his subsequent discussions before the article was published.

Harding makes a good living, like many others, working on the fringes of the intelligence world, in particular selling four books of poorly researched and generally untruthful scare stories. Harding has a history of embarrassing himself and his employer, *The Guardian*, with a succession of fake Spygate stories. His most infamous scoop about GCHQ the British NSA was seemingly based on CIA leaks, are being

---

[413] ibid

[414] Ibid.

probed by Senator Chuck Grassley. Harding falsely accused Paul Manafort of meeting Julian Assange in the Ecuadorian Embassy in London.

At the same time as the other approaches, on March 4, 2017 Harding showed up at a meeting of the highly respected Study Group on Intelligence at the Royal United Services Institute based in Whitehall, London. The building is close to 10 Downing Street and the Houses of Parliament. I was not there because I had just given birth. Harding approached Christopher Andrew who was a speaker that day. Their conversation was overheard by numerous witnesses. Harding was loudly claiming there was collusion between Donald Trump and Russia, and he and Andrew publicly discussed me.

Andrew bizarrely invited the conspiracy theorist Harding to speak at the Cambridge Intelligence Seminar and the episode appears in Harding's crazy book "Collusion." Chris keeps conspiracy theorists away from his seminar. It is not clear to me why he thought inviting Luke Harding to showcase wild theories to a serious Cambridge group was a good idea. It is especially odd as the two corresponded angrily over email about Halper's fake stories about Gen. Flynn and myself. Andrew told Luke Harding he was a conspiracy theorist.

On March 4, Harding put a range of patently false accusations about me to Andrew based on Halper's lies: Harding said I had an affair with President Trump's ex-National Security Advisor General Flynn, I was a member of Russian intelligence, my research came from the GRU on the orders of Putin and I worked for the Russian state. To protect himself, Andrew sent me an extract from emails where he attempts to debunk the claims:

. . . in fairness to Svetlana Lokhova, please draw to his (Nick Hopkins, his colleague) attention the two important sources which we have discussed, and he appears to have neglected.

Your knowledge of Russian history enables you to see the brilliant originality of SL's reinterpretation of the origin of the Terror (see her chapter in Andrew and Tobia) and why it is entirely natural and not in the least sinister for others interested in the Stalin era to engage in email correspondence with her. The chapter, which identifies all its sources, also helps dispose of the conspiracy theories of "privileged access" which you mentioned to me. Nick tells me that, in addition to emails, she continued to "have contact" with Flynn after the Cambridge seminar. SL has confirmed that she did not. Nick has had phone conversations with her partner David North. They have been an inseparable couple since before the Flynn seminar, and I trust that they will have the opportunity in Nick's article to explain that SL had no further non-email contact with Flynn after his visit....This material is quite sufficient to dispose of conspiracy theories about SL somehow serving some Russian interest.

Luke Harding has never approached me. let alone pitched any of these vile accusations directly. Eventually, Harding's sidekick and *Guardian* writer Nick Hopkins, contacted me by email. One of the bizarre antics of all the Spygate journalists is to pretend they know nothing about the subject when they contact their target. In reality they have written a string of stories with bias. In the case of Hopkins, he wrote fiercely pro-Christopher Steele pieces in his paper for months. The "journalists" must believe you are too dumb to research them and know their tricks. They have no interest in listening to the truth as they are working on the next article in a pre-pack chain of stories. They pretend to offer an opportunity to tell your side of the story. On March 22, 2017, I received the following email from *Guardian* reporter Nick Hopkins:

We are researching a story about General Michael Flynn and the circumstances that led to his appointment as President Trump's NSA last November, and the concerns this appeared to generate within the American intelligence community. As you know, the Wall Street Journal published a story a few days ago which named you as someone who had contact with General Flynn in 2014. At the time, General Flynn was head of the DIA. An extremely sensitive post. The WSJ reported that General Flynn did not report your meeting to the Defense Department, which the WSJ suggested was unusual, as you were—and remain—an expert on Russian intelligence, and he was, primarily, America's "top spy" . . . Our story intends to reflect the meeting in Cambridge, which, we understand, was being discussed by American and British intelligence officials in the period just before General Flynn's appointment. We understand this was one of a number of episodes US officials were assessing to determine what they suggested, if anything, about General Flynn's suitability for such a security-sensitive position. General Flynn's spokesman has told us that the meeting with you in 2014 was "incidental" and nothing more.

His email went on to say:

I wanted to give you an opportunity to give an on the record comment about the story in the WSJ, and also to address the nature and longevity of your connection with General Flynn, which appears to have raised questions, perhaps entirely unfairly, about his suitability for the NSA post.

Earlier the same day, without telling me Hopkins emailed Professor Christopher Andrew as follows:

We have been told, by multiple sources, both here and in the US, that American intelligence officials were fretting about General Flynn ahead of his appointment as NSA. These concerns were based on his alleged behaviors in the previous two years, which included his trips to Russia. Their fears, whether they were justified or not, also included an assessment of his connection to a woman named by the WSJ as Svetlana Lokhova . . . We have other material that suggests the meeting in Cambridge was the start, not the end, of their correspondence. Your own piece in the Sunday Times suggested a connection which endured beyond the seminar, and to the casual reader (as I was at the time), a naive behavior rather unbecoming and of the head of the DIA. You have told Luke—quite forcefully, I understand—that we would be quite wrong to suggest that anything untoward happened in Cambridge. Nor will we. But we do intend to set out the broad fears of US intelligence officials and explain why they were as concerned as they seemed to be, even if these anxieties might have been misplaced.

As can be seen from his email, Hopkins never put Luke Harding's crazy allegations to me; they simply printed the crazy allegations. Hopkins was asking a British historian - me, who had met General Flynn once at an academic dinner three years prior "to address the nature and longevity of your connection with General Flynn, which appears to have raised questions about his suitability for the NSA post."

My partner rang Nick Hopkins and pointed out I was on the verge of litigating, unless they took down their article, with the *Wall Street Journal* and not to repeat the libels. Hopkins got cross when the conversation did not go in the direction he wanted.

Appropriately on April Fool's Day, April 1, 2017, *The Guardian* printed a front-page story in the UK that US and UK spy chiefs had fears over Gen. Flynn's appointment. The article began with the false and defamatory statement, "US and UK officials were troubled by Moscow contacts and encounter with woman linked to Russian spy agency records" and proceeded to name me. The false and outrageous allegation that was already debunked was never put to me. *The*

Guardian knew the premise for the story was false after they communicated with Christopher Andrew.

This front-page story by *The Guardian* generated enormous publicity, with other newspapers reprinting it, and posting my photograph. I became the subject of a sustained and nasty media harassment campaign, which included journalists knocking on my and my neighbors' doors. I had to flee. There was massive danger to my safety and it was totally irresponsible of *The Guardian* to effectively name me as a Russian spy and a traitor.

I received credible death threats and the police became involved. Luke Harding knew the likely consequences of printing his story and did not care. I had to go into hiding with my two-month-old child for the next several years. Halper appears several times in the Luke Harding article as a "source close to US intelligence" and one of "multiple sources, who spoke on the condition of anonymity", who said the CIA and FBI were discussing this episode, along with many others, as they assessed Flynn's suitability to serve as National Security Adviser."[415]

Harding is one of the leading proponents of the failed "Russian Collusion" narrative. Famously Sen. Diane Feinstein read parts of his fake article based on "weird and incorrect leaks" into Congressional testimony and asked Clapper if was true. Despite his claims to the contrary, he is a long-term collaborator with Christopher Steele, the compiler of the wholly fake and discredited "Steele dossier."

As previously mentioned, later in November 2017, Luke Harding published a long book called *Collusion* working with Christopher Steele. An entire chapter of Harding's book is devoted to Gen. Flynn titled "General Misha." Harding was apparently paid $700,000 in book

---

[415] https://www.theguardian.com/us-news/2017/mar/31/michael-flynn-new-evidence-spy-chiefs-had-concerns-about-russian-ties

advances and foreign rights to produce a breathless apology for the discredited Christopher Steele according to a well informed source in the publishing industry. The ever-delusional Harding paints a picture of Steele as a super-spy.

It is no coincidence Halper used the "agency" friend Harding and *The Guardian* as catalysts to promote and amplify the false and defamatory statements about me, General Flynn, and by this stage the disproven "collusion" between the Trump campaign and Russia. Could there be a dark web of close connections between, Stefan Halper, Christopher Steele, Richard Dearlove and Luke Harding? Dearlove has never stepped forward to publicly deny any of the false allegations made about me.

Harding, in turn, is networked into the collusion truthers social media channels and in particular the outrageous Louise Mensch.[416] The plan was that this social media network would amplify and distribute the story. Mensch was also anxiously tweeting with WSJ journalist Rob Barrie about the details of their false story on Gen. Flynn.[417]

When I was once booked to appear at a literary festival at Henley, a genteel town on the River Thames, Harding, it transpired, was the next author on stage after me. Fearless Luke was so scared of meeting me in the flesh he confessed to a local reporter he was hiding.[418] This is the man who has made a fortune boasting of his battles with Putin's fearsome security services. I think we have the measure of Luke Harding.

---

[416] Tweets in possession of the author.

[417] ibid

[418] https://www.henleystandard.co.uk/news/henley-on-thames/131491/awkwardness-averted.html

The Guardian tried very hard to imply I had "special access" to documents in possession of the "GRU—Russia's military spy agency." Any historian of intelligence would love to have access to these records, but it is impossible. The *Guardian* article falsely stated *"US intelligence officials had serious concerns about Michael Flynn's appointment as the White House national security adviser because of his . . . encounter with a woman [Lokhova] who had trusted access to Russian spy agency records."*

It is clear that there is no such official intelligence product. As Rep. Devin Nunes has explained, the House Intelligence Committee demanded to see all intelligence documents in February 2017, including British ones supplied under the "Five Eyes" agreement. The then-chairman Nunes has repeatedly said none were shown to them. *The Guardian* further falsely reported that "US and British intelligence officers discussed Flynn's "worrisome' behavior"; that "multiple sources, who spoke on the condition of anonymity, said the CIA and FBI were discussing this episode, along with many others, as they assessed Flynn's suitability to serve as national security adviser" and that "the Cambridge meeting was part of a wider pattern of "maverick" behavior which included repeated contacts with Russia." These quotes are all examples of Cambridge Club "RUMINT," Halper's lies dressed up to look like official product. The Guardian eventually admitted that *"we also wish to make clear, for the avoidance of doubt, that there is no suggestion that Lokhova has ever worked with or for any of the (sic) Rusisan intelligence agencies."*

 The *Guardian* article went viral as was the plan. It was shared via Twitter by virtually every major news network on April 1, 2017. Up to the present day, it has been republished hundreds of thousands more times. The *Guardian* article was universally understood to imply I was an agent of Russian intelligence and I and General Flynn engaged in behavior that caused "US intelligence officials" "serious concerns."

After a long struggle in which I approached virtually every libel and defamation attorney in London, I eventually found a pro-bono lawyer to start a legal action for defamation against *The Guardian*. After rounds of pointless legal argument over a few months by letter, *The Guardian* published the following clarification in and under their article, we "wish to make clear, for the avoidance of doubt, that there is no suggestion that Lokhova has ever worked with or for any of the (sic) Rusisan intelligence agencies." What was the point of ruining my life?

On March 31, 2017, and April 2, 2017, several British newspapers such as the *Daily Mail* and *The Telegraph* followed up the *Guardian* article and published explosive back-to-back stories about General Flynn and myself. "Disgraced Trump aide and questions over his meeting with Cambridge historian at Intelligence Seminar raised concerns among British and US security chiefs" and "Cambridge University dragged into row over Donald Trump's ex-spy chief's links to Russia." The *Daily Mail* and *The Telegraph* articles had no original sources. They rehashed Stefan Halper, Christopher Andrew, the *WSJ*, and of course *The Guardian*/Harding.

The articles repeated and republished the false and defamatory statements made in the *WSJ* article and *The Guardian* article to a much wider audience. The *Mail* article, for instance, was liked 15.9 million times on Facebook.

The Daily Telegraph falsely stated, "Mr. Flynn, a former lieutenant general in the US army, struck up a friendship at a Cambridge dinner with a Russian ..academic whom he then sought to enlist as a translator on an official trip to Moscow."[419] The *Telegraph* further falsely stated, "Mr. Flynn's encounter with Miss Lokhova was exposed in February 2017 by Andrew." Neither the *Daily Mail* nor *The Telegraph* cited any sources for their fabricated statements. As with each and every one of the other defamatory articles, the information was accepted as true and republished without any attempt to fact-check.

I complained to the toothless UK newspaper regulator about these two articles and my complaints were upheld much later. The only solution is to suggest I work with the newspaper to agree to some additions or amendments that would go online. Sadly, pursuing libel claims in the UK is an expensive project. Under the threat of litigation the Guardian retracted part of their story long after the damage was done.

Palmer Reports

The way the media spreads disinformation is a trickle down to the bottom. On April 2, 2017, *Palmer Reports* published another article, titled "Michael Flynn invited female Russian operative Svetlana Lokhova to accompany him to Moscow." The second *Palmer* article republished the false and defamatory statements that originated with Halper and Andrew and repeated in the *Guardian* article. *Palmer* stated, "Now it's being reported by The Guardian that the woman is indeed some kind of Russian operative—and that Flynn later attempted to travel back to Moscow with her." *Palmer* further stated more extraordinary evidence free accusations that:

> The woman in question is Svetlana Lokhova. She and Flynn first met at conference in the United Kingdom. Intelligence officials in Flynn's position are required to report incidental contact with someone from a hostile nation, due to the frequency with which

---

[419] https://www.telegraph.co.uk/news/2017/04/01/cambridge-university-dragged-row-donald-trumps-ex-spy-chiefs/

foreign operatives try to use such "incidental" interactions as a way of obtaining information or recruiting people. Shortly afterward, Flynn began acting so erratically on the job at the Defense Intelligence Agency that he had to be fired. He then maintained his contact with Lokhova. Based on the extremely rare access which Vladimir Putin granted Svetlana Lokhova to GRU spy records, which have only been seen by two or three people in recent years, it's become evident that she's either a Russian government operative or a Russian spy or she has close connections with Russian spy. What's not clear is whether Gen. Flynn knew she was a Russian operative when he invited her to accompany him on his next trip to Moscow, asking her to act as his translator.[420]

The New York Times

As part of the same operation, on March 4, 2017, *New York Times* reporter Matthew Rosenberg emailed me as follows: "Hi—I cover intelligence and national security for The New York Times. I'm eager to speak with you about Lt. Gen. Flynn, who I am told you met at Cambridge in 2014."

 After I sent my blanket denial statement to the *NYT* reporter, Rosenberg later told me he was given the wrong information about me. He told me he soon "found out" it was not I who arranged the payment for General Flynn's trip to the Russia Today Gala dinner in Moscow in December 2015. I had never heard that allegation before. I spoke with Rosenberg, who was friendly and volunteered a great deal of information.

Rosenberg told me—and this has later been confirmed to others— Halper was the source of a series of accusations about General Flynn and me. At this stage Rosenberg claimed he did not believe the affair allegation. Although far from a fan of Gen. Flynn, he knew the general

---

[420] https://www.palmerreport.com/news/svetlana-lokhova-michael-flynn-russia-moscow/2150/

and his wife were a famously loyal couple. On that basis I agreed with Rosenberg that *The New York Times* would publish an exclusive interview in the United States with me. I agreed on a similar approach in the UK with the BBC.

On May 12, 2017, the BBC published a detailed interview with me. I explained the truth for the first time about what happened at the Cambridge dinner in February 2014 and my limited and infrequent email interactions with General Flynn.

I forwarded the BBC story to Matthew Rosenberg at *The New York Times*. Rosenberg said he believed my story and was going to publish an interview to clear my name. I kept pressing him to publish, but he always had some lame excuse why he could not. In addition to sending him the BBC story, I gave Matt Rosenberg an extensive interview and provided detailed written answers to questions he posed. I explained to Rosenberg the outrage I felt that "journalists" were being told I was a Russian spy, the numerous inaccuracies in the *WSJ* article, and I informed him point-blank I had no connection to Russian intelligence. I told in detail the journalist the "accurate story" behind my history book. After receiving my written statement, Rosenberg shelved the story.

The reason Rosenberg and the *NYT* shelved the story was they knew about the plan to start a formal Special Counsel investigation into "Russian collusion." The truth would have been inconvenient for the FBI. The FBI counterintelligence operation, of which Halper and the *NYT* were important parts, succeeded in creating and sustaining the false impression of "collusion" between members of the Trump campaign and Russians. This false narrative established a basis for investigating the invented "collusion."

Chapter Nineteen: President Trump Triumphant!

What shall we then say to these things? If God be for us, who can be against us?

—Romans: 8:31

You know what I did? A big favor. I caught the swamp. I caught 'em all. Let's see what happens. Nobody else could've done that but me.

—President Donald J. Trump

I was puzzled by the timing of the continued press attacks on General Flynn, given he had resigned from his White House position. The articles were carefully timed to coincide with ex CIA Director John Brennan's testimony to Congress planned for March 28, 2017. Rep. Devin Nunes (R-CA), the chair of the House Intelligence Committee, abruptly canceled the appearances on March 24, 2017. The planned public hearings were to be with former DNI director James Clapper, former CIA Director John Brennan, then FBI Director James Comey, and former Acting Attorney General Sally Yates. A new coup effort was under way a mere three months into the new administration. The Chair of the House Intelligence Committee Nunes had unwittingly prevented a show trial of the new President on bogus Russian collusion charges. That show trial was to appear later in various forms when the Democrats took over the House after the 2018 mid-term election.

The Brennan hearing was part of the committee's investigation into Russian interference in the 2016 presidential election, including whether the Trump campaign colluded with Russian operatives. It seems the *Wall Street Journal* article was designed to set the scene publicly and add the details John Brennan could not say in an unclassified setting. The *Guardian* article was to appear after the hearing to add more fuel to the fire. The hearing was going to be widely reported and Brennan was to pretend to speak guardedly in Congress. It was important the press played a huge part in pushing names and details into the public arena.

Through the hearings and press channels the public heard lies that their president appointed a Russian asset to the highest national security position in the country. The effect was designed to be devastating for Donald Trump. The hope was that the cabinet and the Republicans in Congress would act and ask the president to step down. Unknowingly, Rep. Nunes saved the presidency by canceling the knock-out testimony of the coup plotters. The plotters wanted to showcase in their testimony the lie that Donald Trump was unfit and inexperienced for high office. They fed false stories to the press about how Donald Trump was a national security risk.

Brennan did not name publicly the US individuals who were apparently detected communicating with Russian officials. He added, "Russian agencies" routinely seek to gather compromising information, or "kompromat," to coerce treason from US officials who "do not even realize they are on that path until it gets too late." Brennan's intelligence likely came from Halper. Halper later told *The New York Times* in May 2018 that Gen. Flynn was possibly compromised by Russian intelligence. Halper claimed he was "alarmed" by General Flynn's "apparent closeness" with me and a warning was passed to the American authorities."[421]

In his testimony before the Committee, Brennan was expressly referring to the innocuous contacts I had with General Flynn. Brennan's damning *kompromat* was none other than the false alleged affair between General Flynn and me. Brennan passed on Halper's false "intelligence" about General Flynn and me to the FBI to be used to trigger the counterintelligence operation against President Trump. There is no doubt Gen. Flynn was the person the ex-CIA Director Brennan was referring to in his testimony. Greg Miller of *The Washington Post* said so in his report of the hearing. It was once again *The Washington Post* who were comprehensively briefed.

The pre-placed questions offered by the Democratic members of the House Intelligence Committee are illuminating. Rep. Eric Swalwell asked Brennan if any of the Trump campaign advisors failed to report their contacts with Russians or sought to conceal them. He knew the answer to that question. It had been published in the Wall Street Journal!

The Rolling Coup

The Deep State coup plotters colluding with the Democrats and the press seized on Gen. Flynn's resignation in February to push forward with the rolling coup attempts. An early attempt was when acting FBI Director Andrew McCabe tried to persuade the vice president that Donald Trump may have appointed General Flynn, a Russian asset to be his National Security Advisor. The plan was for Vice President

---

[421] https://www.nytimes.com/2018/05/18/us/politics/trump-fbi-informant-russia-investigation.html

Pence to lead a cabinet revolt to force Donald Trump to step down. In his book *The Threat*, Andrew McCabe describes the meeting where he left Pence to leaf through his Gen. Flynn dossier, which mainly contained Halper intelligence gems. The section is titled *"Tiny Shakes of No."*

> The opening passages were not very interesting or germane and Pence was saying things like, Oh, this is fine. No problem with this. Fine, fine, fine. I said, Keep reading. He reached the part that we had been focused on, and immediately his face changed. His expression turned very cold. It hardened. His reading became very focused. His head shook, but barely—tiny shakes of no. He spoke very little. He said a few things along the lines of I can't believe this, and this is totally opposite, and It's not what he said to me.[422]

This coup attempt by McCabe and Co. collapsed when Gen. Flynn resigned. On May 9, 2017, President Trump fired FBI director, James Comey. "Had I not fired James Comey, who was a disaster, by the way, it's possible I wouldn't even be standing here right now," Donald Trump said in February 2020. "We caught him in the act. Dirty cops. Bad people."[423]

This was exactly the excuse the plotters wanted. Within days of the firing, the FBI opened an investigation into whether their own President Trump was secretly working on behalf of Russia against American interests. They had no evidence of collusion despite investigations and months of electronic surveillance. They shifted to building a case for President Trump obstructing their failed investigation. It was a whole new crime. As Halper predicted in a

---

[422] Andrew G. McCabe, *The Threat: How the FBI Protects America in the Age of Terror and Trump* (New York: St. Martin's, 2019), Page 203.

[423] https://www.foxnews.com/politics/trump-in-impeachment-victory-speech-claims-he-wouldnt-be-standing-here-if-he-didnt-fire-comey

BBC radio interview the "question on the table" is whether the firing of Comey "constitutes an obstruction of justice."[424]

Lacking the numbers to control the House, the plotters could not arrange an impeachment. Instead, they focused on trying to force a Nixon-style Watergate resignation. The second soft coup was attempted during May 2017. The plotters wanted to sound out members of the Trump cabinet to gauge if there was sufficient appetite to remove the president for unfitness to hold office. They hoped to use the pretext of the justified firing of FBI Director James Comey to claim the president was obstructing an investigation.

Although Deputy Attorney General Rod Rosenstein denies it, FBI Deputy Director Andrew McCabe says he even offered to wear a wire to record the president.[425] The coup fizzled out before it really got going. Instead, on May 17, 2017, Deputy Attorney General Rod Rosenstein appointed Robert Mueller as Special Counsel to investigate the alleged collusion between the Trump campaign and Russia. Halper was a secret witness to the Mueller inquiry.

On May 18, 2017, Halper fanned the flames of the conspiracy he created with his lies about General Flynn and me and made a revelatory admission on BBC radio. Halper told the world all about the operation against the president. He told the BBC there was a "sense" that the FBI's inquiry into Russian collusion was moving in the direction of Watergate. That was the FBI's intention. Halper disclosed, "[i]t has clearly gathered a fair amount of momentum. It is the topic of continued discussion and analysis in Washington." As part of the propaganda, Halper misrepresented that "people are deeply concerned about the erratic nature of this White House." Halper claimed there

---

[424] https://www.bbc.co.uk/programmes/p05381/m

[425] https://www.cnn.com/2019/02/17/politics/mccabe-fbi-rosenstein-wire/index.html

was "a frustration that the country is lacking a coherent and focused leadership" and a "broad sense that this president may not have the proper skills for this job."[426]

The confidential source—Stefan Halper—revealed on international radio his intimate involvement in the true goal of the FBI counterintelligence operation: to overthrow President Trump in a rolling soft coup.

New York Times Article May 2018

Recognizing he would soon be exposed in the media as a shady, deceptive FBI informant, Halper approached his confederates at *The New York Times*. Halper's main contact is seemingly the FBI go-to journalist Adam Goldman. Goldman is a key part of the propaganda team at *The New York Times* who "reported" on Russia collusion. His partner is the heavily rumored ex-CIA spy Mathew Rosenberg. Rosenberg in his own words speaks regularly to Christopher Steele.[427]

Goldman and Rosenberg served as a medium, a vessel through which Halper, Steele and the FBI leaked information to the public about Gen. Flynn and myself. The pair are leading lights among the "mainstream media" who seemingly serve at the pleasure of the FBI and CIA, and leak classified information in the guise of reporting "news." Goldman and Rosenberg were integral parts of the counterintelligence operation to defame me and Gen. Flynn and to destabilize the Trump administration. Goldman, Rosenberg, and the *New York Times* acted in

---

[426] https://www.bbc.co.uk/programmes/p05381 7m

[427] Mathew Rosenberg CNN with Don Lennon June 4, 2019. https://www.realclearpolitics.com/video/2019/06/04/nyts_matthew_rosenberg_christopher_steele_concerned_he_will_be_thrown_under_the_bus.html

furtherance of the conspiracy against President Trump by laundering Halper's stories through the storied *New York Times* newspaper, which gave them an air of legitimacy. Illustrating just how small the Russia collusion truthers are is that Adam Goldman used to work with David Ignatius at the *Post*.

The purpose of the *New York Times* article was to taint me as a potential witness of Halper's wrongdoing so that I would be disbelieved. I have been falsely reported by Halper and Steele of having connections to Russian intelligence to US authorities and an affair with Gen. Flynn.

On May 18, 2018, the *New York Times* published an article written by Goldman, Rosenberg, and Mark Mazzetti. The purpose was to "get out front" of the news about Halper's role as an FBI spy, to distract readers from the truth, and to promote the FBI narrative that Halper was only used (paid) to "investigate" Russian ties to the Trump campaign, not to spy on the campaign. Although the *Times* did not mention Halper by name in the article, he was the FBI "informant" identified in the headline and the "source" referenced throughout the story who provided "intelligence" on Trump campaign officials.

The *New York Times* knowingly published numerous false statements by Halper, copying exactly the false "witness" account Halper gave the FBI previously in 2016 about Gen. Flynn and me:

> The informant [Halper] also had contacts with Mr. Flynn, the retired Army general who was Mr. Trump's first national security adviser. The two met in February 2014, when Mr. Flynn was running the Defense Intelligence Agency and attended the Cambridge Intelligence Seminar, an academic forum for former spies and researchers that meets a few times a year. According to people familiar with Mr. Flynn's visit to the intelligence seminar, the source

[Halper] was alarmed by the general's apparent closeness with a Russian woman who was also in attendance. The concern was strong enough that it prompted another person to pass on a warning to the American authorities that Mr. Flynn could be compromised by Russian intelligence, according to two people familiar with the matter. Two years later, in late 2016, the seminar itself was embroiled in a scandal about Russian spying. A number of its organizers resigned over what they said was a Kremlin-backed attempt to take control of the group.[428]

From the array of detail—e.g., "February 2014," "Cambridge Intelligence Seminar," "academic," "Flynn," "Russian woman," "in attendance"—it is obvious to any reader the *NYT* article was about me. In fact, after publication of the article, Twitter users quickly posted links to prior reporting naming me.

The *New York Times* intended to doxx me. In publishing the false statements in the article, the *New York Times* completely disregarded my written statement given to Rosenberg a year earlier. The reporters made no attempt to contact me prior to publication on May 18, 2018.

The article falsely stated Halper was at the dinner with General Flynn in February 2014. He was not. The *New York Times* admits the Halper was not at the Cambridge dinner but falsely claim he was at the Seminar before. Quite how this squares with the FBI intelligence is one for the *New York Times* to explain. This admission puts the *NYT* sharply at odds with the *Wall Street Journal* and *Washington Post*.

The *New York Times* coordinated its attack upon me and General Flynn with MSNBC. On May 18, 2018, Goldman appeared on the *Rachel Maddow Show*, where the star of the show, the collusion queen

---

428 https://www.nytimes.com/2018/05/18/us/politics/trump-fbi-informant-russia-investigation.html

Maddow, repeated the false and defamatory statements published in the article. Goldman confirmed Halper was an FBI informant and was the "source" for the article:

> MADDOW: Adam, you also at the end of your piece tonight have a very provocative description about contacts between this same informant and General Mike Flynn, who went on to be Trump's national security adviser and is now awaiting sentencing after having pled guilty in the special counsel's investigation. In 2014, you say this informant had met with Gen. Flynn when Flynn was running the defense intelligence agency at the time. Flynn attended the academy agency. According to people familiar with Flynn's visit to the Seminar, the source was alarmed by General Flynn's apparent closeness with a Russian woman who was also in attendance. The concern was strong enough that it prompted another person to pass on a warning to American authorities that Flynn could be compromised by Russian intelligence. What can you tell us about that incident and what that meant for Flynn going forward in terms of the attention on him from the FBI?
>
> GOLDMAN: Well, that certainly—from the informant's standpoint that was certainly a moment he took note of. It's not clear if that information that went to the American authorities actually triggered a counterintelligence investigation, but it certainly would have been logged by authorities.
>
> MADDOW: "New York Times" reporter Adam Goldman, thank you for joining us on such short notice, and congratulations on this late-breaking news.
>
> Congratulations.
>
> GOLDMAN: All right. Thank you. Bye.
>
> MADDOW: Thanks. I will say Flynn is—if this anecdote about Michael Flynn from 2014, sources alarmed by his closeness with a

Russian woman at an intelligence seminar, reporting it back to US intelligence authorities about whether or not he's compromised.[429]

Between May 18, 2018 and the present, this *NYT* article was republished by CNN and other mainstream media outlets, and by the *Times* and many others to millions via Twitter.

The *Washington Post* Article: June 5, 2018

The *Washington Post* also coordinated its attack upon General Flynn and me with MSNBC. On May 18, 2018, Halper's former student Robert Costa appeared on the *11th Hour with Brian Williams*. Costa admitted he knew Halper was a "longtime intelligence source that has now been used as part of the Mueller investigation." Just like Goldman, however, Costa claimed Halper was "not a mole."

On June 5, 2018, the *Washington Post* published a story written by Tom Hamburger, Halper's former student Robert Costa, and Ellen Nakashima, titled "Cambridge University perch gave FBI source access to top intelligence figures—and a cover as he reached out to Trump associates." The sources of the *Washington Post* article were of course Halper, Costa, and Richard Dearlove. Dearlove was the only person who has stuck his head above the parapet to defend Halper.

Halper is described in previous *Washington Post* articles as a popular Cambridge academic figure hosting entertaining soirees for students. Cambridge's drab daily market is transformed into a Provençal epicurean heaven selling fine wine and delicious cheese. Costa contributed unlikely fantasies from his student days about Halper serving wine from a Cambridge market stall. Have you ever tasted English wine? Convivial evenings with Halper and Dearlove spilling

---

429 https://www.nytimes.com/2018/05/18/us/politics/trump-fbi-informant-russia-investigation.html

stories of spying while sipping English wine are as likely as a cold day in Hell.

Prior to publication, the *Washington Post* reached out to me by email. The next thing I know the senior *Washington Post* journalist and friend of Fusion GPS, Tom Hamburger, is in Cambridge on a tidy-up mission. No one in Cambridge talked to him apart from Dearlove and of course Halper. The *Washington Post* have a big budget to keep flying reporters across the pond to go after President Donald Trump, General Flynn, and protect their source Halper.

Hamburger tries to interrogate me again over the February 2014 Gen. Flynn dinner. I referred him to his colleague David Ignatius. I told Hamburger that after flying to Cambridge and interviewing sources in 2017, David Ignatius had already determined there was nothing to the story. Prior to publication, Hamburger talked to Ignatius, so he knew from many sources his story was false.

Hamburger tried exploring the Kremlin penetration of the Cambridge Seminar line. I read him Halper's resignation email, proving to the journalist that Halper did not tell the truth. We went back and forth for days as I tried to explain to Hamburger that he is about to publish smears and untruths. He claimed to me he spoke to Dearlove about the dinner but later admitted it was only "sources close to" Dearlove.

I told Hamburger about the Gen. Flynn dinner, "You have revealed you have not had contact with Dearlove. So, if the principals in the story have not confirmed their knowledge/statements personally, then the journalists do not have evidence, but only hearsay, and this should be stressed." I told Hamburger Halper's false allegation about Russian intelligence penetration of the Cambridge seminar was investigated by an outside legal counsel and found "no case to answer." I said, "If anything, there is far more evidence that the FBI through Halper, not

Russia's SVR, had 'penetrated' the Cambridge Intelligence Seminar." I also got out of Hamburger that General Flynn's DIA liaison Dan O'Brien was on the record with *The Washington Post* to confirm "he left 2014 dinner with Flynn and was with him that night: nothing happened." Hamburger suppressed this vital information.

I told the *Washington Post* the story about me and General Flynn was false and that there was evidence Halper was a known liar. Hamburger was a tricky and testy journalist to deal with. He pretended to be new to the story and just wanting to get to the truth. A *Washington Post* journalist who had led the hoax stories from the start was not going to fool me. Hamburger was especially upset when I told him I was never interviewed by a single security agency. He repeated his question with a list of US and UK authorities and I replied no to each one.

It was obvious Hamburger had no interest in getting to the truth. Hamburger told me Dearlove reported me to US authorities. I know a little about Dearlove and in my experience that is not something he would admit to doing as it is a breach of the UK Official Secrets Act to expose an ongoing counterintelligence operation. I challenged Hamburger. He went quiet before eventually admitting the source was maybe "a friend" of Dearlove.

Prior to publication, Hamburger sent me a copy of my May 27, 2018 interview in which I roast Halper with *The Sunday Times* of London (see below). I verified to the *Washington Post* reporter that my statements to the *Times* were accurate and the truth. They suppressed those from their article.

The *Post* article Hamburger wrote named Halper and described him as a "a longtime source of information for US intelligence and law enforcement personnel."[430] Hamburger completely ignored the facts stated in the May 27, 2018 interview given by me to *The Sunday Times* of London. Hamburger reported many statements as "facts" that are falsehoods, including that Halper "attended" the February 2014 dinner and Halper and Dearlove were "disconcerted by the attention the then DIA chief showed to a Russian-born graduate student [me] who regularly attended the seminars."

There was no mention of the fact his colleague Ignatius interviewed everyone at dinner a year before and there were no concerns. So, despite the six-page article of May 2018, *The Washington Post* found no place for and suppressed vital information: Halper has history of lying. He did not tell the truth about his resignation, made up stories of Kremlin penetration of Cambridge, and lied about General Flynn and me. The *Post* article was republished millions of times via Twitter.

The *Sunday Times* Article

On May 27, 2018, the leading British Sunday newspaper published an interview with me in advance of my first book being published in the UK. It started with the obvious statement:

"'I can't deny I'm a Russian,' says Svetlana Lokhova, whose name rather gives the game away. 'And I can't deny I'm a woman.'"[431] The reporter kindly described me as "brilliant researcher at Cambridge University." I was about to publish a startling book on a previously undetected network of Soviet spies that infiltrated American

---

[430] https://www.washingtonpost.com/politics/cambridge-university-perch-gave-fbi-source-access-to-top-intelligence-figures--and-a-cover-as-he-reached-out-to-trump-associates/2018/06/05/c6764dc2-641e-11e8-99d2-0d678ec08c2f_story.html

[431] https://www.thetimes.co.uk/article/svetlana-lokhova-im-a-mum-under-siege-not-mata-hari-bkggndttq

universities in the early 1930s. The *Times* pictured me at "only 37 as someone who should be looking forward to an academic future filled with promise, prizes and prestige. Instead she has fled her London home for the sanctuary of a friend's house 600 miles away."

The *Times* understood I'm an author, not a practitioner of intelligence. I said, the actor "Sir Alec Guinness is not a spy just because he played George Smiley [the John le Carré character]." I found myself trapped at the center of a sexual, political, and potentially criminal scandal owing to Halper's lies.

The *Times* tells my story:

[She] was 10 years old when the curtain came down on Soviet-style communism. She remembers the Moscow of her childhood as a poor, grim, menacing city. 'They were horrid times for Russians,' she says. Yet she was able to acquire her first pair of jeans (from the Salvation Army) and remembers 'drinking Coca-Cola while walking in the street. It was absolutely brilliant. I found myself in a brave new world, and I embraced it.'

At 18, with the help of the British Council, she applied for a place to read education and history at Cambridge. Even though her English was at that point sketchy, she was accepted and had to embark on intensive language lessons. . . . 'I had become a huge admirer of Britain. I wanted to get out of Russia, I wanted a future and the future was in the West.'

"It was in the early 2000s that she attended a lecture by Christopher Andrew entitled *The Secret World.* She says, 'He was talking about Kim Philby [the Cambridge traitor]. Of course, we all signed up for his course.'

"It was Andrew who encouraged her to approach some then recently opened Russian archives and she spent 'a very long time' in other communist-era archives. 'Bloody awful places, cold, no electricity, they won't allow you to wear a coat. My book was born of years of going through every bit of paper, I'm just the first person who was able through luck and persistence to get to material describing Soviet intelligence.' She had remained in contact with Andrew, who encouraged her to resume her research. She is now a British citizen and an archives-by-fellow (a kind of junior fellow) of Churchill

College, Cambridge. 'I owe everything I've achieved to this country,' she says quietly. 'I just don't understand how I've become the enemy.'

"She has made formal complaints about Halper's behavior to Magdalene College and to her constituency MP, and has written to [then-Prime Minister] Theresa May. 'Either I'm a Russian spy and there are genuine concerns, or Halper is crazy and a liar.' . . . As my afternoon with Lokhova unfolded, it quickly became clear that she regards herself as "collateral damage" in the rush to pin something fatal on Trump. She blames Halper for dragging her into the collusion affair to the point where she is beginning to despair that she can extricate herself undamaged. She was a Russian woman with a postcard at a dinner with a general who was close to Trump. [432]

NBC and Nance

My article in *The Sunday Times* attracted the attention of NBC. One of their contributors is former CIA Director John Brennan. In late May 2018, after Halper was exposed as an FBI spy, they contacted me by email. A producer, Anna Schecter, represented to me the network wanted to do a program exposing Halper.

Schecter claimed the program would help clear my name and would hold "a powerful (if repugnant) man to account" and would also hold America's "top law enforcement agency to account." Schecter proclaimed, "we will set the record straight, and right a wrong. It will be all the more powerful if NBC does it . . . because it's the most watched network." Schecter stated she was "passionate about righting this wrong and telling your story, which exposes Halper's true character, and calls out the FBI for relying on a slanderer who cares much more about telling a juicy yarn than the truth. This is a breach of justice full stop."

---

[432] Ibid.

Schecter further stated in the email. "[a]s a woman, and a professional woman, I shudder at the notion of a fallacious story about sleeping with Flynn and spying no less not just told around Cambridge but given to the press and reported as fact. I and my team in the investigative unit will take this story and its important implications very seriously and I believe our agencies (FBI and CIA) will be better for the fact that we shine a bright light on an unreliable and loose-lipped informant prone to inventing stories."

This is NBC, the home of Rachel Maddow and Malcom Nance. Nance in particular has an extreme bias and has demonstrated prejudice against General Flynn and President Trump. On April 1, 2017, Nance called me a "honeypot." A "honeypot" is a spy (typically attractive and female) who uses sex to trap and blackmail a target. His tweet read "Fun Fact: The Intelligence community informally describes cheap honeypot temptresses who collect thru sex employed by GRU/KGB (FSB) as 'Svetlanas'. 'Natasha's' were trained smart agents who used brains."

I decided to see if NBC would air the interview as Schecter seemed genuine. In light of Adam Goldman of *The New York Times*'s and *The Washington Post*'s suppression of the facts, I was deeply skeptical of NBC, but Schecter was adamant the truth would be told to the largest audience possible. Her network promised to make that happen.

Of course, NBC was concealing its ulterior motive from me. They were not interested in publishing the truth or holding Halper accountable. Rather, NBC was determined to defame and discredit General Flynn and me, and to blindly promote the "Russian collusion" narrative. The phone calls from Schecter after May 2018 went from fact-checking to interrogation-type questions to twisting. Then, I noticed I had some odd new followers on Twitter including Ken

Dilanian (who is known to have a "closely collaborative relationship with the CIA") and Matthew Alexander the producer of the *Rachel Maddow Show*.

Schecter called me and concealed there were others on the line. It struck me, from the tone of the questioning that there were more than just me and Schecter in the conversation. I asked her directly if Ken Dilanian was listening to the call and feeding her questions. Schecter abruptly ended the call. She then called me back from her mobile phone a few minutes later. Schecter sounded distressed and said she was being pressured by her colleagues. She said she believed me but said a colleague at NBC with "twenty-five years veteran of intelligence" was laughing and saying, "everyone at the CIA knows Flynn had an affair with Lokhova." I wonder who that was? NBC never filmed the interview.

Conclusion: "I Am Not a Russian Spy"

*For in much wisdom is much grief: and he that increaseth knowledge
increaseth sorrow.*

Ecclesiastes 1:18

*Blessed are they which are persecuted for righteousness' sake: for theirs is
the kingdom of heaven.*

Matthew 5:10

*"Now, this is not the end. It is not even the beginning of the end. But it is,
perhaps, the end of the beginning."*

—Sir Winston Churchill

*They were spying on, a term I don't particularly like, but on what the
Russians were doing. Trying to understand were the Russians infiltrating,
trying to gain access, trying to gain leverage or influence — which is what
they do.*

—James Clapper

*"History keeps her secrets longer than most of us. But she has one secret that
I will reveal to you in the greatest confidence. Sometimes there are no
winners at all."*

—John le Carré

T he timeline below shows that during Spygate Stefan Halper was
more than just a source; he was central to Spygate.

September 2015: Stefan Halper is awarded a $245,000 contract by the Pentagon's Office of Net Assessments for a "China Russia" study. The ONA was later described by Gen. Flynn's attorney Sydney Powell as a CIA "slush" fund.

December 2015: Gen. Flynn travels to Moscow and is photographed with Vladimir Putin. OCONUS lures approved. Halper begins drawing down expenses on his ONA contract.

January 2016: The "Lokhova operation" begins. Halper associate Christopher Andrew, a University of Cambridge professor, invites British academic Svetlana Lokhova to dinner on behalf of Halper. Lokhova declines to attend. The former Bush aide used Lokhova to dirty up National Security Advisor Gen. Michael Flynn in a sustained media campaign serving as the basis of an investigation of Gen. Flynn. Halper provides his stories to John Brennan who forwards it to the FBI.

February 2016: Halper's first of his three taxpayer paid trips to United Kingdom. Halper spread lies to members of Cambridge Intelligence Seminar about Svetlana Lokhova's supposed links to Russian intelligence.

March 2016: The "George Papadopoulos operation" begins when a Maltese professor, Joseph Mifsud, meets Papadopoulos.

May 2016: Australian High Commissioner Alexander Downer meets Papadopoulos and much later passes information to US State Department, which is the excuse to open Crossfire Hurricane in July. Trump campaign adviser Stephen Miller is invited to participate in a July symposium at the University of Cambridge arranged by Halper's academic department. Miller declines.

June 2016: The "Carter Page operation" begins. A Halper associate at Cambridge, Steven Schrage, invites Trump campaign adviser, Carter Page, to the July symposium. Page accepts.

July 2016: Halper's second expenses-paid trip to the United Kingdom where he first meets with Page at the Cambridge symposium on July 11, 2016. Downer also speaks with Page, who is sitting next to him during the keynote address delivered by former Secretary of State Madeleine Albright. Halper granted a second larger contract of $455,000 by the ONA.

August 2016: Halper reports his "eyewitness" account to the FBI who open a counter intelligence operation on Gen. Flynn. Halper invites Page to visit him in Virginia. Contacts between the two increase as the FISA application is being drafted. Halper emails Trump campaign Co-Chair Sam Clovis and arranges to meet with him.

September 2016: Halper writes to Papadopoulos, inviting him to London. Both Halper and Azra Turk a US government undercover-investigator and "honey trap" seek to elicit information from him about the Trump Campaign.

October 2016: Halper has a second recorded meeting with Carter Page just before the successful FISA application. FBI meet with Steele in Italy to offer him a significant reward for dirt on Gen. Flynn.

November 2016: After announcement of Gen. Flynn's appointment as NSA; Halper's lies are communicated by Christopher Steele via Sen. John McCain to James Comey of the FBI. Halper's concoctions used as predicate for the FBI surveillance of Gen. Flynn. The House Intelligence Committee briefed by the Intelligence Agencies that "nothing unusual" during in 2016 Presidential election.

December 2016: Halper and Steele brief the US and UK press on allegations about Gen. Flynn and Lokhova. The *FT* article falsely claims Kremlin penetration of the Cambridge Seminar. Halper associate and former head of MI6, Sir Richard Dearlove, reportedly meets with former MI6 agent Christopher Steele.

January 2017: Flurry of coup related activity; Lies, Leaks and Investigation. Start of House Investigation into "Russian Interference." Publication of Intelligence Community Assessment based in big part on Steele and Halper's "intelligence". Publication of Steele dossier. Ambush FBI interview …

February 2017: Gen. Flynn resigns. Christopher Andrew writes a newspaper article regarding Gen. Flynn. Lokhova approached by multiple US media outlets who were briefed by Halper false stories about her supposed relationship with Gen. Flynn. Allegation of "inappropriate contact" (affair) put to multiple individuals including the legal representatives of Gen. Flynn.

March 2017: Halper campaign targeting Gen. Flynn and Lokhova continues with articles in *The Wall Street Journal* and *The Guardian*. Brennan Congressional testimony delayed.

May 2017: Brennan delivers delayed testimony to Congress. Brennan makes allegation that a top Trump campaign advisor later, identified by *Washington Post* as Gen. Flynn, has been compromised by Russian intelligence. Mueller inquiry opens.

September 2017: Halper speaks with Carter Page for the last time; the FISA warrant on Page expires.

March 2018: Halper identified as a key player in Crossfire Hurricane operation by Chuck Ross of the *Daily Caller*.

May 2018: FBI and DOJ leaks to *The Washington Post* and *The New York Times* partially reveal Halper's role in the Crossfire Hurricane investigation. Halper's false allegations regarding Gen. Flynn and Lokhova appear in the *Washington Post* and *New York Times*.[433]

Fight or Flight?

As a family, we made a decision in 2017 to fight Halper's false accusations. The decision came at a huge and unexpected personal cost. Halper's actions have cost me my career and my livelihood. I struggled hard for five years through teaching undergrads, contributing papers, and lectures to establish myself at the University of Cambridge, and owing to Halper's lies, I have become persona non grata. I was associated with a scandal perceived as doing harm to the reputation of the University. Nothing matters more in Cambridge than that.

Somehow the University authorities felt it was my fault the Stefan Halper affair was crashing down around them. I was also sold out and betrayed by my supervisor Professor Christopher Andrew. The University authorities sent several emissaries to me to find out what I might do next. The University wanted to ensure I would not write a tell-all book implicating them. Bizarrely their message was stark. One of the emissaries, Dr. William Foster, wrote the following email to me showing how serious the consequences of Halper's activities are to the reputation of the University:

> The delay in my reply was so I could let you know the result of my deliberations about continuing or not with intelligence history. I decided in the end that while my intellectual interest in intelligence as part of foreign policy history remains strong, there would be

---

[433] With thanks to Lee Smith.

insurmountable problems in trying to work with many of those who have been and remain in this field.

As deputy and often acting head of the largest college in Cambridge or Oxford, I have a specific responsibility that goes well beyond whatever my own scholarly interests might be—and that is to safeguard the academic integrity and standards of the University of Cambridge generally. For me to continue in this research field, in light of the situations of which I am now aware, would be inconsistent with these responsibilities to protect academic standards.

It is regrettable, but I believe nonetheless true, that no matter who may or may not have been responsible for the various controversies that have (very publicly) swirled around the Cambridge Intelligence Seminar in recent years, that intelligence studies pursued in this University will be tainted by these controversies for a long time to come—and certainly well beyond my retirement date. So, I feel I have no choice but to move on professionally. . . .

 Chris Andrew left in his wake an "academic Chernobyl"—toxic to anyone remaining in the area—is shared by many fellow academics in our Faculty and beyond. As I'm sure you'll understand then, . . . severe interpersonal conflicts that staying in this field here in Cambridge would inevitably involve. There is also the second and equally important factor that while Chris was responsible for defining the field in the 1980s and 90s, because he exerted (and apparently still does via his ongoing seminar) absolute control here, we here in Cambridge have never advanced beyond the original Chris Andrew approach and methodology. As a result, Cambridge has fallen well behind . . . Cambridge has gone from the intellectual cutting-edge to a hopeless backwater.

The message was clear: "Don't cause any trouble in Cambridge and go to work somewhere else." The University offered no carrot to me, just a very big stick. I wrote several formal complaints to the Vice-Chancellor who never replied to an email or even acknowledged my many phone calls. When I was in Cambridge, my old friends and acquaintances just avoided me. One distinguished Professor and head of a major faculty whom I have known since I was a teenager, tried so hard to avoid me he almost fell off his bike, saying, "I cannot talk to you, because Putin will find out."

I was ostracized by the "Cambridge Club" when the allegations broke in 2017. In February 2017, I contacted Dearlove for his help about the outrageous allegations circulating about the Seminar. According to Andrew, Dearlove had dealt with the first round of scandals in December 2015. Despite several emails and messages I never heard back from Dearlove. For a while I could not believe he would be involved in such a mess. But then Dearlove began to give interviews where he defended the actions of Christopher Steele and his close friend Stefan Halper.

It emerged that Dearlove was meeting with Christopher Steele in early fall and again in December 2016 and the pair talked through the main allegations of the dodgy dossier. Knowing one lying, leaking "confidential source" is unfortunate; to know both and defend them could be seen as more serious. Dearlove has been effusive in his praise of both Steele and Halper. He has described Steele as the "go-to man on Russia" and Halper as a "patriot and a good academic."

In interviews, Dearlove remains a believer in the veracity of some of the allegations in the Steele dossier. Most odd was an interview which Dearlove gave to a virtually unknown UK publication *Prospect*. In a wide-ranging interview rich with pregnant comments given on April 13, 2017, he made this one revealing comment:

What lingers for Trump may be what deals—on what terms—he did after the financial crisis of 2008 to borrow Russian money when others in the west apparently would not lend to him.[434]

Dearlove has not given up on his support for Halper and Steele.

I lost my home in the United Kingdom; forced out by incessant intrusive press attention and fears over my personal safety. Irresponsible journalists in the UK came knocking on my door, even disturbing my neighbors and showing my picture. The pressure resulted in online threats and culminated in a credible threat with the British Police involved. My address was published online.

The media pursuit was relentless. Media outlets used every angle to try and trap me into giving them ambush interviews. The press campaign to publicize my first book launch was abandoned.

Every time there was an incident, which was blamed on Russia, such as the Brexit referendum result, I became the subject of renewed and unwanted press attention. The tension led to the cancellation of my UK publishing contract as I was considered too controversial and damaging the brand. As for my American publisher, they ran a mile. They would not even acknowledge the receipt of my completed manuscript they had commissioned. Before the scandal my editor was utterly anti-Trump to the point of being unable to talk about anything else. After the articles appeared he just disappeared.

The Second Watergate

On the day Special Counsel Robert Mueller was appointed, the remaining FBI Confidential Source Stefan Halper gave an illuminating

---

[434] https://www.prospectmagazine.co.uk/magazine/interview-richard-dearlove-europe-intelligence-mi6

interview about his views of President Trump to the BBC on May17, 2017. Describing himself as a Nixon White House veteran, Halper misrepresented that "people in Washington are deeply concerned about the erratic nature of this White House." Halper claimed there was "a frustration that the country is lacking a coherent and focused leadership." Halper stated there was a "broad sense that this president may not have the proper skills for this job." He added, the "question on the table" is whether the firing of Comey "constitutes an obstruction of justice." Halper finished by forecasting a second Watergate: that is, the removal of President Trump.

Halper revealed on international radio the true goal of the FBI counterintelligence operation: to overthrow President Trump in a soft coup. This was a new attempt involving obstruction of justice and an alternative to removal for incapacity under the 25th Amendment. Halper knows with absolute certainty that there was no collusion between the Trump Campaign and Russia because he made it up. He created the stories himself and then investigated them for the FBI and CIA.

To remove Donald Trump, who was always the ultimate target, Halper had to hope the president would be taken out quickly by his own cabinet. John Brennan's revelations a mere 5 months into the new administration were key. A coup attempt was in full flower from the recycling of Halper's "intelligence" on General Flynn on May 23, 2017. In the event, Halper had to wait for the Special Counsel inquiry. Halper was a witness to the Mueller Inquiry according to his own lawyer's advertisements.

After all of my nightmares created by Halper, it later transpired that the British Security Services never had any interest in me. There were neither any whispers about me nor issues with me before or after Halper's so-called revelations.

By pursuing defamation action in the UK, I achieved limited retractions of the false newspaper stories. My way is to tell the truth as widely and loudly as possible by giving factual interviews. America media seemed impossible to crack. I worked with a small number of journalists who would listen to me such as Chuck Ross of the *Daily Caller*, who broke the false narrative of the Stefan Halper story.

There has been a whispering campaign against me—by, no doubt, those with most to lose through exposure. They seek to destroy my character by insinuating I am somehow an agent of Russian disinformation. It is ironic that those who earned a fantastic living peddling the Russian collusion conspiracy theory now say those like me who are revealing the truth are the agents of Russia.

The Fox News Interview

Just ahead of the final release of Special Counsel Mueller's Report, Security Correspondent Catherine Herridge, then of Fox News, contacted me. I was overseas keeping a low profile from the media. From a distance, I could observe the extraordinary injustices perpetrated on those caught in their net.

Had he interviewed me, what I had to tell Robert Mueller about Spygate was as destructive to his narrative as it was true. Despite interviewing over 500 witnesses including Halper, the Special Counsel never reached out to me. Mine was one of three stories Representative Nunes used to illustrate why the whole Mueller inquiry was a sham:

> What I'm going to be looking for is there's three specific areas where I think there was some type of setup involved," Nunes said. "The first is involved with Gen. Flynn," Nunes said. "Gen. Flynn was

supposedly entrapped, was meeting with a Russian woman. I want to know what really happened there because we are just now finding out about this and we need a lot more information on what really was general Flynn doing. It's a big deal if somebody within our intelligence agencies were accusing a three star general of having some type of Russian fling. It's serious stuff. I want to get to the bottom of that.[435]

The most serious allegation of the whole collusion hoax was that the Russians could have compromised the US intelligence chief. All of America's greatest secrets might have been revealed to a hostile foreign power. Where was the reaction and the high-level investigation? There was nothing.

At his testimony in front of the House Intelligence Committee, Robert Mueller was unable to answer the question from Rep. Devin Nunes as to why he never spoke to me. Mueller would not answer even the simplest questions citing an ongoing investigation. Rep. Nunes concluded "we still don't have any Russians. We don't know who the Russians were who supposedly colluded with the Trump campaign. Why? Because there were none, and that's what we said two and a half years ago."

It transpired that the revelatory moment for Rep. Nunes was the newspaper articles about the affair between a three-star General and a supposed Russian spy. It was a big deal. Rep. Nunes went to look for the intelligence, the investigation of this serious matter, and discovered there was precisely none. The game was up. Rep. Nunes knew Spygate was a hoax, a total sham. So, he asked Robert Mueller on July 24, 2019:

---

[435] https://www.washingtonexaminer.com/news/devin-nunes-looking-for-some-type-of-setup-in-3-areas-of-muellers-report

NUNES: The first Trump associate to be investigated was General Flynn. Many of the allegations against him stem from false media reports that he had an affair with the Cambridge Academic Svetlana Lokhova and that Lokhova was a Russian spy.

Some of these allegations were made public in a 2017 article written by British intelligence historian Christopher Andrew.

Your report fails to reveal how or why Andrew and his collaborator, Richard Dearlove, former head of Britain's MI6, spread these allegations. And you failed to interview Svetlana Lokhova about these matters. Is that correct?

MUELLER: I'm going to get—not going to get into those matters to which you refer.[436]

So that is it—the extent of the official interest in General Flynn as a Russian asset.

Getting my short, taped interview onto the *Tucker Carlson Show* on April 4, 2019, was a major step forward exposing Spygate. The process took a month. Catherine Herridge is very thorough as a reporter who checked and double-checked every part of my story. The actual segment was filmed twice in the middle of the night. I was in Asia, and the recording quality over Skype was awful. The booming sound added an air of unnecessary mystery. I answered the questions factually and slowly. I was not a spy and met General Flynn once and was never alone with him—ever.

The response to the broadcast interview from the American public was electric and heartwarming. I have a huge place in my heart for every ordinary American who came forward to offer me support. We share a common strong moral sense of right and wrong. I discovered there was

---

[436] https://www.washingtonpost.com/politics/transcript-of-robert-s-mueller-iiis-testimony-before-the-house-intelligence-committee/2019/07/24/f424acf0-ad97-11e9-a0c9-6d2d7818f3da_story.html

a huge demand for my story from a large group of Americans with an untapped hunger to learn the truth about Spygate. I was encouraged by the support of the ordinary and decent American citizens who feel a strong outrage that something went wrong, very badly wrong with their political system in 2016. It has been my journey to help right that wrong in the writing of this book.

In the year that has passed since the interview, I have learned a great deal about America and its ways. There is a long tradition of foreigners traveling around America as observers. They all became admirers of the indomitable spirit of the American people and marvel at their achievements. However, like me they are mystified by the politics—and sports!

Americans are poorly served by their media. The US press is gagged by its corporate interests and obsessive political polarization. The challenge for me today remains as formidable as it was three years ago in getting my message out. The vast majority of the media is closed to me because of their anti-Donald Trump bias. They label me a "Trump supporter" because they don't like what I have to say.

Frankly, that is wrong. I first and foremost want to tell the Truth. Harm was done to me and others and I am exposing it. Halper, plus the former CIA and FBI leadership, came to my country, England with their dirty politics and involved me; I did not invite them. Sadly, whatever the injustices of my case, it is treated by the US "liberal media" as political and toxic. Thank goodness then for social media warriors who inhabit Twitter and Parler. Increasing numbers of inquiring minds have steadily chipped away at the narrative of the Deep State.

I have spent my adult life studying intelligence successes and failures as an academic. The events of 2016 demonstrated that Washington's

Deep State abused the law enforcement and intelligence structure for their political goals. Using "national security" as an excuse, elements of intelligence agencies acted with apparent impunity and will hopefully be brought to account.

A cadre within the intelligence community perverted their foreign-counterintelligence surveillance powers, based on nothing more than a Halper-created fantasy that Donald Trump was an agent of the Kremlin, which in turn fed on their visceral hatred of the man. They covertly used the work of only two sources to justify monitoring an American political campaign and, later, a US presidential administration.

Spygate began as a low level operation to fix an election; to push Hillary Clinton across the victory line. The initial goal was to provide the evidence of a Russian intelligence operation needed to start an FBI investigation. There were never any Russians so Halper and Steele invented them to order. The efforts intensified from July 2016 onwards, as the election became too close to call. The aim switched to obtaining a FISA to stage an "electronic break in" of the Trump campaign. Leaking the existence of an investigation into the Trump Campaign was planned as an October surprise to influence the outcome of the election.

After the election, the fake evidence and the accompanying investigation became pivotal in the attempts to overturn the result and rolling coups. The coup plotters invested heavily in a bogus investigation that was based on a lie. The fabricated evidential base concocted against the key target, Gen. Flynn was leaked to the press to generate a storm to drive President Trump from the White House.

Since 2016 the Deep State has staged a cover up, including suppressing Halper's false evidence against the General to sustain his prosecution. It was not until April 30, 2020 that the Department of Justice released the false testimony. The Deep State needed to convict Gen. Flynn, even jail him to protect their fiction and conspiracy. The long suppressed fake intelligence report by Halper, recycled by Christopher Steele, is the foundation of sand on which Spygate was built.

The FBI "sources", Halper and Steele, were so dirty and their lying and leaking behavior so wrong no one conducting a real investigation would have let either of them anywhere near it. Even in plotting and scheming, corrupt elements in the FBI proved themselves inept, achieving nothing. The election of Donald Trump set in train the first coup in the history of the United States; ruining lives and wasting millions of taxpayers' dollars.

The politicization of law enforcement and the intelligence services is a threat to us all, whatever our politics. Where is the accountability? Not from Democrat politicians who defend the most outrageous behavior, because it resulted in the Trump-Russia investigation. In 2014 the same Democrat politicians were attacking the CIA when they were the victims of surveillance but they are now silent. With rare exceptions, Republicans are largely unwilling to confront the issue.

Conservatives are national security and law-and-order hawks by nature —defenders of the status quo and not revolutionary reformers. They will not drain the Swamp. So, here is the dilemma: the immense powers of the intelligence apparatus are deemed essential to protecting the United States. The public rightly are reacting to the abuse of power by demanding accountability.

The public weariness has grown into anger as the guilty evade accountability so far. It is only the Trump Campaign advisors who were subjected to groundless surveillance or prosecuted. In stark contrast, former government officials who misled investigators, judges, and lawmakers have so far evaded prosecution. Let's hope this does not continue.

The Trump-Russia investigation was a deliberate abuse of power, especially in the use of Stefan Halper. The former FBI and DOJ leadership used a FISA surveillance warrant to conduct a counterintelligence and criminal investigation that lacked a predicate. The warrant was the tool used to hunt for some crime that might render Donald Trump unelectable and once elected, removable. The abuse was politically motivated as the administration deliberately created a non-existent Russia collusion to justify surveillance of the opposition party's political campaign. The abuse did not end with the election but continued for two more years. It has mired the Trump administration by limiting its ability to govern effectively by causing GOP losses in the "mid terms" handing control of the House to the Democrats.

The Investigation

At the point of this writing in early summer 2020, America awaits the eventual outcome of Attorney General William Barr's investigations into Spygate. John Durham, the US Attorney in Connecticut, is reviewing the origins of the Russia Inquiry. Attorney General Barr has signaled his concerns about the Russia investigation during prior congressional testimony, particularly the surveillance of Trump associates. He commented recently on John Durham's progress saying that "I'm very troubled by it. What has been called to my attention so far, but I'm not going to characterize it beyond that."[437]

---

[437] https://www.realclearpolitics.com/video/2020/06/09/
ag_barr_very_troubled_by_durham_probe_familiar_names_tried_to_sabotage_trump_campai
gn.html

AG Barr put the cat firmly among the pigeons with his statement "I think spying did occur."[438] Barr has satisfied himself that Stefan Halper was a spy. As he succinctly put it: if you wear a wire to secretly record another individual, what else can you be called? The question is did the FBI, or others have legal grounds for deploying Halper and what were the events leading to the decision to deploy a spy against individuals in a political campaign? John Brennan may have made himself the key suspect because he has stated he was passing intelligence to the FBI well before July 31, 2016.

 Very little has been said in the media about the details of the probe due to the secrecy of the ongoing investigation. America has high hopes for the impending release, and many people believe the probe will result in accountability and restore faith in the justice system. At CPAC 2020, leading Republican Doug Collins expressed his assumptions about the probe, saying:

> Durham is investigating. Attorney General Bill Barr has expanded his reach into the intelligence community," adding that the US Attorney has "grand juries" along with "everything else" for his investigation. "When he's ready to charge people, he'll charge people.

I am not alone in seeking justice and accountability. In 2016 sixty-three million American voters put their trust in the electoral system to support Donald Trump's candidacy; they deserve better. They remain victims of the conspiracy.

Halper

As for Halper, he is fuming. He lurks in the shadows flush with taxpayer's money, refusing to explain himself while claiming illness. Halper is protected by the intelligence agencies' codes and practices

---

[438] Morgan Chalfont, "Barr says 'spying' took place on Trump campaign," *The Hill* (April 10, 2019).

designed for real sources who put themselves at risk. Publicly, Halper got Dearlove to state that Halper acted at all times as "a patriot," but then he hides behind "legal immunity" to avoid questions. As I, amongst others, expose him, he attacks us with threats to our livelihoods. In Halper's vision of the world, he is the victim—a distinguished academic and loyal American.

New Information.

Since I completed writing this book, the pace of exposing Spygate is picking up at a pace. Finally, with declassification of pivotal documents my long held suspicions are now confirmed as facts.

Three releases of de-classified documents in April and May 2020 are of enormous significance. They are the FBI closing statement of January 4, 2017 which contains Halper's "eyewitness" account to the FBI, David Kramer's testimony to Congress showing the co-ordination between Halper and Steele and the Gen. Flynn tapes.

The newly released documents prove that the FBI opened a counter intelligence operation into a senior Trump advisor, Gen. Flynn in the middle of a political campaign on the word of a known liar. The FBI investigated a top security clearance holder, a former intelligence chief for potentially being a Russian spy based on "intelligence" so preposterous it would not pass muster as the plot for a bad spy thriller.

The documents demonstrate that the close co-ordination of Halper and Steele after the election to re-cycle that lie to keep the bogus FBI investigation alive and launch a fresh round of surveillance. The FBI had earlier in October 2016 offered significant financial incentives to Steele to dig dirt on Gen. Flynn. The Halper lie about the affair likely travelled back to James Comey via a circuitous route involving a former British Ambassador, Sir Andrew Wood, David Kramer, Christopher Steele and finally Sen. John McCain. The lie spurred a fresh round of FBI surveillance on the National Security Advisor designate going about his job. The FBI were waiting for the opportunity to pounce. Based on the false Halper story, they wanted to suggest Gen. Flynn was acting against the interest of America because he was a Russian asset compromised by his affair with me. In the style of "The Spy Who Came In From The Cold" Halper and Steele plotted it all:

> I can see them working it out, they're so damned academic; I can see them sitting round a fire in one of their smart bloody clubs. But how could they know about me; how could they know we would come together?' 'It didn't matter – it didn't depend on that. They chose you because you were young and pretty. They only had to put you and me in contact, even for a day, it didn't matter; then afterwards they could call on you, send you the money, make it look like an affair even if it wasn't."

> 'They used us, They cheated us both because it was necessary. It was the only way.

> What do you think spies are: priests, saints and martyrs? They're a squalid procession of vain fools, traitors too, yes; sadists and drunkards, people who play cowboys and Indians to brighten their rotten lives.'[439]

Finally, the Gen. Flynn transcripts show that the General did not lie to the FBI. Instead, someone leaked the supposed details of the classified call between Gen. Flynn and Ambassador Kislyak to the media and suggested that a "crime" occurred, a breach of the Logan Act! Meanwhile the FBI ambushed Gen. Flynn in the White House while purportedly seeking his help in investigating the leakers. Instead of investigating the actual crime of leaking a highly classified

---

[439] John Le Carre.

information, the FBI eventually proposed prosecuting Gen. Flynn for supposedly lying and obstructing an investigation!

The "crime" Gen. Flynn has been relentlessly persecuted for since 2017 was born from Halper's lie, perpetuated by liars and its fruit was a failed prosecution based on lies. The lie gave life to the coup, the attempt to impeach President Trump on the bogus charge of obstructing a fabricated prosecution of a non existent crime.

America can now see it all. Spygate is exposed!

To be continued...

Made in the USA
Las Vegas, NV
21 July 2022